Norfolk

timeout.com / norfolk

143

135

Contents

30

130

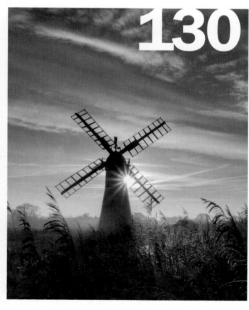

Holkham Beach see p31

ABOUT THE GUIDE

This is one of a series of Time Out guidebooks to cities and regions across the globe. Written by local experts, our guides are thoroughly researched and meticulously updated. They aim to be inspiring, irreverent, well-informed and trustworthy.

Hearts

We use hearts ❤ to pick out venues, sights and experiences in Norfolk that we particularly recommend.

Telephone numbers

All phone numbers listed in this guide assume that you are calling from within Britain. If you're calling from elsewhere, dial your international access code, then 44 for the UK; follow that with the phone number, dropping the first zero of the area code.

Opening times

At the time of writing, the country was still under lockdown due to the Covid-19 pandemic. This has been a particularly challenging time for the hospitality industry who have suffered unprecedented restrictions for over 12 months. Opening times may continue to be subject to government measures for some considerable time.

Part of the charm of the countryside is that it's not like the city. But this means you need to be aware of opening times: places shut up shop for the winter months, or only open at weekends, and some shops still shut for lunch. If you're eating out, many places still stop serving lunch at 2pm sharp and dinner at 9pm. If you're making a journey, always phone to check first. This goes for attractions too, especially outside the summer holiday season. While every effort has been made to ensure the accuracy of the information contained in this guide, the publisher cannot accept any responsibility for errors it may contain.

Maps

The map at the start of each chapter is from the 1:250,000 Ordnance Survey OpenData.

Feedback

We hope you enjoy the guide. We always welcome suggestions for places to include in future editions and take note of your criticism of our choices. You can email us at guides@timeout.com.

Introduction

Norfolk offers a breathtaking variety of countryside: from open heath to wild marshland, and miles of magnificent coastline, including shingle spits and dune-backed sands. There are walks and cycle trails galore, and a huge number of wildlife and nature reserves. Exploring the towns and villages – Norman churches, smart Burnham Market, independent Sheringham – brings rewards too. There's a vibrant cultural scene, from Norwich's Foster-designed Sainsbury Centre to many smaller museums, galleries and arts events, and plenty of historic houses and landscaped gardens. And the pubs, cafés and restaurants just get better every year, with local produce increasingly celebrated.

Norfolk is one of Time Out's regional guides covering Britain. We've used our local knowledge to reveal the best of the region, and while we've included all the big attractions, we've gone beneath the surface to uncover plenty of small or hidden treasures too.

Festivals & Events

FEBRUARY

World Wetlands Day
www.worldwetlandsday.org, www.rspb. org.uk, www.broads-authority.gov.uk, www.norfolkwildlifetrust.org.uk. Date 2 Feb.

Events are held throughout the Broads, Britain's most important wetland, to celebrate World Wetlands Day, which marks the signing of the Convention on Wetlands in 1971. Contact the RSPB, the Broads Authority or the Norfolk Wildlife Trust for more information.

King's Lynn Mart
Date Feb.

A huge funfair in the centre of King's Lynn. *See p17.*

UEA Live
01603 456161, www.uealive.com. Date Feb-May.

Previously known as the University of East Anglia's Literary Festival, UEA Live showcases the works of some of world's most critically acclaimed writers in a series of readings and talks throughout the spring. The 2021 line-up (held online only due to government restrictions) included Zimbabwean novelist Tsitsi Dangarembga and Nigerian-born poet and performer Inua Ellams.

MARCH

King's Lynn Fiction & Poetry Festivals
01553 691661, www.lynnlitfests.com. Date Mar (Fiction), Sept (Poetry).

New and established writing talent. *See p17.*

APRIL

1000 Guineas & 2000 Guineas
0844 579 3010, www. newmarketracecourses.co.uk. Date late Apr/early May.

Two of the biggest fixtures in Newmarket's calendar are held over the QIPCO Guineas weekend: the 1000 Guineas (on the Sunday, for fillies only) and the 2000 Guineas on the Saturday. Hooves thunder down the Rowley Mile, while excited punters throng the stands. For more on Newmarket's busy racing calendar, check online.

MAY

Poetry-next-the-Sea Festival
www.poetry-next-the-sea.com. Date 2nd weekend May.

This mini literary festival sees national and international poets performing alongside East Anglian talents in the beautiful seaside setting of Wells-next-the-Sea on the north Norfolk coast.

Norfolk & Norwich Festival
01603 531800, www.nnfestival.org.uk. Date 2nd-half of May.

Norfolk's biggest arts festival, held every May, offers a vibrant, impressively diverse programme of music, theatre, dance, circus and visual arts.

Fairy Fair
www.fairylandtrust.org/fairy-fair-2020. Date late May.

Held at Bradmoor Woods (West Acre PE32 1FQ), the fair is organised by the Fairyland Trust, which helps families learn about nature and conservation through workshops and crafts (potion-mixing and wand-making might feature). A similar event, Real Halloween, happens in late October.

Saracen Horse Feeds Houghton International Horse Trials
www.musketeer.co.uk. Date last week May.

See the world's leading riders compete at this four-day event at Houghton Hall, in north-west Norfolk. Falconry displays, bouncy castles and other entertainments are laid on to amuse non-equestrian-minded visitors.

JUNE

Three Rivers Race
www.3rr.uk. Date 1st weekend June.

Boats race along the Rivers Ant, Bure and Thurne, in the northern Norfolk Broads. *See p125.*

British Touring Car Championship
www.btcc.net. Date mid Jun.

One of the ten rounds of this fast and furious touring car racing series takes place at Snetterton Circuit in Thetford.

Royal Norfolk Show
01603 748931, www.royalnorfolkshow. co.uk. Date late June (cancelled in 2021 due to government restrictions).

The largest two-day agricultural show in the country, Royal Norfolk, held at the Norfolk Showground in Norwich, offers more than just livestock (although the farming industry is a large part of the equation). Sample some of Norfolk's finest produce in the food hall, have a go at archery in the countryside area or admire the work of around 150 local artists in the exhibition marquee.

Wymondham Music Festival
www.wymfestival.org.uk. Date late June-early July.

Founded in 1996, this annual music festival brings a fortnight of concerts, recitals and workshops to the market town of Wymondham. Highlights include a jazz picnic by the River Tiffy and the town busking day.

JULY

Festival Too
07765 248152, www.festivaltoo.co.uk. Date early July. The 2021 festival is cancelled, although some festival activities may take place later in the year; check the website for up-to-date information.

Free music festival in King's Lynn. *See p17.*

World Snail Racing Championship
www.snailracing.net. Date 3rd Sat July (but cancelled in 2021).

The undisputed highlight of Congham Fair, the World Snail Racing Championship is a hotly contested event. Around 200 snails are entered every year; the current record was set in 1995 by a gastropod named

Archie, who completed the 13-inch course in a blistering two minutes.

King's Lynn Festival

01553 764864, www.kingslynnfestival. org.uk. Date mid to late July.

A fortnight-long celebration of music and the arts, with plenty of big-name performers. See p17.

Sandringham Flower Show

01485 545400, www. sandringhamflowershow.org.uk. Date late July (but cancelled in 2021).

Attracting more than 22,000 visitors, Sandringham Flower Show is a highlight on the horticultural calendar. There are glorious show gardens, plant displays, stalls and talks; in the main arena, motorcycle stunts, dog and horse displays and a military band keep the crowds entertained. All profits go to charity.

Worstead Festival

www.worsteadfestival.org. Date late July (cancelled in 2021).

The largest village festival in Norfolk, in Worstead, near North Walsham. See p110.

Langham Street Fayre

www.langhamnorfolk.com. Date last weekend July, alternate years.

A biennial street fair (on even-numbered years – it was first held in 1974) in the village of Langham, north Norfolk. The main street is lined with stalls, raffles, games and fluttering bunting, and festivities culminate with a hog roast and dancing at the Bluebell pub.

AUGUST

Reepham Summer Festival

www.reephamfestival.co.uk. Date early Aug (but cancelled in 2021).

A diverse array of music, from rock to pop, world music to punk, at this one-day event, plus arts and crafts, street entertainers and plenty of stuff for kids. Reepham is about 12 miles north of Norwich.

Hunstanton Kite Festival & Classic Car Rally

www.hunstanton-rotary.org.uk. Date mid Aug.

Swooping kite displays and hands-on kite-based activities take place in the main ring, while stalls offer crafts and refreshments. Leave time to admire the resplendent line-up of gleaming classic cars and vintage Harley-Davidsons.

Cromer Carnival

www.cromercarnival.co.uk. Date 3rd week Aug (but cancelled in 2021).

The week-long shindig in the seaside resort of Cromer, with carnival day on the Wednesday, is one of the biggest carnivals in the county. Events run from fireworks and a fancy dress ball to the much-disputed knobbly knees contest.

North Norfolk Music Festival

01328 730357, www. northnorfolkmusicfestival.com. Date mid to late Aug.

The North Norfolk Music Festival continues to entice top-level classical musicians to come and play in the region. Concerts are held in two churches, in South Creake and Burnham Norton (South Creake only in 2021).

Aylsham Show

07717 860756, www.aylshamshow.co.uk. Date bank holiday Mon.

More than 60 years old, the Aylsham Show is a vast, one-day agricultural event, held on the National Trust estate of Blickling Hall. The day's entertainments include show jumping, floral displays, dog agility shows and the children's sack race. In the morning, the more serious business of selecting prize-winning animals – cattle, sheep, goats, horses and ponies – takes place.

Barton Broad Regatta

01692 630593, www.bartonbroadopen regatta.co.uk. Date bank holiday Mon.

A flotilla of yachts take to the water at Barton Broad. This is one of several regattas that take place on the waterways in the Broads each year.

SEPTEMBER

British Superbike Championship

www.britishsuperbike.com. Date early September.

Snetterton Circuit, in Thetford, plays host to a round of the UK's road-racing superbike championship. It's one of the fastest and most exciting stages of the competition, with riders reaching speeds of almost 200mph.

King's Lynn Heritage Open Day

www.kingslynncivicsociety.co.uk. Date 2nd weekend Sept.

A chance to see inside buildings that are usually closed to the public. *See p17.*

King's Lynn Poetry Festival

01553 691661, www.lynnlitfests.com.

New and established writing talent. *See p17.*

East Anglian Game & Country Fair

01263 735828, www.ukgamefair.co.uk. Date late Sept.

Variety is the spice of life at this two-day, family-friendly event, held at the Euston Estate near Thetford, just off the A11. Clay shooting, archery instruction, dog jumping and ferret racing are all on the agenda, along with trade stalls and displays in the main arena.

OCTOBER

Norwich Beer Festival

www.norwichcamra.org.uk. Date last week Oct.

More than 200 real ales from Britain's independent breweries are on sale at this week-long festival, alongside 25 types of English cider and perry, and a selection of draught and bottled brews from further afield. The venue is atmospheric medieval surrounds of St Andrew's & Blackfriars' Hall in Norwich.

Beccles Carnival

www.becclescarnival.co.uk. Date mid Aug.

There has been a carnival at Beccles for well over a century. The procession usually takes place on the Sunday; other attractions include a battle of the bands, a funfair, and fireworks on the Monday. .

King's Lynn & the Wash

West Norfolk gets a raw deal. While near-neighbour north Norfolk lords it over the county with a reputation for glorious beaches, gastronomic delights and an outstanding coastline, the Wash is more likely to be thought of – if it's thought of at all – as a vast mudflat stretching between Norfolk and Lincolnshire. Yet this stretch of coast is magical, from the underrated and unsung charms of King's Lynn and the resort pleasures of Hunstanton ('sunny Hunny') on the coast to the delights of gorgeous villages such as Castle Rising on the 46-mile Peddars Way cross-county trail. There's a huge amount here for the visitor willing to forgo metropolitan pleasures for a few days and instead explore a piece of Norfolk that's as timelessly beautiful as anything the north coast has to offer.

KING'S LYNN

This gem of a medieval town rewards the intrepid visitor who's willing to try the handle on a 15th-century panelled door just to see what's on the other side, or to nip down an unlikely looking alley in the hope of finding an unexpected watchtower. Doing the former on Queen Street will reveal **Thoresby College**, a beautiful 16th-century priests' college sited around a rectangular courtyard with a glorious old Judas tree at its centre; while nipping down King's Staithe Lane and taking a right through a private car park will bring you to the door of **Clifton Tower**, a five-storey Elizabethan building that is now a privately owned family home. You can't get into the college, and the tower is open only sporadically (see www.cliftonhouse.org.uk for details), but they are both part of the joy of wandering around King's Lynn.

It's fitting that such rewarding exploration lies at the heart of a town once home to George Vancouver – who in the 18th century mapped 5,000 miles of North America's west coast (and circumnavigated the island that would later be named in his honour) – and to Samuel Gurney Cresswell, the Arctic explorer who was the first man to sail the Northwest Passage. The relaxed charms of this manageable town can easily keep you busy for hours.

Medieval magic

The major historic sites are all centred in the area around **Purfleet Quay** and **South Quay**, adjacent to the River Ouse. This is where you'll find the aforementioned buildings, as well as elegant private courtyards and quadrangles – such as **Hampton Court** (Nelson Street), built in the 14th century as a private merchant's house; **Clifton House** (Queen Street), with its spiralling barley-sugar mahogany columns; and the **Hanse House** (St Margaret's Place), once owned by the lucrative and influential Hanse League of German merchants.

11

The Wash

Just opposite the quay is **Saturday Market Place**, where, as you might expect, a market is held on Saturdays. It's also the site of one of the loveliest churches in Norfolk, and one of the largest town churches in the country: **St Margaret's**. A limestone beauty founded in the 11th century, it sports a fetching three-storey leaning tower dating from the 12th, 13th and 14th centuries.

The medieval wonders continue 100 or so yards beyond St Margaret's, with the **Trinity Guildhall** – now the Town Hall – to the west, marked by a fetching flint and stone chequerboard fascia. It's home to the excellent **tourist office** (01553 763044) and the **Stories of Lynn museum** (01553 774297, www.storiesoflynn.co.uk, *see p18*), tracing 800 years of the town's history and showcasing some of its most impressive historic artefacts. Venture to the east and you'll reach **Greyfriars Tower**, just off

St James Street, founded by the Franciscans in 1230 and a rare survivor of the Reformation thanks to its importance as a marker guiding ships into port. Carry on to the end of St James Street and you reach the **Walks** park, the town's historic and extensive public green space that houses the imposing **Red Mount Chapel** (*see p18*) in its centre.

Other don't-misses await on the north-western side of town. The classical building just north of **Purfleet Quay** that would send Prince Charles into paroxysms of delight is the **Custom House**; designed by local architect Henry Bell as a merchant's exchange house in 1685, it was celebrated by Nikolaus Pevsner as 'one of the most perfect buildings ever built'; currently closed to the public.

From here, head north on King Street and wander into the **King's Lynn Arts Centre** (no.29, 01553 764864, www.kingslynnarts.co.uk) to

Things to do

Trinity Guildhall, King's Lynn *see p12*

KING'S LYNN

Walking tours

King's Lynn's dedicated Red Badge guides enthusiastically volunteer their services, donating fees to conservation projects in the town. They offer a range of imaginative walking tours, among them the excellent Historic Lynn, charting the development of the town from 1100 to the present day, 'The darker side of Lynn', visiting sites that reflect the grimmer aspects of Lynn's history, including tales of murder, treason, hangings and witchcraft. It's not all old stuff, though: find out, for example, which recent blockbuster movie was shot in the town (such as the star-studded *Personal History of David Copperfield*, filmed in 2019). The guides can often get you inside buildings not usually open to the public. To book go to www.kingslynntownguides.co.uk, call 01553 774297 or enquire at the tourist office.

Alternatively, the tourist office has maps for self-guided walks, such as Hanseatic King's Lynn, charting the town's prestigious and lucrative union with the Hanseatic League, and the Maritime Trail, which takes in wharfs, quays and merchant houses along a two-mile route.

HUNSTANTON & OLD HUNSTANTON

Hunstanton Water Sports

North Promenade, Hunstanton, PE36 6BF (01485 534455, www. hunstantonwatersports.com).

Well-established outfit offering a variety of classes in kitesurfing, paddleboarding, windsurfing and powerkiting, from two-hour taster sessions (from £40) to two- and three-day courses. You can also hire the kit or buy it from their online shop.

Searles Sea Tours 💜

Central Promenade, Hunstanton, PE36 5BH (01485 534444, www.seatours.co.uk). Tours Mar-Oct 11am-6pm daily. Rates 30min Coastal Tours £8, 1hr Seal Safari £16. Advance booking advisable.

Taking a trip to the sandbanks or along the coast to the lighthouse and striped cliffs of Old Hunstanton is a great way to appreciate the unique coastline and marine life of the Wash. And doing it on the *Wash Monster* – a landing craft used by US troops in Vietnam – is enormous fun whether you're five or 50. It's just one of the Searles fleet; there's a wide range of regular tours on various vessels.

Hunstanton Beach

check out its programme of comedy, theatre, music, dance, film and visual arts. Part of it is located in the largest surviving medieval guildhall in Britain.

Head further north still and you'll reach vast **Tuesday Market Place**, an elegant Georgian square that's curious for the fact that it has no shops on it (barring one small chemist). It once thrummed to the noise of vendors who filled the entire space; now they rarely fill a third of the square, but good farmers' market produce can still be had here on Tuesday, along with picnic food, jams and Women's Institute goodies. For the rest of the week, it's used as a car park. Head across the square and east along St Nicholas Street to reach St Nicholas's Chapel (*see p18*) – England's largest parochial chapel, just off St Ann's Street.

Once you've taken in all this medieval splendour at close quarters, catch the foot ferry (every 20 minutes from the quayside, 07583 122950) across the Ouse to admire the town's spires, towers and wharfs from the start of the Fen Rivers Way at West Lynn. A short walk from here brings you to St Peter's Church, famed for its rare medieval seven-sacraments font.

Many visitors will enjoy a nose around the **Old Granary** (01553 775509, closed Sun) on King's Staithe Lane. This 'centre for antiques and collectables' is a warren of rooms stuffed with everything from gigantic architectural ironmongery to 1970s hippie-chic clothing and tableware – all at surprisingly good prices.

A wealth of self-guided walks that help you to explore this lovely town with ease are available from the tourist office. Better still, enrol on a guided walk (*see p14*). The volunteer guides will bring medieval history alive for you – as well as opening all those doors and nipping down those alleyways you might otherwise have missed, unless your name's Vancouver.

Where to eat & drink

Many of King's Lynn's eating options are in attractive spots. The **Bank House Hotel** (*see right*) holds pride of place, looking on to both the Ouse and Purfleet Quay; it's worth making a detour to sample its Modern British cuisine. **Riverside** (27 King Street, 01553 773134), located in a timbered building behind the Arts Centre with views over the Ouse, is a pleasant, upmarket restaurant that's particularly good for snacks and lunch, as is the dark and atmospheric Crofters Coffeehouse inside the arts centre itself.

Marriott's Warehouse (01553 818500, www.marriottswarehouse.co. uk), housed in a converted Hanseatic warehouse on South Quay, does meals, snacks and drinks inside or at quay-side outdoor tables, but for real open space, stock up on picnic fodder at **Norbury's Fine Foods** (20-21 Tower Street, 01553 762804, closed Sun and Mon) and head to the nearby Walks park.

Where to stay

Small independent hotels and B&Bs abound in King's Lynn, offering varying degrees of comfort, and prices that reflect the variety. The rambling **Victorian Fairlight Lodge** (79 Goodwins Road, 01553 762234, www.fairlightlodge.co.uk), a little way away from the old town's hustle and bustle, has spacious, light-filled rooms at good prices. **The Grange Hotel** (Willow Park, South Wootton Lane, 01553 673777, www.thegrange hotelkingslynn.co.uk) is a more traditional establishment, as is the **Maranatha Guest House** (115-117 Gaywood Road, 01553 774596, www. maranathaguesthouse.co.uk); both offer good value.

This handsome 18th-century town house and former bank in the heart of historic King's Lynn faces across the Purfleet towards the Custom House on one side and the Ouse on the other. It has an appealing riverside terrace as well as a bar and dining room that is intimate without being intimidating. The 12 guest rooms are decorated with lovely fabrics and old finds that ensure each has its own character; all have very comfortable beds and Wi-Fi. The restaurant does modern brasserie food well with a daily changing menu. Indulgent afternoon teas are served at the weekend, and their Sunday lunch is talk of the town. And, given the town's explorer and maritime heritage, it feels fitting to stay in the house in which Arctic adventurer Captain Samuel Gurney Cresswell died.

Old Granary see p15

Dukes Head Hotel
5-6 Tuesday Market Place, PE30 1JS (01553 774996, www.dukesheadhotel. com). Rates in high season from £109 double incl breakfast.

Set in a beautiful Georgian building, this elegant hotel has 80 light and spacious guest rooms tastefully decorated in calming, muted shades with details of colour and plush king-size beds and Wi-Fi. The location, on the huge and very pretty Tuesday Market Place, is bang in the middle of town.

Old Rectory
33 Goodwins Road, PE30 5QX (01553 768544, www.theoldrectory-kingslynn. com). Rates £88 double incl breakfast.

A beautiful, rambling Georgian ex-rectory with modern rooms, all with Wi-Fi, large comfortable beds and lots of tasteful neutral tones.

Stuart House Hotel
35 Goodwins Road, PE30 5QX (01553 772169, www.stuart-house-hotel.co.uk). Rates in high season from £99. Plenty of offers online.

Just down the road from the Old Rectory, Stuart House has 18 lovely rooms – some dripping with rich brocades and deep vibrant colours, others in contemporary tones with deft and original touches. It's a great place to stay if you're happy to take a stroll across town to reach the sights – though with its own restaurant and a CAMRA-listed bar with cosy fire, it would be easy not to venture out at all.

NORTH TO HEACHAM
Heading north on the A149 from King's Lynn, the smart suburbs quickly give way to open countryside that positively undulates (who said Norfolk was flat?) – particularly as you near **Castle Rising** ♥, a pretty little village topped by what appears from a distance to be a small hill. On closer inspection, it turns out to be earthworks surrounding the incredibly well-preserved remains of the 12th-century castle (*see p18*),

Five King's Lynn events
King's Lynn Mart
Tuesday Market Place. Date Feb.
For two weeks each year, starting on Valentine's Day, the town's main square turns into a massive funfair. It's the first in the showmen's calendar and a fitting homage to Victorian entrepreneur Frederick Savage, a King's Lynn inventor who brought steam power to fairground barrel organs then roundabouts, swings and other rides.

King's Lynn Fiction & Poetry Festivals
01553 691661, www.lynnlitfests.com. Date Mar (Fiction), Sept (Poetry).
Emerging and established contemporary poets and writers from around the world talk about their work in an informal and original setting with plenty of opportunities for the public to meet participants.

Festival Too
07932 114901, www.festivaltoo.co.uk. Date end June/early July.
King's Lynn's annual free contemporary music festival, established in 1985, provides big-name headline acts as well as three weekends of street entertainment and family activities. The 2021 festival has been cancelled due to Covid-19 although some activities may take place later in the year.

King's Lynn Festival
01553 764864, www.kingslynnfestival.org. uk. Date mid to late July.
The fortnight-long festival of music and arts – established in 1950 – is an eclectic and enjoyable celebration, drawing big names in classical music and literature. Many of the events take place in wonderfully atmospheric settings, including St Nicholas's Chapel, St Margaret's Church and St George's Guildhall.

Heritage Open Day
www.kingslynncivicsociety.co.uk. Date Sept.
The second weekend in September sees many buildings usually closed to the public open their doors. Alongside the more famous historical buildings that can often be difficult to access – the Town Hall, Clifton House and Thoresby College, for example – Open Day regulars include the art deco Majestic Cinema and the Victorian Burkitt Homes almshouses. A vintage bus is on hand to ferry people to more far-flung sites of interest.

Places to visit

KING'S LYNN

Lynn Museum
Market Street, PE30 1NL (01553 775001, www.museums.norfolk.gov.uk). Open 10am-4pm Tue-Sat; noon-4pm Sun (Apr-Sept only). Admission Apr-Sept £4.70; £4 reductions. Oct-Mar free.

The much-talked-of life-size replica of Seahenge, a Bronze Age timber circle discovered on the beach at Holme in 1999, isn't as impressive as it could have been, but this small museum is otherwise a pleasure to explore, not least for the insight into local engineer and inventor Frederick Savage and the development of his steam fairground rides.

Red Mount Chapel & The Walks
The Walks (01553 774297, www.west-norfolk.gov.uk). The Walks: open at all times. Red Mount Chapel: May-Sept 1-4pm Wed, Sat, Sun. Admission free.

The impressive late 15th-century chapel for pilgrims on their way to the shrine of Our Lady in Walsingham is the second most important pilgrimage site in England after Canterbury. It stands in the centre of the Walks, an 18th-century park that is a gorgeous spot for a stroll.

St Nicholas's Chapel 💙
St Ann's Street, PE30 1LR (01553 774471, www.stnicholaskingslynn.org.uk). Open 10.30am-4pm Tue-Sat. Admission free.

The largest parochial chapel in England, founded in 1146, is a real stunner. Most of the building dates from the early 15th century; it houses some terrific 17th- and 18th-century merchant memorials, but it's the structure that really takes your breath away – from the stone star-vaulted porch to the beautiful wooden ceiling decorated with angels, all topped by George Gilbert Scott's 19th-century spire.

Stories of Lynn
Saturday Market Place, PE30 5DQ (01553 774297, www.storiesoflynn.co.uk). Open 10am-4.30pm daily (last admission 4pm). Admission £3.95, £1.95-£2.95 reductions, £9.85 family. Sun joint ticket available for Stories of Lynn and Lynn Museum.

The Stories of Lynn charts 800 years of the town's history. The highlight in the Treasury is the lavishly decorated King John cup from the 14th century. The Old Gaol House, with its ducking stool and leg irons, is popular with children who can dress up as gaolers and prisoners and explore the dark dungeons. On Tuesdays and Sundays visitors can also take a free tour around the first floor of King's Lynn Town Hall.

True's Yard Fisherfolk Museum
North Street, PE30 1QW (01553 770479, www.truesyard.co.uk). Open 10am-4pm Tue-Sat. Admission £3; £1.50-£2.50 reductions.

Commemorating the fishing way of life in two beautifully restored Victorian fishermen's cottages – the only remainder of the once teeming North End fishing community – this little museum includes a smokehouse and a tearoom.

NORTH TO HEACHAM

Castle Rising Castle 💙
Castle Rising, PE31 6AH (01553 631330, www.castlerising.co.uk). Open Apr-Oct 10am-6pm daily. Nov-Mar 10am-4pm Wed-Sun. Admission £5; free-£4 reductions.

Hyperbole such as 'one of the most famous and important 12th-century castles in England' often sets visitors up for disappointment, but Castle Rising, or Castle D'Albini, really is spectacular. Heading towards the ticket-office-cum-shop, an impressively steep earthwork – in some places 120ft high – and deep (empty) moat surround and conceal a well-kept castle keep, which, when it comes into view, is breathtaking. The main section of the roof is gone, but all the walls and some of the rooms are fully intact, and the sense of medieval life is palpable.

Sandringham Country Park
Sandringham, PE35 6EH (01485 545400, www.sandringhamestate.co.uk). Open 24hrs daily. Admission free.

Once part of the Queen's private estate and covering nearly 600 acres, this wooded country park is a lovely spot, with two waymarked nature trails, as well as a fascinating sculpture trail and plenty of paths for walkers and cyclists. The visitor centre contains a restaurant, a café and a gift shop, where you can pick up souvenir mugs and produce from the estate's farms.

Sandringham Estate
Sandringham, PE35 6EN (01485 545400, www.sandringhamestate.co.uk). Open daily Apr-Sept. House 11am-4.45pm, Oct 11am-3.45pm; Gardens Apr-Sept daily 10.30am-4.30pm, Oct 10.30-3.30; Museum 11am-5pm daily; Visitor Centre all year 10.30am-5.30pm daily. Admission House, museum & gardens £17.50; £8.50-£15.50 reductions; £42.50 family. Museum & gardens only £11.50; free-£10 reductions; £28.50 family.

The Queen's winter residence, a vast Victorian mansion, makes an intriguing day out. A number of ground-floor rooms are open to the public, their contents a strange mixture of styles that create the kind of home your gran would have if she'd been given tat by heads of state for the last 50 years and didn't have any taste. Does the Queen really do the jigsaws of herself that are piled in the drawing room? You could ask one of the friendly and informative guides, who love to tell stories about what the royals like to do when they're in residence. Visitors can also stroll through the extensive gardens and visit the museum in the old stable block, which includes a collection of vintage royal motor vehicles. Admission includes access to Sandringham Country Park.

Snettisham Park
Park Farm, Snettisham, PE31 7NG (01485 542425, www.snettishampark.co.uk). Open Feb-mid Dec 10am-4pm daily. Admission check website for details.

Very much geared towards children, Snettisham Park encompasses 150 acres of farm and woodland. A highlight is the large herd of deer, which can be viewed on the 45-minute 'safari' by tractor and covered trailer. Other livestock include sheep (visit March to September to bottle-feed the orphaned lambs), piglets and kid goats, as well as rabbits, guinea pigs and newly hatched chicks. There is also a play area equipped with pedal tractors and sit-on diggers. Pony grooming and rides are also available (not on Saturdays), and there are wildlife, archaeology and farming trails. You can bring your own picnic and eat it under the trees in the orchard, or buy lunch and cakes at the tearoom. The gift and farm shop sells everything from soft toys to fresh venison.

Snettisham RSPB Nature Reserve ★
Beach Road, off the A149, nr Snettisham (01485 210779, www.rspb.org.uk). Open 24hrs daily. Admission free.

The Wash is the most important estuary for birds in the UK, supporting more than 300,000 of them, thanks to a mix of marshland, shingle, mudflats and lagoon. The happy convergence of all these habitats at Snettisham Beach makes this stretch of coast the best place to see waterfowl in huge numbers. Two of Britain's great wildlife spectacles take place here: at big tides, when tens of thousands of wading birds wheel over the mudflats and pack on to the islands in front of the reserve's hides; and at dawn and dusk, when the skies fill with pink-footed geese. Even if you're not interested in the birds, the reserve makes for a great walk with expansive views across the Wash.

HUNSTANTON & OLD HUNSTANTON

Hunstanton Sea Life Sanctuary
Southern Promenade, off Seagate Road, Hunstanton, PE36 5BH (01485 533576, www. sealsanctuary.co.uk). Open 10am-4pm daily. Admission £18.95, free-£15.75 reductions (cheaper online); advance booking advised.

With a seal and fish hospital, otter and penguin sanctuaries and an underwater tunnel, this is seriously good educational fun for kids – and most adults will find themselves cooing over the convalescing marine animals brought here from around Britain's shores, or the small colony of Humboldt penguins bred here. Star attractions are the rescued seal pups, and there's also an aquarium where you can get close to the likes of bamboo sharks, seahorses and skate.

which are a joy to explore. Clambering down the hill, it becomes apparent that there are further delights in the village itself. Simple, elegant **St Lawrence's Church**, for example, contains 17th-century furniture and some Norman elements (such as the west front and font), and a 15th-century 20-foot cross nearby. And if you manage to find the warden of the Grade I-listed single-storey red-bricked almshouses near the church, there's a good chance you'll be able to see the remarkable interiors of this Jacobean building and maybe even meet one of the inhabitants, the ladies of Trinity Hospital or Bede House, founded by the Earl of Northampton in 1614.

To this day the ladies still adhere to the conditions imposed on the recipients of the Earl's largesse – namely being single, able to read, at least 56 years old and not a 'harlot, scold, drunkard or frequenter of taverns, inns or alehouses'. They still attend church every Sunday wearing their scarlet cloaks and badges of the Earl of Northampton, adding a distinctive black steeple hat to the outfit once a year (on founder's day). Presumably, they stop for a post-church chat at the quaint local café **Castle Rising Tea Rooms** (*see p22*) rather than the **Black Horse Inn**, the equally quaint village pub.

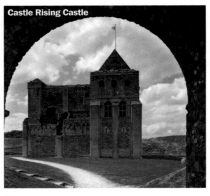
Castle Rising Castle

From Castle Rising, the A149 wends its way past the tiny village of **Wolferton** – signposted near Sandringham and a must for royalists. Here you can snap the site of **The Royal Station** (www.wolfertonroyal station.co.uk), which operated from 1862 (when Queen Victoria bought Sandringham Estate as a Norfolk retreat for Edward VII) until the 1960s (when it closed). It's fun to imagine all the royals and dignitaries who've stopped here – even Rasputin, apparently. It has been lovingly restored and is now a private residence (although owner Richard Brown does open the garden and platform to visitors). **Sandringham Estate** itself (*see p19*), where the Queen and the late Duke of Edinburgh spent many a Christmas, is open to the public in high season, while adjoining **Sandringham Country Park** (*see p18*) is open all year.

The next stop of any note is **Snettisham**♥, a pretty little village with a rambling second-hand bookshop, **Torc Books** (9 Hall Road, 01485 541188; open 10am-4pm Fri and Sat, and at other times by appointment); a couple of excellent eating places – the award-winning **Rose & Crown** (*see p22*) and Michelin-listed **The Old Bank** (*see p22*); and a gorgeous 14th-century church, **St Mary the Virgin** – look out for rare flying buttresses on the 175-foot spire. All these make Snettisham a good place for an overnight stay, particularly as it's close to the glorious beachside **Snettisham RSPB Nature Reserve** (*see p19*) – one of the most important twitchers' sites in the country, and a terrific place for a walk even if you wouldn't know a wading bird from a sparrow.

Just before **Heacham** is popular **Norfolk Lavender** (01485 570384, www.norfolk-lavender.co.uk). 'England's premier lavender farm' is so good at marketing itself – pictures

Rose & Crown *see p22*

of purple lavender fields stretching to the horizon, for example – that coachloads of visitors stop off here. What they find is a small field of lavender bounded on two sides by main roads, a herb garden, a tearoom, a gift shop and a farm shop. But there's more: cross the little wooden bridge to the **Animal Gardens** (open 10am-4pm daily, adults £6, concessions £5) and you'll enter a wondrous space, with a pretty pond, meadow garden, rose garden and woodland walk bordering a delightful rare breeds centre. Chickens predominate, but what chickens – you're unlikely to have seen such breeds before, some with glorious colours, others boasting plumage fabulous enough to make Gypsy Rose Lee green with envy. Wallabees, pigs, goats and more exotic animals also feature.

Heacham itself has few sights, though an interesting memorial to Pocahontas features in **St Mary's Church**. The Algonquin Native American princess, presented here in a Jacobean hat and neck ruff, had numerous ties to the area, saving the life of King's Lynn man Captain John Smith when she was just 12 years old and marrying John Rolfe of Heacham Hall in Virginia at 19. Sadly, she died after returning with him to England three years later in 1614. From here it's a few short miles to Hunstanton.

Where to eat & drink

The villages along the Wash contain some lovely spots in which to eat and drink, from quaint village pubs such as Castle Rising's **Black Horse Inn** (01553 631333, www.theblackhorseinn castlerisingnorfolk.com) to top-class country hotel restaurants such as **Congham Hall** (*see p22*), where aperitifs are served with dainty canapés in a cosy lounge full of squishy sofas and chesterfields.

Castle Rising Tea Rooms & Gardens♥

Castle Rising, PE31 6AF (01553 631211).
Open 8am-7pm.

Sited in the former post office, this picturesque tearoom does a roaring trade to visitors who come to see the castle, then stay for a good range of daily specials, lunch and snack items as well as own-made cakes and scones, all served in a pretty interior and at even prettier garden tables. Dinner options – typically home-made pies and quiches – are listed on the specials board. All the furnishings and accessories on display are available to buy at Castle Rising Barn (01553 631500, www.uniquegiftsandinteriors.co.uk).

Old Bank

10 Lynn Road, Snettisham, PE31 7LP (01485 544080, www.theoldbankbistro.co.uk). Open 6-8.30pm Wed; noon-1.30pm, 6-8.30pm Thur, Fri, Sat; noon-2.30pm Sun. Closed Mon, Tue.

This small, family-run bistro restaurant has a modern, imaginative menu that uses locally sourced seasonal ingredients. There's a set-price lunch menu, a seven-course tasting menu in the evening and traditional Sunday roasts. And judging by the awards and Michelin listing, they are getting it right.

Rose & Crown♥

Old Church Road, Snettisham, PE31 7LX (01485 541382, www.roseandcrownsnettisham.co.uk). Meals served noon to 8pm Mon-Sat, all-day menu and takeaway.

This lovely 14th-century inn sprawls beguilingly, with seemingly unending rooms – some elegant dining spaces, others tiny snugs with huge fireplaces that look like they've been there for centuries, complete with locals to match. The three pretty and always busy dining rooms offer an appealing and selective gastropub menu that doesn't get fancy, instead serving hearty stalwarts such as steaks and bangers and mash, plus a good selection of fish dishes. There's something for everyone, and the desserts are delicious. Upstairs, 16 airy rooms (£160-£170 double incl breakfast) make you feel like you're at the beach, with bright paintwork and striped throws on the huge beds. Sister hotel to the **Bank House Hotel** (*see p16*) in King's Lynn.

Where to stay

Snettisham's **Rose & Crown** (*see left*) is a great place to stay, as is the lively and friendly **Red Cat Hotel** (01553 631244, www.redcathotel.com) in North Wootton.

Appleton Water Tower

Near Sandringham House, PE31 6BB (01628 825925, www.landmarktrust.org.uk). Rates £1,508 per week, minimum stay 3 nights.

This two-bedroom Landmark Trust property near Sandringham is a glorious structure: a red-brick, octagonal water tower designed by Robert Rawlinson in 1877. Each of the three floors contains just one room, and the building is topped by a water tank and a roof terrace, from which, on a clear day, you can see the Wash.

Congham Hall♥

Lynn Road, Grimston, PE32 1AH (01485 600250, www.conghamhallhotel.co.uk). Rates £174-£424 double incl breakfast.

This beautiful Georgian manor has amusing illusions of grandeur (you can charter a private jet at reception), but the 26 rooms are nicely appointed, the house comfortable and intimate and the grounds lovely. New rooms, arranged around a courtyard, offer a more modern alternative to the ones in the main house. There's a 12-metre indoor swimming pool with floor-to-ceiling windows and a luxury spa which includes a sauna, steam room and bio-sauna. A walk after a very good breakfast reveals an orchard, a pretty herb garden and a wide number of activities: croquet, tennis or golf are all offered, with equipment available at reception. The setting, in 35 acres of tranquil, rolling (well, as rolling as Norfolk gets) countryside is delightful. As befits a country hotel, dinner here is a big deal: lots of modern French/English haute cuisine served in a bright, elegant space that's intimate rather than intimidating, by friendly staff who keep obsequiousness to a minimum.

Heacham Manor Hotel
Hunstanton Road, Heacham, PE31 7JX (01485 536030, www.heacham-manor. co.uk). Rates £139-£199.

Another country hotel, this time with an eye to modernity. Outside, the Grade II-listed 16th-century farmhouse is all traditional gables and manicured parkland; the interior has been restored and converted into a luxury, boutique-style hotel, with individuality to the fore. Some of the 45 rooms are four-postered, dark and cosy, others are bright and contemporary, while others still are in comfortable self-catering barn cottages.

Sandringham Camping & Caravan Club
Double Lodges, Sandringham Estate, PE35 6EA (01485 542555, www. campingandcaravanningclub.co.uk). Rates from £8.10 per pitch.

Tell your friends you've slept at Sandringham by camping among the trees at this pretty woodland site within the royal estate, run by the estimable Camping & Caravanning Club. The pitches are large, facilities are plentiful and clean, the posh-looking shop sells a decent range of goods at reasonable prices, and there are lots of great walks.

HUNSTANTON & OLD HUNSTANTON

'Sunny Hunny' has a claim to fame, being England's only east coast resort that faces west. That may not sound like much, but it is quite peculiar, and rather thrilling, to watch the sun set from the east coast, particularly when it's setting over land (Lincolnshire, just across the Wash). Fortunately, the town's charms go further than just this geographical quirk.

An archetypal Victorian seaside resort, Hunstanton's rather austere buildings of dark brown local carrstone look down on a triangular green (with a bandstand for summer concerts), a wide expanse of sandy beach and the rump of a **pier**. Rebuilt after a 2002 fire, the latter no longer stretches out into the sea; it does,

however, house an amusement arcade, a diner and bar and a ten-pin bowling centre. In summer, you can take pony rides on the sands or explore the coast and see the seal colonies in **Searles Sea Tours** (*see p15*).

You won't find much in the way of fine dining or high fashion in Hunstanton, but prices are low and there's a fair range of shops, plus a market on Wednesday and Sunday at the Southend car park on the seafront. And although on first sight the town feels a bit tatty and tawdry, a couple of hours in and you begin to fall for the place; for the crazy golf course on **Cliff Parade**, for **World of Fun** on St Edmund's Terrace, 'England's largest joke shop', and even for the permanent funfair on the **Southern Promenade**, with its carousel, dodgems and other old-fashioned delights that hark back to a day when rides weren't named after drinks brands or made into films.

The **Hunstanton Sea Life Sanctuary** (*see p19*) next door and the Boston Square Sensory Park just behind the bowling green offer more natural but equally enjoyable entertainment. Hunstanton also has a theatre, the **Princess** (13 The Green, 01485 532252, www.princesstheatre hunstanton.co.uk), where professional pantos play in winter and a varied menu of films, amateur dramatics and easy-listening music is offered the rest of the year.

Leaving Hunstanton on the A149, you soon come to the altogether less brash village of **Old Hunstanton**, where carrstone houses, an antiques, arts and crafts centre, an impressive medieval church and two clifftop pitch-and-putt courses offer enough entertainment for a pleasant afternoon. The sandy beach is peaceful and uncrowded, and the village shop, **Old Hunstanton Stores** (38 Old Hunstanton Road, 01485

533441, closed Sun pm), has become a foodie attraction, with its deli selling a rich array of local grub.

Away from the main hub is the beautiful 14th-century church of St Mary the Virgin; of more interest to young children is the duck pond opposite. **Le Strange Old Barns** ♥ (Golf Course Road, 01485 533402, lestrangeoldbarns on Facebook) looks like a sprawl of unappealing crafts shops from the outside, but inside there are genuinely thrilling antique finds to be had, and workshops house potters and jewellery makers.

Down on the beach, you can explore the stunning **candy-striped cliffs** – layers of Norfolk carrstone and red and white chalk dating back to the Cretaceous period – and try to find a 135-million-year-old fossil at their base.

Hunstanton's unmanned **Tourist Information Point** (The Coal Shed Gallery, 5 Le Strange Terrace, PE36 5AJ) has information on local events and attractions, including a map of three heritage trails: it's a thoroughly enjoyable way to explore the town centre, Old Hunstanton and the cliffs.

Where to eat & drink

This northernmost part of the coast is close to some of the fine dining to be found on Norfolk's north coast, which has also resulted in a trickle-down effect for this area. So there are plenty of great pubs in which to enjoy a pint and very good British food, often made with local ingredients – Sedgeford's **King William IX Country Inn & Restaurant** (01485 571765, www.thekingwilliam sedgeford.co.uk), for example, as well as a handful of more upmarket options, among them the **Caley Hall Hotel** (see p25) and **Le Strange Arms Hotel** (01485 534411, www.abacushotels.co.uk), both in Old Hunstanton.

Fishers Traditional Fish & Chips
2-4 Greevegate, Hunstanton, PE36 6BJ (01485 532487, www.fishershunstanton. co.uk). Open 11.30am-8pm Mon-Sat, 11.30am-7pm Sun.

This traditional chippie (eat in or take away) does a range of other meals too, including steak and kidney, burgers and a one-foot-long battered sausage, fitting the bill for a family feed.

Neptune ♥
85 Old Hunstanton Road, Old Hunstanton, PE36 6HZ (01485 532122, www.theneptune.co.uk). Dinner served 7-9pm Tue-Sat; lunch served 1 Sun a month. Booking essential.

Since 2009 Chef Kevin Mangeolles has retained his Michelin star for the lovely Neptune, an 18th-century coaching inn that replaces traditional olde worlde interiors with a refreshing New England style. He sources as much as he can locally, using Brancaster lobsters, local lamb and game and fruit from nearby Drove Orchards to deliver a menu that's as inventive and refreshing as the decor. There are four spick-and-span bedrooms (£290 double incl breakfast and 3-course dinner), as well as self-catering Neptune Cottage, which has three bedrooms (£550-£990 per week).

Salad Bowl Café & Ice Cream Parlour
Cliff Parade, Hunstanton, PE36 6DX (01485 534768). Open Mar-Oct 10am-4pm daily. Feb, Nov, Dec 10am-3pm weekends only.

Catch a fabulous east coast sunset from the pretty Salad Bowl Café, situated on the cliff at the end of the promenade just past the sailing club. Good ice-cream, sandwiches and snacks should keep everyone in the family happy.

Where to stay

Seaside B&Bs of dubious quality are plentiful in Hunstanton, but so too are owners who realise that nylon bedspreads don't always cut the mustard; the **Burleigh** (01485 533080, www.theburleigh.com) is a

Hunstanton cliffs

good example. If you'd prefer to be out of town, the **Neptune** (*see p24*) is cosy and gorgeous, while **Lakeside** (07768 496256, https://lakeside-old-hunstanton.business.site) – a converted Victorian waterworks with its own lake – is on the outskirts of Old Hunstanton.

Caley Hall Hotel

Old Hunstanton Road, Old Hunstanton, PE36 6HH (01485 533486, www. caleyhallhotel.co.uk). Rates £135-£185 double incl breakfast.

This is a good option in Old Hunstanton, with 38 bedrooms in a sprawling and handsome manor house. Family rooms, dog-friendly rooms and wheelchair-accessible rooms are all available. There's also a fine restaurant, bar and attractive outdoor terrace.

Golden Lion Hotel

The Green, Hunstanton, PE36 6BQ (01485 532688, www.bespokehotels.com/the-golden-lion). Rates £129-£164 (2-night minimum stay) double incl breakfast.

There are sea views from most of the 29 rooms at this impressive hotel perched next to the sea. Bold colours make a refreshing change from the neutral tones of so many hotels.

Lodge

Old Hunstanton Road, Old Hunstanton, PE36 6HX (01485 532896, www. thelodgehunstanton.co.uk). Rates £140-£180 double incl breakfast. Self-catering cottage £825-£2,200 per week.

The village location, proximity to Old Hunstanton Beach, nice furnishings and decent restaurant make the 16-roomed Lodge a great base for exploring Norfolk's west coast. There's also a bar and a garden room. A self-catering four-bedroom cottage, with a garden and a barbecue area, is also available.

North Norfolk Coast: Holme to Holkham

Nothing prepares you for the sheer scale and spectacular beauty of the 47-mile stretch of coast from Holme-next-the-Sea right round to Cromer. Holkham Beach is the star in this western half of the coastline, and a lure for location scouts: it's appeared in (among others) *The Eagle Has Landed*, *Shakespeare in Love*, *Never Let Me Go* and, more recently, *Annihilation*, with Natalie Portman. It's a knockout even on the dullest and dampest of days, when the palette of colours runs from dove grey to slate and the beach is perfect for long contemplative walks. But the rest of the coast is no less glorious: sand dunes, saltmarsh and nature reserves teeming with birdlife predominate, and there are plenty of coastal and rural footpaths to explore. Head inland to find equally rewarding landscapes, pretty sights and some excellent eating and drinking – particularly in gorgeous villages such as the Massinghams, or East Rudham and the Creakes, or the six villages that make up the Burnhams, complete with six medieval churches. A couple of grandiose stately homes also demand attention.

HOLME-NEXT-THE-SEA TO HOLKHAM

Holme-next-the-Sea

The attractive village of Holme-next-the-Sea marks the transition from the seaside resort style of Hunstanton and the Wash, with its coachloads of daytrippers taking in Sandringham and taking home Heacham lavender bags, to the more untamed isolation of the North Sea coast. It's a sweet village where chalk and flint cottages give way to golf links and a vast sandy beach that's a fine taster of what lies east. The gently undulating dunes are accessed via a boardwalk, and there's a shop selling Norfolk-made ice-cream, but little else, making for a lovely day at the seaside if your preference is for minimal amenities and a lot of sand between you and the next windbreak.

There's a choice of long-distance walks: the famed Peddars Way, following the course of a Roman road, begins – or ends – here; and the section of the Norfolk Coast Path that runs west from Holme to West Runton. Less completist hikers might prefer the range of guided walks organised by the Norfolk County Council and the Ramblers' Association (see www.countryside access.norfolk.gov.uk for details), or the numerous shorter walks along both long-distance paths. The coast path, in particular, is easily accessible thanks to the frequent CoastHopper bus service (CH1), which allows you to walk one way and return by bus (run by Sanders Coaches, 01263 712800, www.sanderscoaches.com, for timetables). If you're driving, the A149 runs the length of the coast from Holme all the way to Cromer.

Brancaster *see p30*

Brancaster Beach Norfolk
Brancaster Beach Norfolk

Burnham Market *see p30*

A couple of miles east of Holme lies the 35-acre Drove Orchards (Thornham Road, 01485 525652, Drove Orchards on Facebook, closed mid Jan-Mar), worth visiting for its farm shop – a great place to buy apples and freshly pressed juice from the orchards, as well as a huge range of other local produce.

Thornham to Brancaster

Next door to Holme, **Thornham** is typical of the area; it's a tiny village with small cottages of clunch (a type of chalk), reddish-brown carstone and knapped flint on the High Street and more imposing homes down the lanes, plus a café, village shop, post office and two family-friendly pubs, the **Lifeboat Inn** (*see p32*) and the **Orange Tree** (*see p34*). Both offer accommodation, making the village a nice base for wild and windswept Brancaster Bay, just a mile away across the marshes and creeks. They may look bleak and desolate but this land teems with wildlife, and the area is a huge draw for birdwatchers.

A couple of miles east, the equally typical **Titchwell** is notable for the RSPB's **Titchwell Marsh Nature Reserve** (*see p40*), but most people head on to Brancaster. Here, homes ranging from the bijou to the pseudo-stately line the winding road leading to the excellent, unspoilt beach. Bar a snack shack opposite the car park, there's nothing here but sea, sky, marsh and one of the country's best golf links. Among golfing cognoscenti, the **Royal West Norfolk club** (*see p82*) is famous for having a waiting list that's longer than St Andrews', but for the rest of us, the area is more famous for its mussels. During the season, bags of tender little bivalves are sold from fishermen's cottages in **Brancaster Staithe**, as well as from **Letzers Seafood** (the fabulous Crab Hut Brancaster Staithe Harbour, 07582 916652, www.letzersseafood.

co.uk, closed Nov-Mar), on the harbour, where you can also buy more exotic seafood, including lobster and crabs in baguettes and impressive seafood platters.

The coastal path runs around the pretty harbour and close to the excellent **White Horse** pub (*see p36*), and there are some atmospheric walks across the marshes – to the National Trust-owned remains of the Roman fort at **Branodunum** (www.nationaltrust.org.uk), or a mile to Burnham Deepdale, where the backpackers' hostel and campsite at Deepdale Farm (*see p34*) is filled with walkers and families.

The Burnhams

A short detour inland leads to rather smart **Burnham Market**♥, the largest of a clutch of villages known as the Burnhams. In the 13th century, the River Burn was navigable by sea-going boats as far as Burnham Thorpe, now almost three miles inland. Silting of the river led to a decrease in the commercial importance of the Burnhams, but in the past 30 years there's been a curious and profound transformation in the fortunes of Burnham Market. It's a handsome old place with a long, tree-lined green at its centre and is at the very heart of north Norfolk's gentrification, with the impact being felt on towns and villages along the coast. Many of its properties are now second homes to folk from outside the county, and the newcomers' money has allowed some of Norfolk's most interesting shops to flourish.

Quality food is a highlight. Gather the ingredients for a picnic at the first-class deli **Humble Pie** (Market Place, 01328 738581, humblepiedeli on Facebook, closed Sun), the traditional **Groom's Bakery** (Market Place, 01328 738289, closed Sun) and **Satchells Wines** (North Street, 01328 738272, www.satchellswines.com, closed Sun).

Gurneys Fish Shop (Market Place, 01328 738967, www.gurneysfishshop. co.uk, closed Sun winter) is great for smoked fish, and **Tilly's Café** (Market Place, 01328 730300, closed Sun) is a must for cakes and pastries.

Food apart, there are two bookshops: **Brazen Head** (Market Place, 01328 730700, www.brazenhead.org.uk, closed Sun winter) for second-hand books, and **White House** (Market Place, 01328 730270) for new books and maps – not to mention the weekend Burnham Market Book Festival each November. Other shops sell clothes, antiques and gifts; galleries include the **Fairfax** (Market Place, 01328 730001, www. fairfaxgallery.com, closed Mon, Sun), which has contemporary painting, sculpture and ceramics, and **Burnham Grapevine** (Overy Road, 01328 730125, www.burnham grapevine.co.uk, closed Sun), sister gallery to the excellent Grapevine in Norwich.

The other five villages that make up the Burnhams are smaller and, except for their churches, unremarkable. The round-towered churches of **St Mary** in Burnham Deepdale and **St Margaret** in Burnham Norton are both worth a look; the latter, in particular, is outstanding in both its structure and hilltop setting, and features a notable 15th-century painted wine-glass pulpit.

The little village of Burnham Thorpe, just east of Burnham Market, is the birthplace of Horatio Nelson. There's little here to mark the fame of this local boy made good, though Nelson held a farewell party at the village pub (now called the **Lord Nelson**, *see p44*) before returning to sea in 1793. If you detour here to pay homage, follow his example, then take the B1155 to rejoin the coast road, which you reach just west of Holkham.

Holkham

The land for miles around this area is owned by the Coke family (pronounced, with typical Norfolk linguistic idiosyncracy, 'Cook'), the Earls of Leicester. The grounds of the family's stately pile, **Holkham Hall** (*see p38*), stretch down to the famed **Holkham Beach♥**. If you've ever seen a picture of a north Norfolk beach, it's likely to be this one. At high tide it's the perfect beach: immensely wide, sandy, backed by lovely pine woods and serviced by the Beach Café.

The views are magnificent until the fog rolls in, and then the place acquires an eerie desolation magnified by the sound of unseen birds passing overhead. On a sunny day, sandcastles, swimming and beach games take priority; on windswept ones, walking, horseriding and kite-flying come to the fore. On such days Holkham Beach may appear stark and bleak, but in fact it has an abundance of wildlife and is packed with interest for naturalists: sea lavender covers the salt marsh in the summer, and the dunes host a variety of flowers and grasses. The sand dunes are also popular with nesting birds – when necessary, sections of the beach are cordoned off to give colonies of little terns some space and a chance to rear their offspring.

The car park is just off the main coast road opposite the entrance to the Hall; pay, park and then walk along the boardwalk, through the woods, to the beach. Turn left at the end of the boardwalk and after about 20 minutes you get to the part of the beach used by naturists; turn right and the sand stretches away into the distance. If you keep walking, after about two miles you arrive at **Wells-next-the-Sea**, identified by a jaunty row of beach huts. The colourful cluster comes as a surprise after the bare expanses of Holkham, and marks the beginning of a busier stretch of the coast, but one that's just as understated and enchanting.

Where to eat & drink

Local delicacies such as Holkham Estate venison, Morston and Brancaster mussels and Wells crabs and lobsters are made much of in the area, and were treasured even before gentrification set in.

Most of the hotels and inns with rooms have excellent food too, including the **Hoste Arms**, the **Victoria**, the **White Horse**, the **Ship** and **Titchwell Manor**; *see p36* for all. For refreshments after a walk on Holkham Beach, there's the Courtyard Café at Holkham, or The Lookout, at the top of Lady Anne's Drive. which has stunning views over the Holkham National Nature Reserve.

Jolly Sailors

Main Road, Brancaster Staithe, PE31 8BJ (01485 210314, www. jollysailorsbrancaster.co.uk. Open noon-11pm daily; food served noon-9pm daily.

Highly likeable as a pub (serving its own-brewed beer in a congenial old bar), the Jolly Sailors also has a pretty garden and children's play area, all of which makes it a top choice for families. They're sure to find something they like from a menu that includes pub classics, a wide range of stone-baked pizzas and burgers, as well as daily specials such as pulled pork and smokehouse prawns. The 312-foot-long maltings that once stood here, built using blocks salvaged from the old Roman fort Branodunum, is long gone, but the brewery still produces ales, all served here.

Lifeboat Inn

Ship Lane, Thornham, PE36 6LT (01485 512236, www.lifeboatinnthornham.com). Open 8am-11pm daily. Lunch & dinner served noon-9pm daily.

Thirteen spick-and-span, good-sized rooms (£190-£200 double incl breakfast; good discount for online and advance booking), most of them with views out

Holkham Beach *see p31*

over Thornham harbour and the sea, make this a good option for a night or two. The 16th-century smugglers' inn is full of character and does a mean pile of mussels, served in one of the three bars, the pretty conservatory or the slightly more formal restaurant. Two menus are on offer: the pub-style Sail Menu with the likes of scampi, ribs or beer-battered fish and chips, and the more formal Main Menu. Sunday lunch is served from noon to 6pm.

Nelson

Creake Road, Burnham Market, PE31 8EN (01328 738321, www.the-nelson. com). Open 8.30am-11pm daily. Food served noon-9pm daily.

First recorded as a pub over 400 years ago, The Nelson has a bar, a restaurant and some outdoor tables – great for a post-beach walk pint – plus seven B&B rooms. Dishes range from local fish and seafood to chef's own chicken or prawn curry, served in light, bright surroundings.

Orange Tree 💜

High Street, Thornham, PE36 6LY (01485 512213, www.theorangetreethornham. co.uk). Open 8am-11pm Sun-Thur; 8am-midnight Fri, Sat; 8.30am-10.30pm Sun. Breakfast served 8.30-10am Mon-Fri; 9-10am Sat, Sun. Food served noon-3.30pm, 5.30-9pm Mon-Fri; noon-9pm Sat, Sun.

A pretty whitewashed pub set amid extensive gardens, serving a Modern English menu featuring tempting and inventive dishes such as black pearl scallops served with chorizo, black pudding and pea purée, or Norfolk razor clams. The slick, smart decor extends to the six bedrooms (£135-£195 double incl breakfast).

Where to stay

Deepdale Farm

Burnham Deepdale, PE31 8DD (01485 210256, www.deepdalefarm.co.uk/ camping). Rates Hostel £21-£26 per person. Camping £14 for a standard tent pitch to £110 for a luxury safari-style tent sleeping 4.

Three shops and galleries

Creake Abbey Studios

North Creake, NR21 9LF (07801 418907, www. creakeabbey.co.uk). Café open 9am-4pm Wed-Sun (5pm in the summer holidays); some of the shops open daily.

A huddle of converted barns near the ruins of Creake Abbey (see p40) houses a small range of studios and shops selling an array of arts, crafts, old and new homeware, clothing and a fabulous array of local food and drink. The Abbey Café has outdoor tables and a good range of hot and cold food (to eat in or take away), and on the first Saturday of each month a local food fair and farmers' market is held in the barn.

Norfolk Living

55 Market Place, Burnham Market, PE31 8HD (01328 730518, www.norfolk living.co.uk). Open 10am-5pm Mon-Sat.

Stylish home and garden accessories in a handsome (and very tempting) Georgian setting that seems to go on forever; once through the shop there's a courtyard to explore too. Great for (extravagant) gifts.

Real Ale Shop 💜

Branthill Farm, Wells-next-the Sea, NR23 1SB (01328 710810, www.therealaleshop. co.uk). Open Summer 10am-6pm Mon-Sat; noon-4pm Sun. Winter 10am-4pm Tue-Sat; noon-4pm Sun.

Just off the B1105 and set in a malting barley farm owned by the Holkham Estate and farmed by local tenant farmers. The farm supplies 14 Norfolk brewers with much of the malt necessary to make an impressive 60 bottle-conditioned ales, and all of them are sold in this enticing shop. The farm also offers self-catering accommodation for two in Canary Cottage (£400-£525 for seven nights).

This environmentally friendly farm, right in the heart of an area of outstanding natural beauty, has a family-friendly campsite, as well as self-catering private rooms with both en suite and shared facilities in the Stables and Granary. It's a quiet, well-equipped site, with friendly, helpful staff. A strict noise policy in the late evening means that party animals don't bother with Deepdale, and the caravan ban keeps it cosy (campervans and motorhomes are permitted). At the time of writing, some services were not available due to government restrictions.

Hoste Arms 💜

The Green, Burnham Market, PE31 8HD (01328 738777, www.hostearms.co.uk). Rates £190-£550 double incl breakfast.

The revamping in the 1990s of this 17th-century inn on Burnham Market Green paved the way for the village's gentrification. Now a member of the City Pub group, the hotel was one of the Guardian's top 10 country hotels in the UK and has featured in The Times Cool Hotel Guide. On top of the 45 beautifully appointed rooms – some of which are situated in nearby Vine House – the Hoste Arms is known for its food, served in a candlelit wood-panelled dining room, or al fresco in the sheltered walled garden. Admiral Lord Nelson stayed here regularly and used the historic bar as a recruiting post, although he wouldn't have had the luxury of fitness centre, beauty spa and a 20-seat cinema.

Ship Hotel

Main Road, Brancaster, PE31 8AP (01485 210333, www.shiphotelnorfolk.co.uk). Rates £190-£280 double incl breakfast.

Completely refurbished in 2021 (making the most of locklown), the old pub contains a delightful bar area with a woodburner, a restaurant specialising in locally caught seafood (try the local cured and smoked fish platter) and a garden with space for outdoor dining). The nine beautifully designed en-suite bedrooms have a warm, contemporary fee (some are dog-friendly and some can be combined to make family suites).

Titchwell Manor *see p36*

Titchwell Manor

Brancaster Bay, Titchwell, PE31 8BB (01485 210221, www.titchwellmanor. com). Rates £185-£335 double incl breakfast.

Overlooking the marshes of the RSPB reserve and just steps from the national coast path, Titchwell Manor is an old Victorian farmhouse in a lovely location. After a long windswept walk, you'll be happy to collapse on to a leather sofa in front of the open fire for an afternoon pint or evening aperitif. The 31 bright airy rooms (two with hot tubs) are spread over a number of buildings, chief of which is the big house, where rooms at the front have sea views. The dining room and conservatory serve good Modern European food often featuring local produce; and then there's Eric's fish and chip restaurant.

Victoria Inn ♥

Park Road, Holkham, NR23 1RG (01328 711008, www.victoriaatholkham.co.uk). Rates £200-£310 double incl breakfast.

Located just a few minutes' walk from glorious Holkham Beach, 'The Vic' is a stylish 19th-century inn with 20 generous bedrooms with king-sized beds and gleaming bathrooms spread over two houses (10 are in Ancient House, opposite). Some rooms are dog-friendly. The lovely brasserie-style restaurant uses local produce – often very local, such as Holkham steaks, organic chickens from a farm tenant, fruit from down the road or, in winter, wild game from family shoots.

White Horse

Brancaster Staithe, PE31 8BY (01485 210262, www.whitehorsebrancaster. co.uk). Rates £170-£250 double incl breakfast.

If the fresh, contemporary and beach-style decor of the 15 rooms here (eight of them garden rooms with their own dog-friendly patios) weren't special enough, the location certainly would be, overlooking the marshland coastline of Brancaster Bay out to Scolt Head island. An engaging conservatory restaurant with a sun deck terrace offers a wealth of coastal dishes plus good gastropub standards.

INLAND TO GREAT MASSINGHAM

Given the lack of settlements along this stretch of the coast, gentrification has been forced inland, most obviously to the surrounding Burnhams, but also further afield. At **Ringstead**, **Great Massingham**, **East Rudham** and **South Creake**, gastropubs and inns with rooms – such as the **Crown Inn**, the **Dabbling Duck** (for both, *see p43*) and the **Gin Trap Inn** (*see p44*) – offer great bases from which to explore the area. Villages such as **Sedgeford**, **East Barsham**, **Great Bircham** and the **Weasenhams** are home to medieval churches and pleasant pubs, and are surrounded by picturesque countryside criss-crossed by lots of trails and walks.

Such villages, often containing little more than just a glorious church and a cluster of knapped-flint thatched houses, are in some ways the most appealing; a fine example is Sedgeford, where the round-towered **St Mary's Church** adds a serene grandeur to the village. **Harpley** too is beautifully laid out and features some excellent houses alongside a church, **St Lawrence**, whose delicate angel roof and rustic medieval benches are just two of the features that help create a wonderfully atmospheric space.

But it's not all cute villages; grand halls and mansions can be found near Tatterford, where the Palladian-style **Houghton Hall** (*see p41*) is located, and in **East Raynham**, home to the 17th-century **Raynham Hall** with its famous 'Brown Lady' ghost (Lady Dorothy, the supposedly mistreated wife of 'Turnip' Townshend, the estate's second viscount). She forms a nice link between the two houses, being sister to Britain's first prime minister, Robert Walpole and one of the Walpoles of Houghton Hall.

White Horse see p36

NORTH NORFOLK COAST: HOLME TO HOLKHAM

Places to visit

HOLME-NEXT-THE-SEA TO HOLKHAM

Holkham Hall 💙

Holkham, NR23 1AB (01328 01328 713111, www.holkham.co.uk). Open Holkham Hall Apr-Oct 11am-5pm Mon, Thur, Sun. Holkham Stories Experience and Walled Garden 10am-5pm daily. Admission Hall, Stories & Garden (timed tickets) £22, free-£8.50 reductions, £48 family. Stories & Garden £9, free-£4.50 reductions, £15 family. Stories only £5.50, free-£2.50 reductions, £25 family. Garden only £5.50, free-£2.50 reductions, £25 family. The Hall can only be visited as part of the package.

Home to the Earls of Leicester and the Coke family, this extensive, beautifully proportioned Palladian-style stately home was built during the 18th century on the site of a former family home. It's likely to be familiar to those who saw *The Duchess*, which was shot almost entirely on location here, and it is hugely impressive, from its jaw-dropping marble entrance hall and terrific collection of paintings to its opulent state rooms and servants' quarters. Holkham Stories is an interactive experience that brings alive the history of the estate, while the walled garden, covering six acres and originally laid out in the 18th century, includes a vegetable garden, ornamental garden and some impressive Victorian greenhouses. The 3,000-acre deer park in which the hall is set is worth a visit too, and there are extensive walks through it and

Titchwell Marsh Nature Reserve *see p40*

around the mile-long lake. If you don't want to walk, there are cycles and boats to hire and a ropes course through the trees.

NWT Holme Dunes ♥
Just west of Holme-next-the-Sea, PE36 6LQ (01485 525240, www.norfolkwildlifetrust.org. uk). Open 10am-5pm daily. Admission £4. In Jul and Aug, the £5 beach car park day ticket rises to a whopping £10.

Just at the point where the Wash meets the North Sea lies this exceptional Norfolk Wildlife Trust reserve, comprising a vast tract of mud flats, foreshore, sand dunes, scrub, pines, marsh and reedbeds. These all combine to make Holme Dunes one of the coast's most attractive landscapes, with a tangible air of fragility and emptiness. Of course, it's not empty at all; 320 species of bird have been seen from the three hides overlooking grazing marsh, pools and numerous paths, but even if you don't spot any of them, it's a wild and wonderful introduction to Norfolk's north coast.

Scolt Head Island
Brancaster Bay (0300 060 3900, www.gov.uk/ government/publications/norfolks-national- nature-reserves). Open Summer 24hrs daily. Admission free; cruises may vary.

This offshore barrier island and nature reserve, run by Natural England, can be reached in summer via a ferry from Burnham Overy Staithe (01328 738348, www. burnhamoveryboathouse.co.uk), or on a range of escorted cruises (try Branta on

Places to visit

01485 211132, www.brantacruises.co.uk). The mix of sand dunes, saltmarsh, shingle and intertidal sand and mud flats supports a wide range of birds. Much of the island is off-limits to human visitors in order to protect their nesting habitats, but a short nature trail with interpretation panels is a nice way of seeing this quiet and atmospheric site. You can get a terrific view of the island from Barrow Common and Burnham Deepdale Downs if you want to leave the birds in peace.

Sculthorpe Moor Nature Reserve
Turf Moor Road, Sculthorpe, NR21 9GN (01328 856788, www.hawkandowltrust. org). Open Apr-Oct 8am-5pm daily; Nov-Mar 8am-4pm daily (last entry 1hr before closing). No dogs (except assistance dogs). Admission £6 voluntary donation.

Created and managed by the Hawk & Owl Trust, this lovely reserve in the Wensum Valley is one that children in particular will enjoy. Birds of prey, woodpeckers, kingfishers and masses of insects and mammals are supported by a fertile habitat that includes wet and dry woodland, reed beds, pools and riverbank. A boardwalk with bird feeders, nestboxes and a series of hides should help eager nature fans spot their targets.

Titchwell Marsh Nature Reserve♥
Signposted off the A149, just east of Titchwell village, PE31 8BB (01485 210779, www.rspb. org.uk). Open daily at all times. Admission free.

This RSPB wetland reserve is utterly absorbing, whatever your level of interest (or binocular power). Spanning an area rich in wildlife, thanks to a mix of deserted beach (where ancient peat beds, the remains of an age-old forest, are occasionally exposed), reed beds, saltmarsh and freshwater lagoons, the reserve houses a series of hides with pictures and information to enable close observation of a wide variety of wetland birds. These include marsh harriers and avocets in summer and wigeons and brent geese in winter. You can hire normally binoculars at the visitor centre (although not currently due to government restrictions) where you'll also find a shop and café.

INLAND TO GREAT MASSINGHAM

Creake Abbey
Off the B1355, nr North Creake, NR21 9LF (www.english-heritage.org.uk). Open 24hrs daily. Admission free.

Isolated in the middle of fields with nothing for company but the tasteful and discreet Creake Abbey Studios (see p34) nearby, these extensive ruins of a 14th-century

Augustinian abbey are great for moody, atmospheric pictures and a spot of gothic romance. The existing and impressive church of St Mary is worth a look for its wealth of artefacts and information about the original abbey.

Great Bircham Windmill

Great Bircham, PE31 6SJ (01485 578393, www.birchamwindmill.co.uk). Open Apr-Sept 10am-5pm daily. Admission £6, free-£5 reductions, £20 family ticket.

Lovingly restored to its 19th-century grandeur, when it was one of more than 300 windmills in Norfolk, Great Bircham is an enjoyable place to spend an hour or two. It bustles with activity and various farm animals; there are pens housing happy-looking goats and sheep. The working mill is fun to climb (the fan deck offers great views), and there's also a bakery (where you can try your hand at baking bread), tea room and gift shop in which to fritter away time and money. Pitch up at the campsite (see *p45*) if you want to stay the night, or book in to one of the shepherds' huts. And for those keen to explore further afield, the mill can provide a range of walking routes.

Houghton Hall💙

Just off the A148, nr Harpley, PE31 6UE (01485 528569, www.houghtonhall.com). Open May-Sept 11am-5pm Wed-Fri, Sun & bank holiday Mon; July-Sept 11am-5pm Wed-Sun. Admission Walled Garden and Stables £10; Exhibition & Gardens £18, under 18s free. In 2021 visits are limited to the Walled Garden and Stables; entry to the state rooms and gallery spaces of the house will be for visitors to the Tony Cragg sculpture exhibition only.

Four miles west of the village of Tatterton, this palatial, Palladian-style hall was built in the 1720s by Britain's first prime minister, Sir Robert Walpole, with spectacular furniture and interiors designed by the coach painter turned stately home and furniture designer William Kent. From its pale golden exterior of Aislaby stone (quarried in North Yorkshire and transported by sea from Whitby to King's Lynn) to finely carved mahogany woodwork and sumptuous furniture, art and porcelain inside, Houghton is almost equal in splendour to Holkham

Hall. It also boasts a walled garden that shouldn't be missed. New Houghton, the village built to replace the original Houghton (demolished because it spoiled the views from the house), lies just a mile away.

Raynham Hall is only very occasionally open to the public, usually by organised tour (check at 01328 862133, www.raynhamhall.com/open-days).

The villages lucky enough to have popular inns with rooms often thrive and draw other businesses too. At **East Rudham**, a pretty village centred around a large green, the popularity of the **Crown Inn** (*see p43*) spawned **Jane's Coffee Corner** next door, for example. All stripy tables and beach umbrellas on the outside and bright floral homeware inside, this is a lovely café serving home-made snacks and light lunches as well as fairy cakes and cream teas. The **Creake Abbey Studios** (*see p34*) in North Creake offer fun browsing of art, design, crafts, clothing and food, and just a couple of miles east the **Real Ale Shop** (*see p34*) stocks an impressive 60 Norfolk-brewed beers.

Further south, the village of **Great Massingham** is one of the county's most attractive, with a huge green divided by little roads, a dizzying array of ponds (thought to be the fishing ponds for a long-gone 11th-century Augustinian abbey) and a famed son in Robert Walpole. He was educated here and built the majestic **Houghton Hall**. An atmospheric RAF wartime airfield near the village adds an unusual dimension, its dilapidated control tower calling to mind JG Ballard's tales of a dystopian future as well as echoing a sad past that saw the loss of 600 servicemen based here during World War II. Picturesque **St Andrew's**, in nearby **Little Massingham**, was the church of the RAF servicemen, and the graveyard has a number of simple but moving war graves.

A few miles east in **Weasenham St Peter**, fans of the *Today* programme might want to pay homage at presenter John Timpson's graveside; he settled in the village after 16 years on the show – though nearby **Rougham** offers more general interest in the church of **St Mary**, where there's a lovely screen and a plethora of brasses.

Dropping south from here brings visitors to one of Norfolk's greatest medieval sites, at **Castle Acre** (*see pp172-173*) but heading back north towards the coast – possibly along the county-long trail Peddars Way, which bisects the area from Swaffham further south back to Holme on the

Dawn at Holme-next-the-Sea

coast – **Great Bircham** rewards exploration. There's a working windmill with a bakery (*see p41*) and, at **St Mary's Church**, a war graves plot for British, Commonwealth and German servicemen.

Beyond here the rolling folds of the **Ringstead Downs** valley, the largest area of chalk grassland in Norfolk, stretches to the village of Ringstead; best seen perhaps from the **Norfolk Wildlife Trust site** (NWT Ringstead Downs, 01603 625540, www. norfolkwildlifetrust.org.uk), just off the Ringstead/Sedgeford road. It's a beautiful valley and part of the north Norfolk strip of Area of Outstanding Natural Beauty that stretches 40 miles from here to **Mundesley**; even if you don't walk any other stretch of the Peddars Way, the two miles between Ringstead and the ancient trail's end at Holme shouldn't be missed.

Where to eat & drink

Crown Inn♥
The Green, East Rudham, PE31 8RD (01485 528530, www.crowninnnorfolk. co.uk). Open 8am-11pm daily. Lunch served noon-2.30pm daily. Dinner served 6-9pm Mon-Fri, Sat; noon-8pm Sun.

Another good Norfolk country pub/ restaurant that combines traditional period features with modern-day comfort. The bar prides itself in its selection of real ales while the friendly restaurant does modern pub food well – check the specials board. Upstairs are six small but comfortable and beautifully appointed rooms (£95-£135 double incl breakfast).

Dabbling Duck
11 Abbey Road, Great Massingham, PE32 2HN (01485 520827, www. thedabblingduck.co.uk). Open daily although at time of going to press the pub was serving a limited menu; regular lunch and dinner opening hours will return as soon as government guidelines permit.

Four Norfolk ice-creams

Dann's Farm
Pound Farm, North Tuddenham, NR20 3DA (01362 638116, www.dannsfarm.co.uk). Open 9am-5pm daily.

The Dann family is understandably proud of its award-winning gooseberry and elderflower sorbet, but don't discount other ice-cream flavours made with local produce, such as lavender or toffee and fudge. There are flavours for diabetics too, and even 'pupsicles' for your canine companions. The ices use eggs, fruit, milk and cream from the Dann's farm at North Tuddenham, near East Dereham, where you can buy the full range of flavours to take home.

Norfolk Country Fresh Cream
www.lakenhamcreamery.co.uk.

Traditional batch methods are used by Lakenham Creamery to produce a range of 29 ice-cream flavours; try award-winners such as rhubarb and custard, rich butterscotch or French vanilla, or, our favourite, coconut and cream: velvety, coconutty and luscious enough to transport you straight to the Caribbean.

Parravanis
www.parravanis.co.uk.

The Parravanis family has been making ice-cream in Norfolk for more than a century. Although they are now based across the River Waveney in Beccles, Suffolk, the firm uses fresh local milk to create an adventurous range of 40 ice-creams (including coconut and chocolate, Italian marmalade and more traditional fruit-based versions) plus gelati and sorbets, which are sold from vans, a mobile ice-cream parlour and in farm shops throughout East Anglia.

Ronaldo's
www.ronaldo-ices.co.uk.

Available in most of the coastal resorts, including Cromer and Sheringham, Ronaldo's uses Norfolk produce – apples, strawberries, raspberries, blackberries and gooseberries – wherever possible. Try the blueberry, which contains fruit from King's Lynn's Fairgreen Farms, then have a go at re-creating the rich, colourful ice-cream by picking your own berries at the farm.

Bircham Windmill Campsite see p45

A sweet blue and white pub facing the huge green, the Duck's name comes from the village's many ponds. Inside, worn leather armchairs, scrubbed country tables and big fires make it the kind of place you could happily spend the day, eating pints of prawns, big bowls of moules marinière and above-par pub favourites such as burgers and traditional puds. There are eight guest bedrooms, six classic pub rooms with wrought-iron beds and crisp white linen, and three slightly bigger garden rooms with king-sized beds and spacious bathrooms. Spick-and-span self-catering Duckling Cottage, sleeping six, is a few doors down.

Gin Trap Inn

6 High Street, Ringstead, PE36 5JU (01485 525264, www.thegintrapinn. co.uk). Food served 5-9pm Mon-Thur; noon-9pm Fri-Sun.

This pretty 17th-century coaching inn is a firm favourite with locals and visitors, and it's easy to see why. You'll find friendly staff, a traditional warm and cosy space (plus a lovely walled garden) and a menu that includes refined, imaginative dishes as well as pub classics and Sunday roasts with all the trimmings. There are ten stylish guest rooms (£125-£175 double incl breakfast) and three cottages, all individually designed, and with excellent facilities.

Kings Head Hotel

Great Bircham, PE31 6RJ (01485 578265, www.thekingsheadhotel.co.uk). Open daily. Breakfast served 8-10.30am; lunch noon-2.30pm; afternoon tea 2.30-5.00pm; dinner 5.30-8.30pm.

Contemporary dining and bedrooms in a gorgeous whitewashed Grade II-listed 19th-century coach house make the Kings Head a good inland base: it's handy for the coast, but away from the hustle and bustle. Quality Modern British food is served in an elegant restaurant and courtyard, while the 12 individually styled rooms (£105-£190 double incl breakfast) are luxurious.

Lord Nelson

Walsingham Road, Burnham Thorpe, PE31 8HL.

There are around 200 pubs in Norfolk bearing the name of the Trafalgar hero, but this one, in his birthplace, was positively shrine-like, with memorabilia adorning much of the whitewashed space, and lots of Lord Nelson souvenirs for sale behind the bar. Built in 1637, the classic boozer closed down in 2016 but, was eventually bought by the Holkham Estate who have renovated the iconic venue and hope to re-open it soon.

Ostrich Inn

1 Fakenham Road, South Creake, NR21 9PB, (01328 823320, theostrichinnnorfolk.co.uk). Open noon-11pm daily. Lunch served noon-2pm, dinner served, 6.30-9pm daily.

A charming location in an equally charming village makes the Ostrich a good pint pit stop, even before factoring in the menu, which offers gastropub staples done well: fresh salmon tartar for starters, marinated fillet of mackerel or confit duck leg for mains. Enjoy it all in a cosy library room warmed by a log burner. There are four bedrooms (£140-£200 double incl breakfast) and a two-bedroom self-contained cottage just along the road.

Rose & Crown

Nethergate Street, Harpley, PE31 6TW (01485 521807, www. roseandcrownharpley.co.uk). Open/food served noon-9pm Mon-Sat; noon-6pm Sun.

Scrubbed wooden floors and a bright modern interior decorated with local artwork set the Rose & Crown apart from a run-of-the-mill village pub, and so does the food. The menu ranges from well-prepared and appealing pub dishes (homemade steak and kidney pudding, game cobbler, fish and chips, using local ingredients where possible) plus the odd dash of more international fare. There's a good range of wines by the glass, plenty of local ales, and an attractive garden for summer supping, all set in one of the area's prettiest villages.

Where to stay

As well as the B&Bs and campsites listed here, many of the inns listed above offer accommodation, including the Crown in East Rudham, the Kings Head in Great Bircham, the Gin Trap Inn in Ringstead and the Dabbling Duck in Great Massingham.

Bircham Windmill Campsite

Bircham Windmill, Great Bircham, PE31 6SJ (01485 578393, www. birchamwindmill.co.uk). Rates £25 per pitch for 2 people. Shepherds' huts from £60.

Freshly baked bread for breakfast, and waking to the noise of sheep and chickens are just a couple of reasons to stay at this small, friendly campsite; the gentle whirr of the sails sweeping round as you go to sleep is another. As well as the campsite, there are two shepherds' huts (each sleeping two people). *See also p41.*

Church Farm House

Great Bircham, PE31 6RJ (01485 576087, www. church-farmhouse.com). Rates from £90 double incl breakfast. At time of going to press the house was closed but was set to reopen as soon as government guidelines permit.

A whitewashed period farmhouse on the outskirts of Great Bircham, Church Farm features three light-filled, cosy and comfortable rooms. There are plenty of thoughtful and individual touches, including bright textiles.

Old School

South Creake, NR21 9JE (01328 823778). Rates £80-£120 double incl continental breakfast.

A cross between a B&B and self-catering accommodation, the Old School consists of a huge family room (the ex-headmaster's study) and two interconnecting rooms, all with independent ground-floor access – and that's it. There's no breakfast room (continental breakfast is served in the bedroom) and no lounge, so this is one for people who like peace and quiet, and a quirky place to stay. There's a fridge and microwave and it is dog friendly.

Things to do

Extreeme Adventure

High House, Weasenham, PE32 2SP (01328 838720, www.extreemeadventure.co.uk). Open Easter-Oct by appointment only. Admission quad trekking £70 (minimum age 16); assault course £20 (£5 discount for combined activities).

These quad-trekking safaris take you through beautiful woodland with some of the highest trees in eastern England. The setting, south of Weasenham All Saints and just off the A1065, is impressive. Spend half an hour mastering your quad, then head out in a guide-led group for a one-hour safari. The army-style assault course can be tackled individually or you can compete against a friend. Prepare to get muddy. Less intrepid adults can stay in the covered picnic pavilion, where refreshments are served and a log fire greets you in cold weather.

North Norfolk Paddle Boards

Burnham Overy Staithe (7768 123797, www. northnorfolkpaddleboards.co.uk)

If you have a basic level of paddleboarding and are 14 or over, there is a choice of tours lasting two-three hours (£50) that explore the creeks and salt marshes around Burnham Overy Staithe. Complete SUP beginners (12 and over) can opt for a two-hour taster session (£40) to learn the basics.

North Norfolk Coast: Wells to Weybourne

Where the western half of the north Norfolk coast is a huge empty expanse of sand, dunes and marsh, the eastern half is tamer, tidier and altogether more down to earth. In settlements such as Wells-next-the-Sea, Blakeney and Morston, fishing still plays its part, but as the A149 winds through Salthouse towards the Victorian town of Sheringham, the wide stretches of beach and marsh give way to pebbles and seaside resort pleasures. Inland, the towns of Little Walsingham and Holt are unmissable and offer some great shopping and eating opportunities. Dotted with numerous quaint villages, such as Salle, Reepham, Swannington and privately owned Heydon, as well as hundreds of Norman and Saxon churches, this inland area is great driving and walking terrain, with heath, wood, fen, pasture and even the odd small hill offering something for everyone.

WELLS TO WEYBOURNE
Wells-next-the-Sea

Less than two miles east of Holkham's vast, sparse, pine-backed beach, the little town of Wells-next-the-Sea manages to cram in a beach resort, a fishing port, a picturesque shopping street and a leafy green (the Buttlands, where the carnival is held in summer).

There's a wealth of things to do here, from sampling the fine dining at the **Crown Hotel** (*see p51*) or the **Globe Inn** (*see p51*) to browsing old-fashioned independent shops (butcher, baker, fishmonger, sweet shop, hardware store) along the Staithe, the narrow high street that runs uphill from the pretty quay lined with fishing and pleasure boats. Recently relocated to the Staithe from down the road in Holkham village is **Bringing the Outside In** (*see p60*) and, next door is **GROUND**, a coffee house and eatery. There's a huge range of other cafés and takeaways on the Staithe too, including **Nelson's Coffee Shop** and the **Picnic Hut** (purveyor of Norfolk County ice-cream). Facing the quay, **French's Fish Shop** (10 Quayside, 01328 710396, www.frenchs.co.uk, closed Mon in winter) has been selling fish and chips for more than 75 years; a few doors away the **Wells Deli** (*see p61*) makes a mean crab sandwich.

Wells's sandy beach is a mile from the town centre; in summer, you can travel there on the narrow-gauge **Harbour Railway** (£1.50 each way) that ferries passengers from the harbour to the beachside holiday camp, **Pinewoods**. At low tide it's a long walk out to the water. At high tide the sea rushes in (very fast – sirens sound to alert bathers to the danger of being cut off on the dunes), the beach shrinks dramatically, and crabbing boats flood into the harbour to unload their snapping cargo.

On the outskirts of town is the **Wells & Walsingham Light Railway** (*see p57*). If you're visiting in May, look out

Wells-next-the-Sea *see p47*

for the annual **Poetry-next-the-Sea Festival** (01328 711813, www.poetry-next-the-sea.com).

Stiffkey to Blakeney

East of Wells, the coast road narrows as it passes through the small villages of **Stiffkey** (pronounced 'Stukey') and Morston, reflecting the change of mood to a more rural, homely feel. Look out for seasonal fruit and veg sold from roadside cottages, along with mussels, oysters, honeycomb and – that much sought after Norfolk speciality – samphire. Stiffkey boasts a good pub, the **Red Lion** (*see p56*), and the excellent **Stiffkey Stores** (01328 830489). Stock up on fabulous cupcakes and savoury snacks before heading a couple of miles south to the ruins of Elizabethan Stiffkey Hall.

Morston's creeks are splendid for muddy paddling at low tide, but don't miss the tiny 11th- to 13th-century All

Saints' Church. The tower is actually very early, although the stark brick top is an 18th-century repair after a lightning strike. The 15th-century painted rood screen is a highlight.

Pub-lovers might want to make a small detour inland to the west of Stiffkey to pay homage to the **Three Horseshoes** at Warham (69 The Street, 01328 710547, www.warhamhorseshoes.co.uk), which has retained its classic pub interior, and has well-kept ales, decent food (pies a speciality), and rooms. Or continue along the main coast road to **Blakeney**, where the two narrow streets leading down to the quay contain a handful of shops, pubs and restaurants, including the **Blakeney Delicatessen** (30 High Street, 01263 740939, www.blakeneydeli.co.uk) and **Willi Weston's Fish Shop** (5 Westgate Street, 01263 741112). Here you'll find own-made enticements such as potted shrimps, fresh crab and seafood quiches.

Blakeney is justly famous for its grey **seal colony**, best seen on a boat trip from Blakeney or Morston harbours (*see p57*), but it's also a lovely place to while away a few hours exploring the area's ancient relationship with the sea. In Back Lane, for example, the vaulted cellars of the 14th-century Guildhall were used as a mortuary for drowned sailors in the 19th century, while the small turret on the north-east chancel of **St Nicholas**, a beautiful hilltop church, was for centuries a burning beacon guiding ships into harbour.

Cley-next-the-Sea to Weybourne

Continuing east along the A149, delightfully idiosyncratic **Cley-next-the-Sea** (pronounced 'Cly') makes a great base for hikes. There's no newsagent or grocer, but you will find a deli, smokehouse, lovely bookshop, pretty tearoom and a couple of galleries, including **Made in Cley** (*see p60*). The energetic should take the

lane east of the village down to the shingle beach and from there it's possible to trek to **Blakeney Point** (four miles there and back), keeping a seaward eye out for seals along the way. A more leisurely stroll starts from Church Lane (off the A149 by Picnic Fayre) and runs past Cley's enormous **St Mary's Church**, built in the 13th century, when the village was a prosperous port; the south porch, with its traceried battlements and lovely fan-vaulted roof, is stunning.

You can stock up on picnic goodies at **Picnic Fayre** (The Old Forge, 01263 740587, www.picnic-fayre.co.uk) and find presents for foodie friends at the **Cley Smokehouse** (High Street, 01263 740282, www.cleysmokehouse.com).

Also on the High Street, the Pinkfoot Gallery (01263 740947, www.pinkfootgallery.com) has wildlife-inspired prints, paintings and sculptures, many by local artists.

Just east of Cley, the **Cley Marshes Nature Reserve** (see p52) is another good walking spot – head through the salt marshes and down to the beach. From here you can walk as far as Salthouse for lunch at **Cookie's Crab Shop** (see p51), a pint at the Dun Cow (Coast Road, 01263 740467, www.salthouseduncow.com), a poke around another terrific church (**St Nicholas**), or a pleasurable stroll along the one-time **Salthouse Sculpture Trail**. Although most of the sculptures have now gone, the walk nonetheless provides a peaceful route around this part of the county.

From here it's just a few miles to the more built-up charms of **Weybourne**, home to the **Muckleburgh Collection** (see p52) and the usual collection of tea shop, village store, pub and church backing a pretty and very steep pebbly beach known as Weybourne Hope (or Hoop). For paddling and castle-building, it's best to continue along the coast to the Victorian resort of **Sheringham**, where samphire and smoked fish give way to cotton candy floss and greasy spoons.

Where to eat & drink

Food along this stretch of the coast spans every budget, from shellfish and sandwich shacks on the quay to pubs serving huge pots of mussels, pies and local game (try Warham's **Three Horseshoes**; see p49), and more upmarket restaurants and bistros, such as the **Moorings** (01263 740054, www.blakeney-moorings.co.uk, open for coffees, cakes and lunch from 11am Tue-Sun – eat in or take away; for supper from 6pm Tue-Sat) in Blakeney and **Morston Hall** (see p56) in Morston. Thanks to a

Wells & Walsingham Light Railway see p57

strong emphasis on local produce cooked on the premises, most of what's on offer is great.

Blakeney White Horse

4 High Street, Blakeney, NR25 7AL (01263 740574, www.whitehorseblakeney.com). Open 11am-11pm daily. Food served noon-2pm, 5-7pm Mon-Fri; noon-7pm Sat; noon-4pm Sun.

This 16th-century pub, just up from the quay on Blakeney's quaint High Street, is part of the Admans' empire. Food is accomplished, and there are also local real ales and a good wine list. There's a B&B too: nine light and welcoming en-suite rooms, some with views of the coastal marshes and the sea beyond (£109-£129 double incl breakfast).

Cookie's Crab Shop ♥

The Green, Salthouse, NR25 7AJ (01263 740352, www.salthouse.org.uk). Food served 8am-6pm Tue-Sun (weather dependent, best to call first). No credit cards.

This jewel of a café keeps things simple. Seating is at cramped tables in a garden shed, or outside in a pagoda or beneath parasols. The menu is equally frills-free: a couple of soups (including the smoky kipper and tomato), prawn bisque, seafood platters and takeaway sarnies.

Crown Hotel

The Buttlands, Wells-next-the-Sea, NR23 1EX (01328 710209, www. crownhotelnorfolk.co.uk). Open 10am-11pm daily. Food served noon-2.30pm, 6-9pm Mon-Sat, noon-9pm Sun.

Chris Coubrough's cream and blue, 16th-century coaching inn on Wells's elegant Georgian square is a smart affair. The restaurant serves great British food with Pacific Rim and Mediterranean influences, including plenty of fish. In the adjoining black-beamed bar, things are more low-key; heaped-high sandwiches at lunchtime, plus well-kept local ales and a good selection of wines by the glass. The 20 guest rooms – divided into 'cosy', 'roomy', 'copper bath rooms' and 'family rooms and suites' (£175-£225 double incl breakfast) come with attractive decor and all mod cons.

Globe Inn

The Buttlands, Wells-next-the-Sea, NR23 1EU (01328 710206, www.theglobeatwells. co.uk). Open 9am-11pm daily. Lunch served noon-2.30pm, dinner served 6.30-9pm daily.

Places to visit

WELLS TO WEYBOURNE

Cley Marshes Nature Reserve

Coast Road, Cley-next-the-Sea, NR25 7SA (01263 740008, www.norfolkwildlifetrust. org.uk). Open Mar-Oct 10am-5pm daily; Nov-Apr 10am-4pm daily. Admission £5; free reductions & NWT members. Visitor centre free.

One of Britain's top birdwatching sites has six hides looking out over reed beds and pools, enabling you to spot avocets, bitterns, terns, marsh harriers, oystercatchers and more. The award-winning sustainable visitor centre incorporates a café, shop, observation area and displays on coastal history and stories. CoastHopper buses (01263 712800, www.sanderscoaches.com) stop outside the reserve. Dogs are not allowed in the reserve.

Muckleburgh Collection

Weybourne, NR25 7EH (01263 588210, www.muckleburgh.co.uk). Open 10am-5pm. Admission £12, free-£8 reductions.

Tanks, armoured vehicles, guns, aircraft and military gear by the shedload, are spread across eight exhibition halls. There's also a large gift shop and bookable tank rides. Outside, rusting vehicles and a radar station alongside crumbling concrete dormitories lend a bedraggled air of authenticity to the whole macho affair.

INLAND TO EAST DEREHAM

Gressenhall Farm & Workhouse 💚

Gressenhall, NR20 4DR (01362 860563, www.museums.norfolk.gov.uk). Open Mar-Oct 10am-5pm daily. Admission £13.90, free-£13.20 reductions.

Housed in an imposing workhouse, this social history museum evokes life in rural Norfolk with skill and flair, keeping things lively for children with a rare breeds farm, cart rides and a brand new adventure playground. Interpretive panels, interactive displays and audio-visual material mean there's something for all ages; a dungeon for gore-fixated teenagers, workhouse trails and inmates' stories for the more thoughtful. There are lovely walks in the grounds and a decent tearoom.

Letheringsett Watermill

Riverside Road, Letheringsett, NR25 7YD (01263 713153, www.letheringsettwatermill. co.uk). Closed at time of writing but set to reopen in accordance with government guideles; opening hours and admission fee to be confirmed. Online booking only. Check website for the latest information.

Norfolk's only flour-producing watermill attracts thousands of visitors each year and is a regular on the tourist attractions awards circuit. It's justified; the 217-year-old mill is a lot of fun to explore and the riverside setting is magical. The regular working demonstrations and guided tours (on most weekday afternoons) offer a fascinating insight into the production process. A well-stocked shop sells the spelt flour produced by the mill, as well as 12 other varieties of flour produced from locally grown wheat.

Natural Surroundings

Glandford, NR25 7JN (01263 711091, www.birdventures.co.uk). Open Apr-Sept 10am-5pm daily; Oct-Mar 10am-4pm Tue-Sun. Admission £5, free-£2.50 reductions.

A lovely inland nature resource that has something for everyone, including ponds, wildlife gardens, wildflower meadows and a decent nursery. The tearoom is a must, not least for viewing birds and wildlife close up, thanks to window feeders and nest-box cameras.

Pensthorpe Nature Reserve

Fakenham Road, nr Fakenham, NR21 0LN (01328 851465, www.pensthorpe.com). Open Mar-Dec 10am-4:30pm Wed-Sun during term time and daily in school holidays. Admission £12.95, free-£11.95 reductions (pre-booked slots only while government restrictions are in place).

The one-time home of BBC's *Springwatch* is a vast nature site in the Wensum Valley containing a wide range of areas, among them wildflower meadows, a bug walk and conservation centres. With 171 recorded wild bird species, including avocets, oystercatchers, kingfishers, ringed plovers and marsh harriers, in the sprawling wetlands, gardens and woodlands, it's of particular interest to birdwatchers. To visit some of the more remote areas of the estate which are not accessible on foot (and at an extra cost of £4) you can climb aboard the *Pensthorpe Explorer*, a Land Rover trailer, for a one-hour tour. There are also indoor and outdoor adventure playgrounds as well as a coutyard café and a well-stocked gift shop.

Shell Museum

Church House, Glandford, NR25 7JR (01263 740081, www.shellmuseum.org.uk). Open Easter-Oct 10am-12.30pm, 2pm-4.30pm Tue-Sat. Admission £2.50, 50p-£2 reductions.

Built in 1915 to house a collection of shells assembled over a period of 60 years by Sir Alfred Jodrell, this tiny Dutch-style gem of a building contains thousands of exquisite seashells, fossils, birds' eggs, agate ware, local archaeological finds and the enjoyable tat only local museums ever seem to exhibit. Next to it stands St Martin's church, an equally arresting building that contains elaborate woodcarving, beautiful stained-glass windows and a carillon of 12 bells.

Slipper Chapel

Houghton St Giles, nr Walsingham (01328 820495, www.walsingham.org.uk). Open 8am-7pm daily; reduced opening hours in winter, phone for details. Admission free.

The pretty but unremarkable little 14th-century Roman Catholic Shrine of Our Lady, built as the last wayside chapel for pilgrims on their way to the Walsingham shrine, lies an attractive one-mile stroll from Walsingham. Be prepared to see people walking the route from the chapel to the village in slippers or bare feet, as Henry VIII supposedly did in 1511.

Thursford Collection

Thursford, NR21 0AS (01328 878477, www.thursford.com). Open Apr-Sept noon-5pm Mon-Fri, Sun. Admission £8; under 12s free. Nov-Dec open for the Christmas Spectacular (from £38). Closed at time of writing but set to reopen once government guidelines permit; check website for latest news.

One of the strangest attractions in Norfolk was begun more than 50 years ago by George Cushing, who collected an eye-popping array of steam-powered and mechanical engines, fairground organs and carousels; look out for the steam-powered Venetian gondola ride, but whatever you do don't miss the 1931 Wurliitzer organ.

Its 1,339 pipes create an astonishing array of sounds and effects, best experienced through daily recitals in the Wurlitzer cinema. Dickensian-style shops and cafés add to the olde-worlde theme. Booking is obligatory for the Christmas Spectacular shows.

Walsingham Abbey Grounds

Entrance through Shirehall Museum, Common Place, Walsingham, NR22 6BP (01328 820510, www.walsinghamabbey.com). Open Feb-Oct 11am-4pm Thu-Sat. Admission £5.50, free-£2.50 reductions.

The 12th-century abbey ruins and lovely gardens are part of 20 acres of woodland and parkland, linked via beautiful little bridges and winding paths. Snowdrop walks in early spring are especially popular. The Shirehall Museum, which acts as the entrance to the grounds, houses the old courthouse as well as artefacts, photographs and an engaging history of the village's 1,000-year history.

Five crabbing tips

- Both Blakeney Quay and Wells Quay are ideal spots for crabbing (aka gillying). It's best to crab at high tide, when the sea is near the top of the harbour walls and you won't have far to reach down to grab your catch. Local tide tables can be found online at www.tidetimes.org.uk. Times of high tides are also published in the *Eastern Daily Press* (Mon-Sat) and the *Lynn News* (Tue, Fri).
- You can get a weighted crab line for a few pence at local shops. Don't use a hook – which can get lost and injure seabirds – but simply tie your bait to the line or put it inside the little net provided.
- Instead of expensive bait, buy around £1's worth of bacon bits. These work just as well.
- Buy a landing net. A net is crucial, especially if you're crabbing near low tide: you don't want your snappers to drop off the line before you can haul them up to the quay.
- Use a decent-sized bucket (see-through, if possible), partially filled with seawater, to collect the crabs. When you're done, gently tip over the bucket and allow the little snappers to escape.

... and where to buy the edible kind

- Direct from fishermen's houses along the A149, particularly around Cley, Morston, Blakeney and Sheringham (look out for signs).
- **Cookie's Crab Shop** in Salthouse (see p51) – a wooden shack, a plastic pergola and a few rickety chairs and tables might not look like much, but the huge salads, sandwiches and takeway shellfish here are some of the best in the county.
- In Cromer, **JWH Jonas Fishmongers** (01263 514121) on Chapel Street, or **J Lee Fisherman**, on New Street, for dressed crab.
- The **Old Forge Seafood Restaurant** (see p64) in Thursford always has Cromer crab on the menu – alongside plenty of other local fish and seafood.
- The **Fair Maiden fishmonger** in Happisburgh, where fresh and dressed crabs are joined by lobster and a terrific range of fresh and smoked fish – all the ingredients you need for a seafood salad or stonking fish pie.

The gorgeous Globe is located on the same grassy square as the Crown and is its equal in every respect. The excellent food is Modern British in style, employs as much local produce as possible, and is served as bar snacks and full meals. The 19 contemporary-styled en-suite rooms – from luxury to 'bolthole' (£145-£190 double incl breakfast) – include five on the ground floor for easy access.

King's Arms

Westgate Street, Blakeney, NR25 7NQ (01263 740341, www.blakeneykingsarms. co.uk). Food served noon-2pm, 6-9pm daily.

A wonderfully old-school cosy pub near the Quay that's especially popular with walkers fresh from the salt marshes, who come to refuel on hearty dishes such as steak and ale suet pudding, Norfolk pork sausages and mash, or vegetable lasagne. There's also a board with daily specials and a real fire in the grate. And if you are staying the night, there are four guest bedrooms, two are dog-friendly (from £100 double incl breakfast), and three flats.

Where to stay

As you'd expect from such a popular area, there's a huge choice of accommodation, from cute self-catering cottages (try the pretty blue and white **Quayside cottages** at Blakeney, 01263 741533, www. blakeneycottages.co.uk; or small and sweet **Mach's Shack**, Burnt Street, Wells-next-the-Sea, 01328 711653, www.machrimore.co.uk) to B&Bs such as **Arch House** (50 Mill Road, Wells-next-the-Sea, 01328 710112, www.archhouse.co.uk), or the slightly more upscale **Meadowview Guest House** (53 High Street, Wighton, 01328 821527, www. meadow-view.net). Upmarket options include the luxurious **Blakeney House** guesthouse (High Street, Blakeney, 01263 740561, www. blakeneyhouse.com). In between, lots of great inns such as the **Crown**

Hotel (*see p51*) in Wells, and the **White Horse** (*see p51*) in Blakeney offer excellent accommodation.

Blakeney Hotel

Blakeney, NR25 7NE (01263 740797, www.blakeney-hotel.co.uk). Rates £150-£217 double incl breakfast.

This smart hotel's leisure features are a godsend in wet weather, with spa facilities, a heated pool, a gym and a games room. Sixty spacious rooms, some with balconies and private patios, others with wide-ranging views to the marshy estuary, will appeal to those who prefer hassle-free anonymity to B&B intimacy.

Cley Windmill ♥

Cley-next-the-Sea, NR25 7RP (01263 740209, www.cleymill.co.uk). Rates £189-£310 double incl breakfast.

This 18th-century windmill stands just outside the village, and has supreme views of the reed-rustling salt marshes and the distant sea. Choose from six rooms in the circular mill itself or opt for seclusion in one of four garden rooms, including the former boat house, located across a small courtyard from the mill, and in a converted outhouse. The Dovecote can also be rented on a self-catering basis.

High Sand Creek Campsite

Greenway, Stiffkey, NR23 1QF (01328 830235, www.highsandcreek campsitestiffkey.co.uk). Open Easter-Oct. Rates £30 per pitch for 2 people.

This lovely hillside campsite has fantastic views across the marshes, which are near enough to ensure plenty of birds and wildlife interest. The 80-pitch site (12 with electric hook-up) is clean, has great facilities and friendly, helpful staff. It's a three-mile walk along the coast path to Wells (you can take the CoastHopper bus back).

Kelling Heath

Weybourne, NR25 7HW (01263 588181, www.kellingheath.co.uk). Rates Camping £42-£55 per pitch for 2 people. Lodge or holiday home £940-1,563 per week.

Set in 250 acres of woodland and open heath, Kelling Heath has it all, from a campsite to attractive wooden lodges and luxury holiday homes (both sleeping up to to six). There's also a dizzying range of activities, including star-gazing nights, pond-dipping, cycling, swimming (in an indoor or outdoor pool) and tennis, as well as plenty of entertainment for all ages.

Morston Hall

The Street, Morston, NR25 7AA (01263 741041, www.morstonhall.com). Rates £380-£430 double incl breakfast & dinner.

This award-winning country house hotel in Morston is a bastion of traditional comfort without being overbearingly old-fashioned; think English country house with all mod cons. Most of the 13 guest rooms are pet-friendly, and six are open-plan Pavilion garden rooms. But it's the hotel's gastronomic credentials that are the real draw; Michelin-starred chef Galton Blackiston (who runs the hotel with his wife Tracy) produces a daily changing seven-course tasting menu for dinner, and a four-course set lunch menu on Sundays. His food draws on local produce cooked simply but exquisitely (just let them know if you have any dietary requirements when booking). Non-residents are welcome to eat too.

Old Town Hall House

Coast Road, Cley-next-the-Sea, NR25 7RB (01263 741439, www.oldtownhallhouse. com). Rates to be confirmed; check on the website (the hotel was shut at the time of writing but is set to open when government guidelines permit).

A quietly charming B&B, with four lovely rooms decorated in calming colours with splashes of colour and named after three birds and a smoked herring (sandpiper, kestrel, spoonbill and böckling). Slap-up breakfasts include the likes of kedgeree with locally smoked haddock. A self-catering apartment sleeping two is also available.

Red Lion

44 Wells Road, Stiffkey, NR23 1AJ (01328 830552, www.stiffkey.com). Rates £129-£149 double incl breakfast.

Blakeney see p49

A lovely eco-conscious village inn with big roaring fires, nooks and crannies, and ten light and airy guest rooms plus two suites. The first-floor rooms have balconies and expansive views across the Stiffkey Valley, while those on the ground floor have a terrace and communal garden area; all are quiet and clean. A short walk down the road, self-catering Manor Cottage sleeps up to six people. The food – good-quality pub grub – features local ingredients.

Weybourne Forest Lodges

Sandy Hill Lane, Weybourne, NR25 7HW (01263 588440, www. weybourneforestlodges.co.uk). Rates £365-£995 per week.

This small cluster of timber lodges in a forest glade in the middle of nowhere (well, three miles from Holt and Sheringham) is perfect for a getaway, with no clubhouse or entertainment, just lots of beautiful countryside. Different styles of lodges include large, A-frame Scandinavian buildings and more humble two-person cabins, but all come with heating, games, books, a TV and parking for two cars.

Things to do

WELLS TO WEYBOURNE

Blakeney Seal Trips

Seals can be seen in a number of places along Britain's coastline, but the beauty of the beasts at Blakeney Point is their proximity. At high tide, boats from Morston Quay (try Beans Boats, 01263 740038, www.beansboattrips.co.uk, or Temples Seal Trips, 01263 740791, www.sealtrips.co.uk) take visitors out to a seven-mile shingle spit where a sizeable colony of seals can be viewed at surprisingly close quarters. Carry on to the idyllic coastal village of Blakeney and you can go out to the point on foot, taking a desolate but wonderful two-and-a-half-mile hike along the coast path and back inland to Cley.

Wells & Walsingham Light Railway

Wells-next-the-Sea, NR23 1QB (01328 711630, www.wwlr.co.uk). Open Apr-Oct. Departures hourly 10am-4pm; check website for details. Tickets £5, children under 4 free; dogs travel free when trains aren't busy.

This is the world's longest 10.25in narrow-gauge steam railway, though at a little over five miles long, the half-hour journey is scarcely arduous. The diminutive train pulls its brightly painted carriages (some enclosed, others open-topped or part covered) through the Norfolk countryside to its destination on the outskirts of Walsingham. Refreshments are sold at Wells station.

INLAND TO EAST DEREHAM

Roarr Dinosaur Adventure

Weston Hall Road, NR9 5JE (01603 876310, www.roarrdinosauradventure.co.uk). Open 10am-5pm daily. Admission £18.95 (adults and children over 90cm); £9.48 reductions; children under 90cm free.

This replica dinosaur theme park will obviously delight young visitors, but it's a hoot for grown-ups too. Trek along the dinosaur trail, have a round of Jurassic Putt and take a stroll through the Neanderthal Walk. You can even get chased through the trees by a T-Rex and escape by zip-wire. There is also a water park complete with slides and cannon shoots as well as a splash zone for the smaller children.

Whitwell Station & Reepham Railway

Whitwell Road, Reepham, NR10 4BA (01603 871694, www.whitwellstation.com). Open 10am-4pm daily (from 8am for breakfast on Steam Sundays). Admission Station free; train tickets £3, £1 reductions.

Lovingly restored after being closed for 50 years, Whitwell & Reepham Railway runs Diesel Days (weekends, 10am-5pm on demand) and Steam Sundays (first Sunday of the month noon-4pm). There's a bookshop for train enthusiasts, a café/bar with a garden to relax in and a campsite.

INLAND TO EAST DEREHAM

Wiveton to Letheringsett

Inland north Norfolk has charms that are no less pleasurable than its coastal counterparts; they're just less obvious. The pretty little villages of **Kelling** and **Wiveton** are just a couple of miles from the sea; lovely views can be had from the pub garden at the **Pheasant** (01263 588382, www. pheasanthotelnorfolk.co.uk), set on rising ground in Kelling, and from the **Wiveton Bell** (01263 740101, www. wivetonbell.co.uk). The latter is next to a lovely church in the rolling landscape of Wiveton Downs and just a short walk from the magical **Wiveton Farm Café** (*see p66*).

Glandford too is a delight. It's a model village built at the start of the 20th century by Sir Alfred Jodrell, and contains flint and red-brick Dutch-style gabled houses; **St Martin's Church**, which has a beautiful roof and stained glass; **Birdscapes Gallery** (Manor Farm Barns, 01263 741742, www.birdscapesgallery.co.uk); and Norfolk's oldest purpose-built museum, the tiny and gorgeous **Shell Museum** (*see p53*). Sir Alfred lived at nearby Bayfield Hall (Holt, 01263 713901, www.bayfieldhall.com), now a wedding and events venue. The brick and flint building of the Old Stables houses **Bayfield Hall Antiques and Interiors** (01263 715538, www. bayfieldhallantiques.com), with specialist traders in everything from painted furniture to Persian rugs. Nearby, at 3 Bayfield Brecks, you can find **Bray's Cottage Pork Pies** (phone ahead to buy the mouth-watering pies – 01263 712958, www.perfectpie.co.uk).

This is an area of rolling hills criss-crossed with public paths and bridleways, with something of interest at almost every turn. Just a couple of miles south-west of Wiveton, the village of **Binham** contains the evocative ruins of **Binham Priory**,

plus a nice pub, the **Chequers Inn** (Front Street, 01328 830297, www. binhamchequersinn.co.uk). Nearby **Langham** is home to the biennial summertime **Street Fayre** (www. langhamstreetfayre.com).

Heading slightly further inland, **Letheringsett**'s still-working flour watermill (*see p52*) is consistently voted one of the county's best attractions. Stop for lunch at the **Kings Head** (*see p65*), a rambling beauty of a pub in a lovely garden setting, before popping into the well-stocked farm shop and gallery **Back to the Garden** (*see p60*), just outside the village. From here it's just a mile to the Georgian town of Holt.

Holt ♥

This handsome market town easily gives Burnham Market a run for its money. In some ways it's a better base and a more interesting town; less monied, more youthful and vibrant, with plenty to keep your interest for a weekend, as well as a pleasant escape route to Sheringham via the North Norfolk Railway, aka the **Poppy Line** (*see p79*). Most of the town was consumed by fire in May 1708; one of the few medieval buildings to survive is part of Gresham's public school. Christmas is a lovely time to visit Holt, with many considering the lights to be the best in the county.

The centre is pretty compact, with most shops and businesses on or near the High Street and Market Place, with an antiques enclave around Albert Street. Excellent independent shops range from department store **Bakers & Larners** (8-12 Market Place, 01263 712244, www.bakersand larners.co.uk, closed Sun), which has a fine food hall, to clothing shops such as cult classic **Old Town** (*see p60*) and **Annie & Boo** (01263 712020). In addition, there are vintage shops such as **Past Caring** and great bric-a-brac, homeware and antiques to be found.

EXT TRAIN

DEPARTING

ROM
FORM 1

TO
OLT

EAM | HAULED

RUNNING TODAY

NER B12	BR 9F 2-10-0
-0 8572	92203 Black Prince
2-10-0	BR 4MT
90775	2-6-0 76084

Holt station on the **Poppy Line** see p79

Wiveton Farm Café see p66

The best independent shops

Back to the Garden 💚
Letheringsett, NR25 7JJ (01263 715996, www.back-to-the-garden.co.uk). Open 8.15am-5pm Mon-Sat; 9am-4pm Sun.

Just off the A149, Barney Farm produces a wide range of organic meat, vegetables and fruit and sells it here in a large barn. The huge ceilings and airy space are a far cry from most farm shops, and the café and Restaurant Garden are great places to stop for breakfast, lunch or a snack – meals are made using the shop's impressive range of cheeses, organic meats, deli goods, charcuterie, vegetables and breads.

Bircham Gallery
14 Market Place, Holt, NR25 6BW (01263 713312, www.birchamgallery.co.uk). Open 9am-5pm Mon-Sat.

A great contemporary art space showing and selling the work of some 200 artists and craftspeople, with an emphasis on modern work and a nice range of prices – linos and prints start at around £50. The ceramics and printmaking selections are particularly good.

Bringing the Outside In
Staithe Street, Wells-next-the-Sea (01328 713093, www.bringingtheoutsidein.co.uk). Open 10.30am-4pm Mon, Wed-Sun.

Recently relocated from the original studio space in Holkham village (now housing California beach-inspired Ocotillo), Martin Billing has opened a much larger store in Wells-next-the-Sea, still displaying his ever-changing and no less browsable collection of artefacts, ceramics, tableware, houseplants, textiles, vintage finds and so on. Next door is GROUND, a coffee house and eatery.

Fakenham Chapel Antiques
Old Congregational Church, 14 Norwich Road, Fakenham, NR21 8AZ (01328 851911, www.fakenhamantiques.co.uk). Open 10am-4.30pm Mon-Sat.

Some 20 dealers sell everything from furniture, lighting and homeware to prints, books and jewellery. It's a fun space in which to browse and there's no pressure to buy, just friendly dealers happy to talk about their wares (or about featuring in the BBC's *Antiques Road Trip*) if you want them to.

Gallery Plus
Warham Road, Wells-next-the-Sea, NR23 1QA (01328 711609, www.gallery-plus.co.uk). Open Tue-Sat 10am-4pm.

This appealing art and design shop, gallery and studio is owned and run by Trevor and Joanna Woods, who display and sell a wide range of 2D art including prints, etchings, photos and paintings, as well as 3D pieces such as jewellery and ceramics.

Made in Cley
High Street, Cley-next-the-Sea, NR25 7RF (01263 740134, www.madeincley.co.uk). Open 10am-5pm Mon-Sat; 11am-4pm Sun.

The brightly painted exterior draws you into a warm and welcoming space where you can browse the hand-thrown stoneware pottery for the home and garden (made in the on-site workshop), as well as prints, photography and jewellery.

Old Town 💚
49 Bull Street, Holt, NR25 6HP (01263 710001, www.old-town.co.uk). Open 10am-5pm Tue-Sat. By appointment only until autumn 2021.

This wonderful clothing manufacturer and retailer produces around 50 understated garments every week from its workshop

Two galleries – **Bircham** (*see above*) and **Red Dot** (7 Fish Hill, 01263 710287, www.thereddotgallery.com) – are definitely worth a browse.

There's plenty of food too, with a dizzying range of restaurants and tearooms that span the gamut from good down-to-earth café (**Charlie's** on Appleyard and the **Owl Tea Room** on Church Street) via pub grub (the **Kings Head** on the High Street, and **The Pigs**, *see p65*) to high-quality fare at **Number Ten** restaurant in Bakers & Larners, and **Byfords** (*see p64*), which has rooms at its Posh B&B.

Just three miles south-east of Holt, the extensive ruins of **Baconsthorpe Castle**, a moated and fortified using beautiful British cottons, woollens and linens. Along with a pleasing range of accessories (the handsome ties make great gifts), Old Town offers made-to-order items too. Choose your fabric and garment from a range that includes dresses, jackets, waistcoats and shirts.

Osokozi Gallery

6 Albert Street, Holt, NR25 6HX (01263 711363, www.osokozi.co.uk). Open 9am-5pm Mon-Sat.

A colourful bazaar of goods from all around the globe, ranging from Rye pottery to Afghan glass and Persian ceramics, as well as ethnic and silver jewellery.

Walsingham Farms Shop

Guild Street, Walsingham, NR22 6BU (01328 821877, www.walsingham.co). Open 9am-5pm Mon-Sat; 10am-4pm Sun (closed on Mon in winter).

Local producers and farmers are showcased here, with a tantalising array of fresh and prepared food. The range includes salami from Suffolk, vegetables from nearby allotment holders, honey from Walsingham bees and a mouth-watering range of picnic goodies made in the shop's kitchen.

Wells Deli 💜

15 The Quay, Wells-next-the-Sea, NR23 1AH (01328 711171, www.wellsdeli.co.uk). Open 9am-5pm daily.

The cornucopia of goodies served in this relaxed little deli-café includes a fantastic range of sandwiches (try fresh crab) and takeaway dishes using local meats and fish. There are also warming soups plus cakes and pastries to go with the excellent coffee.

15th-century manor house run by English Heritage, are fun to explore, and you can chart the rise and fall of the once-prominent Heydon family. A couple of miles out of Holt on the A148 towards Cromer, the rare bookseller Simon Finch's unusual **Arts and Crafts house Voewood** (*see p66*) is a must-see.

Little Walsingham to East Barsham

Further inland, to the east, lies Little Walsingham. This handsome medieval village, really more of a small town, has been an important place of Christian pilgrimage for almost 1,000 years. Even now, half a million devout members of the Catholic and Orthodox churches are drawn each year to the modern Anglican shrine of **Our Lady of Walsingham**, the 600-year-old **Roman Catholic Slipper Chapel** (*see p53*), the ruins of the old Priory, and the **Chapel of St Seraphim**, a Russian Orthodox church housed in the old railway station. An enjoyable day can be spent in a variety of ways: wandering the narrow streets, admiring the half-timbered medieval buildings, popping into gift shops (religious souvenirs a speciality) and tea shops (the Walsingham tearoom does a mean pot of char and toasted teacake). For more substantial meals, **The Bull** on the High Street serves good grub. Gather the makings of a great picnic at the **Walsingham Farms Shop** (*see left*), and enjoy it amid the peaceful gardens of **Walsingham Abbey** (*see p53*). A Christmas fair is usually held in the village on the third weekend of November.

Poor old Great Walsingham, by contrast, is a misnomer if ever there was one, but it is worth a stop, not least for an enjoyable crafts and galleries mall at **Great Walsingham Barns** (10am-4.30pm Tue-Sun) and some pretty-as-a-picture cottages. Heading south, park at the **Barsham Arms** pub at East Barsham to check out the amazing battlemented red-brick Tudor manor house occupied by Henry VIII when he made the pilgrimage to Walsingham shrine – the house is closed to the public, but you can get fine views of the famed chimneys, towers, turrets and mullioned windows if you walk up to the rise facing it.

Fakenham & East Dereham

The market town of **Fakenham** is just a few miles further inland from here. The route is crossed by the pretty River Wensum, and further along the A1067 Norwich to Fakenham road is the magical **Foxley Wood**, Norfolk's largest area of ancient woodland. But the town itself offers few diversions or attractions. Its one-time Georgian grandeur is evident in the Market Square, but the place has a somewhat shabby, workaday demeanour. There's the odd architectural delight, such as the cinema, the market cross and old gasworks (now the Fakenham **Museum of Gas**, 07909 890484, www.fakenhamgasmuseum.com), plus a lively Thursday market.

On the outskirts of town, **Fakenham racecourse** (01328 862388, www. fakenhamracecourse.co.uk) makes a nice day out. The nearby **Thursford**

Collection (*see p53*) and **Pensthorpe Nature Reserve** (*see p52*) offer good excursions for families – as does the Norfolk Wildlife Trust site at **Thursford Wood**, about three miles north-east of Fakenham (on the A148 road towards Cromer). The oaks here are some of the oldest in the county and provide refuge for an array of wildlife.

From Fakenham it's a short hop south to **East Dereham**, with a look at the ruins of **North Elmham**'s 1,000-year-old **Saxon cathedral** on the way, but there's little reason to spend much time in the town nearest to Norfolk's geographical centre. It's key attractions are the marketplace, home to some elegant 18th-century houses (marred by insensitive shopfront conversions), a mad Gothic Revival Congregational chapel and, facing it, a corn hall turned into a cinema. **Bishop Bonner's Cottage Museum** of local history (01362 691455, www.derehamhistory.com,

Baconsthorpe Castle *see p60*

check website for opening times) is housed in a very pretty 1502 cottage at the bottom of Church Street. Best of all is the two-towered church of **St Nicholas**, a mainly 14th- and 15th-century structure with a 13th-century chancel and a wonderful font depicting the seven sacraments.

North-east to Reepham & the coast

Heading back towards the coast, a swathe of villages close to each other all reward exploration, whether you're into history, bucolic scenery, architecture or walking. **Swanton Morley**, lying in a hollow near the River Wensum, is famous for being home to the ancestors of Abraham Lincoln (the home of Richard Lincoln, who lived here in the 16th century, is now the Angel Inn). Other favourites include **Elsing**, which contains one of the country's best church brasses (in 14th-century St Mary's) and 15th-century **Elsing Hall**, whose gardens are occasionally open to the public. **Lyng** is pretty as a picture and offers some great riverside walking; **Lenwade** has a highly rated **Roarr Dinosaur Adventure** (*see p57*; and the area around handsome **Swannington** further east offers some wonderful walks through terrain that takes in heathland, woods, fens, meadows and even a small hill.

The nicest area is around the conservation town of **Reepham**, a few miles north-west of Swannington. It's full of quaint thatched cottages and 18th-century brick houses tidily arranged around a neat marketplace, where a weekly Wednesday market is held. The town also contains a pleasing selection of independent shops: **Very Nice Things** has everything from art and crafts to homeware and books; and **Diane's Pantry** is a deli and café. There are two good pubs and a clutch of

Our Lady of Walsingham *see p61*

restaurants and tearooms (including one in what used to be Reepham train station; you can also pick up the long-distance Marriott's Way trail here). Of the two churches sharing the same churchyard, **St Mary** is worth exploring in some detail; highlights include a lovely ironwork door leading to the tower and a rather magnificent tombchest in the chancel.

But it's to **Salle** and **Booton**, just outside Reepham, that lovers of church architecture should head. **St Peter & St Paul** in Salle is built in splendid 15th-century Perpendicular style and is an awe-inspiring sight; it also has a beautiful interior. Booton's **St Michael & All Angels** is altogether more controversial, a Gothic fantasy designed and built in the 19th century by Reverend Whitwell Elwin. He, magpie-like, took elements of all his favourite church architecture to construct a crazy-looking building that's also glorious, not least for its slender twin towers and central pinnacle (*see p74 and p141*).

The final village, **Heydon**♥, is possibly the most attractive, being a privately owned estate village that could be straight out of the pages of an Agatha Christie novel. Ranged around a delightful village green are the 13th-century **St Peter & St Paul Church**, the whitewashed **Earle Arms** (*see right*), a tearoom (*also see right*) and about 30 impossibly pretty houses. A mile away, **Heydon Hall Park** offers some great walks.

Wending your way back to the coast, the charming villages of **Melton Constable** and the **Snorings** (Great and Little) are exactly as their names suggest; sleepy, ancient and picturesque villages that have changed little in the last century, and will probably change little in the next.

Where to eat & drink

Almost every village in this area has a pub; almost all of them are called The Crown, and almost all of them are worth at least a pint stop; some, like **The Crown** in Colkirk (Crown Road, 01328 258714) are even worth eating in. In Holt, try the **Owl Tea Room** (Church Street, 01263 713232, closed Sun) for a snack or the **Lawns hotel** (*see p66*) for a more refined setting. Fish lovers should head to the **Old Forge Seafood Restaurant** (01328 878345, www.seafoodnorthnorfolk. co.uk, bookings only Jan, Feb) in Thursford, on the A148 between Fakenham and Holt, where most of the shellfish (lobsters, crabs, oysters, mussels) comes from Blakeney.

Byfords Café, Deli & Posh B&B♥
1-3 Shirehall Plain, Holt, NR25 6BG (01263 711400, www.byfords.org. uk). Food served 8am-8pm Mon-Sat, 8am-6pm Sun.

Ideally located on the market square, Byfords is usually heaving, and it's easy to see why. The café is as cosy as they come and the food exemplary: a Mediterranean-influenced selection with plenty of local ingredients. Takeaway food is available at the Deli (including a wide range of ready meals), and the 16 rooms in the Posh B&B (£170-£210 double incl breakfast) make stylish use of local materials.

Earle Arms♥
The Green, Heydon, NR11 6AD (01263 687001). Open noon-11.30pm Wed-Sun. Lunch served noon-2pm; dinner served 6-8.30pm Wed-Sun.

This unspoilt, largely unmodernised village is popular with film and TV crews – *Jeeves and Wooster* was shot here, for example. Fittingly, the 16th-century village inn is all gnarled beams and wood panelling. Daily specials are cooked with flair and imagination, with local produce to the fore; book ahead if you want to sample them.

Heydon Village Teashop
The Street, Heydon, NR11 6AD (01263 587211, www.heydonvillageteashop. co.uk). Opening hours to be confirmed once government restrictions are lifted; check on the website.

White lacy tablecloths, crockery decorating the walls and a warm terracotta flagstone floor tell you this is a totally traditional tearoom, and that's before you clap eyes on the gigantic sponges and slabs of chocolate cake. It's a surprisingly large space, with lovely views out to the village green, and staff couldn't be friendlier.

Hunworth Bell
The Green, Hunworth, NR24 2AA (01263 711151, www.hunworthbell.co.uk). Pub open all day Wed-Sun. Food served noon-2pm, 5.30-8.30pm Wed-Sat; noon-6pm Sun.

A beautiful village pub and restaurant that serves Modern British food using locally sourced seasonal ingredients (Cromer crabs, Holkham beef and herbs and veg from the pub garden) in a dining room made cosy with warm tones of terracotta,

St Michael & All Angels, Booton see p63

brick and golden wood, and also on a garden terrace.

Kings Head 💚

Holt Road, Letheringsett, NR25 7AR (01263 712691, www.kingsheadnorfolk. co.uk). Open noon-9pm; food served noon-8.30pm daily.

With its great location, convivial atmosphere, good selection of ales and wines and wide-ranging menu, the Kings Head contines to attract both locals and visitors. Upstairs are four stylish rooms (£120-£150 double incl breakfast).

Pigs 💚

Norwich Road, Edgefield, NR24 2RL (01263 587634, www.thepigs.org.uk). Open daily from 8am. Food served noon-8pm Fri-Sun.

Wise diners take heed: the Modern British food served at this pretty village pub is worth travelling miles for. If the miles clocked up make you feel a tad guilty, you'll feel decidedly virtuous eating the carefully sourced venison sausages, steaks and belly pork – the meat is locally reared, and comes via butchers and farmers who practise good animal husbandry. Snacks, Norfolk tapas (otherwise known as 'iffits'), a piglets' menu and a decent drinks list complete the dining picture. There's a bar billiards table too and indoor and outdoor play areas. The 19 comfortable and contemporary spa rooms are all individually decorated (£220-£290 double incl breakfast).

Wheatsheaf

Church Road, West Beckham, NR25 6NX (01263 822110). Open 11am-11pm Mon-Sat, noon-10.30pm Sun. Lunch served noon-3pm daily; dinner served 6.30pm-9pm.

This sprawling, ivy-clad country pub just a few miles from Holt is a real gem. There's a pretty covered terrace and a large garden. Inside is a cosy beamed bar area and dining room warmed by a roaring wood-burning stove. The food is hearty pub grub with a few more adventurous dishes and is obviously popular – book ahead or risk disappointment. Upstairs are five traditional guest rooms (£103-£167 double incl breakfast).

Wiveton Farm Café ♥
Wiveton Hall, 1 Marsh Lane, Wiveton, NR25 7TE (01263 741001, www.wivetonhall. co.uk). Food served 9:30am-3:30pm daily; wood-fired pizzas served 5pm-sunset Wed-Sun.

In and around a building reminiscent of a large beach shack, brightly painted rickety furniture, flowery tablecloths and pretty mismatched crockery create a distinctly rural Mediterranean feel, as though you're about to sit down for a long leisurely lunch with a large Italian family. And the food is everything you could hope for: a great range of surprisingly delicate and sophisticated daily-changing meals and snacks that use as many ingredients from the farm as possible. The charming shop sells jams and produce made using the farm's own fruits.

Where to stay

The **Kings Head** in Letheringsett (*see p65*), and **Byfords Posh B&B** (*see p64*) are two of the nicest places to stay in the area, but if they're full there are plenty of pleasant alternatives, particularly if you're fond of comfortable, intimate B&Bs. For serious luxury in a unique building, gather together your friends and book **Voewood** (01263 713029, www.voewood.com), a splendid Arts and Crafts mansion with room for 42 guests.

Lawns
26 Station Road, Holt, NR25 6BS (01263 713390, www.lawnshotelholt.co.uk). Rates £125-£165 double incl breakfast.

This elegant house is a great example of Holt's Georgian architecture, and is equally impressive inside, with eight light-filled rooms decorated in period colours to create a real sense of warmth and comfort. There are also two garden rooms with twin beds and walk-in shower. In the pretty dining room, Modern British food (pan-fried sea bass with crispy potatoes and seasonal greens, say) comes nicely cooked.

Quaker Barns
Quaker Barns, School Road, Haveringland, NR10 4QF (07968 872898, www.quakerbarns.co.uk). Rates from £1,125 per week.

Perfect for big groups, these two award-winning barns (Quaker Barn and Hall Barn, sleeping eight and nine respectively) have been beautifully converted into contemporary living spaces available for a two-night weekend through to a week's stay. Pastel tongue-and-groove and wood-burning stoves brighten and warm large rooms that feature a fascinating array of materials, from flint-peppered walls and resin floors to granite worktops and exposed oak beams.

Wensum Lodge Hotel
Bridge Street, Fakenham, NR21 9AY (01328 862100, www.wensumlodge. co.uk). Rates £89-£99 double incl breakfast.

This 18th-century grainstore turned hotel and restaurant has a lovely riverside setting. Inside there are basic rooms and apartments. Don't expect luxury, but it is a decent base for exploring nearby attractions such as the Thursford Collection and Pensthorpe Nature Reserve (for both *see p52*).

Cley Marshes *see p52*

Cromer &
Sheringham

As the north Norfolk coast curves around to the east, rolling dunes and nature-rich marshes give way to decidedly more traditional seaside views and landscapes, particularly in the once-grand Victorian resorts of Sheringham and Cromer. In summer the towns' sandy beaches are packed, but winter is glorious too for windswept walks scored to the explosion of waves against the sea defences. At high tide, the sand is completely covered and only pebbles remain on view, backed by past-their-best hotels and fishermen's cottages. Inland, stately architectural wonders such as Blickling Hall and Felbrigg Hall, numerous round- and square-towered churches of singular design, two fabulous steam railways and the market town of Aylsham mean there's lots to do when you've had your fill of sand, crabs and watery sunsets.

And, finally, the area can lay claim to one very special attribute: the highest point in Norfolk. Take a trip on the Poppy Line or play a round on Sheringham golf course and it becomes clear that the land here is anything but flat, a fact attributable to the rolling nine-mile-long glacial Cromer Ridge that runs beside the coast. The apex of the ridge, Beacon's Hill, is just a 15-minute walk south from West Runton, and at 338 feet above sea level makes for a rare, knee-flexing Norfolk walk. Bring a picnic and enjoy the terrific views.

SHERINGHAM & THE RUNTONS

Sheringham

Arriving fresh from the abundant beauty and affluence of west Norfolk, the faded seaside resort of Sheringham may initially feel like a slap in the face with a cold wet fish, but wander round for half an hour and the quiet charms of this genteel town start to become apparent. It began as a fishing village, and the links with the sea remain – if you're lucky you might hear the Sheringham Shantymen (www.shantymen.com)

singing in the pub one night. The town is easily accessible by train – the Bittern Line runs here from Norwich – but remote enough to have retained its independent shops.

And it has real character, from an esplanade with attractive public gardens, model-boating lake and gleaming pre-war tiled public toilets to fine sea views and a Blue Flag beach backed by sizeable cliffs. Walk along the top for glorious vistas, especially at sunset; head lower down and you'll pass colourful beach huts and small fishing boats. The Norfolk Coast Path runs through the town, but a short

stroll along the front is pleasure enough, particularly at night when you can wander beneath the illuminations. The **High Street** climbing away from the sea is similarly appealing, chock-a-block with cafés, ice-cream parlours and seaside-tat shops that give way to better cafés, bistros, a butcher, greengrocer and, of course, charity shops.

Antiques and bric-a-brac fans can delve for knick-knacks in the **Trading Post** (Wyndham Street) and **Sheringham Collectables** (Melbourne Road), and everything else at the **street market** on Wednesday and Saturday. Food too is wide-ranging, from DIY options such as **Seafare** (Church Street) to the wondrous interiors of **Crofters Austrian restaurant** (High Street), with its blue gingham curtains, dark rich wood, and beams taken from the old North Norfolk railway station.

A growing number of more modern bistros suggests the British hobby of keeping up with the neighbours seems to be having a positive influence, and pubs such as **The Lobster** (High Street) and the **Wyndham Arms** (Wyndham Street) offer excellent horizon-gazing, beer-supping spots. Opposite the Wyndham, a little nugget of history is commemorated by a blue plaque in the diminutive Whitehall Yard. Here, at 8.30pm on 19 January 1915, the first bomb was dropped on Britain in World War I (it didn't explode).

The Runtons

East of Sheringham, the tiny villages of West and **East Runton** offer excellent sandy beaches (reached via lanes off the A149) and little else, making them ideal for the quiet pleasures of sandcastle-building, rockpooling and clambering over sea-defence barriers at low tide, and immersing yourself in the waves at

Cromer see p78

Places to visit

SHERINGHAM & THE RUNTONS

Hillside Animal & Shire Horse Sanctuary
West Runton, NR27 9QH (01603 736200, www.hillside.org.uk). Open Easter-Oct 10am-5pm Sun-Fri. Admission £6, free-£5 reductions; by donation only while government restrictions are in place.

More than 300 horses, ponies, donkeys and mules, including the magnificent Ardennes breed of Shire horse, are looked after here, as well as cows, sheep, pigs and even a couple of ostriches – many of them rescued from factory farms or the slaughterhouse. There are harnessing demonstrations three times a week in summer, but this is definitely not a petting zoo; the emphasis is on the welfare of the animals and campaigning against cruel farming methods. There's an indoor play area for wet days, as well as a gift shop and café. Hillside has another animal sanctuary at Frettenham.

Peter Coke Shell Gallery
West Cliff, Sheringham, NR26 8JT (www. sheringham-preservation.org.uk). At time of going to press the gallery was closed; check website for opening times.

Actor, playwright and sea shell sculptor Peter Coke died at the age of 95 in 2008, leaving behind this fascinating museum filled with more than 180 of his weird and wonderful sea shell sculptures. Inspired by the 'sailor's valentines' sculptures produced by seafarers in the 18th century, the works include incredibly intricate 'flower' arrangements, model garden scenes and finely detailed pagodas – all made from a variety of (often tiny) shells in natural colours.

Priory Maze & Gardens
Cromer Road, Beeston Regis, NR26 8SF (01263 820942, www.priorymazegardens. co.uk). At time of going to press the gardens were closed; check website for opening times.

A quiz trail and enjoyably (but not frustratingly) difficult hedge maze, based on the footprint of the nearby ruined Beeston Priory, will keep youngsters happy. Meanwhile, the grown-ups can delight in the formal gardens, woodlands, meadows and tearoom.

Sheringham Museum at the Mo
Lifeboat Plain, Sheringham, NR26 8BG (01263 824482, www.sheringhammuseum.co.uk). Open 11am-1pm, 2pm-4pm Wed-Sat (opening times to be confirmed after restrictions are lifted; check on the website).

Opened in 2010, this local museum bills itself as a 'place of people and boats'. It is stuffed with fascinating historical artefacts and displays charting the town's changing fortunes as it went from fishing town to Victorian seaside charmer. Perched on the coastline, the location ensures fabulous views.

Sheringham Park
Wood Farm, Upper Sheringham, NR26 8TL (01263 820550, www.nationaltrust.org.uk). Open 9.30am-4.30pm daily. Café Easter-Oct 10am-4pm. Admission free. Parking £6.50

Blickling Hall *see p74*

(at busy times parking space must be pre-booked).

Humphry Repton's fabulous design for this vast park takes in woodlands, parkland and stunning gardens, where the displays of azaleas and rhododendrons (mid May to June) are legendary. There are heaps of walks and paths, but a favourite is to walk through the park to the coast and back to Sheringham along the cliffs.

CROMER

Amazona Zoo
Hall Road, NR27 9JG (01263 510741, www.amazona zoo.co.uk). Open Apr-Nov 10am-5pm daily. Admission £9.90; free-£8.90 reductions.

Big cats roam happily it seems in the feline forest of this ten-acre zoo, where a range

of critters, including snakes, parrots, fish and monkeys, offer a couple of hours of amusement and education for children. The one-time derelict woodland site makes the most of pre-existing habitats; brick kilns are now used as a winter hibernating shelter for bats, for example.

Cromer Church & Tower
30 Cromwell Road, NR27 0BE (01263 512000, www.cromer-church.org.uk). Open June-Sept 9am-5pm Mon-Sat; 9-11.45am, 7-9pm Sun.

St Peter & St Paul boasts the county's highest church tower, at 160ft; if your knees can take it, in the summer you can climb the 172 steps to the top for magnificent views. The lofty interior has some some good modern stained glass, including depictions of lifeboats, the lighthouse and buckets and spades. It is believed that a smuggler's tunnel once linked St Peter & St Paul to Cromer Hall, half a mile away.

Cromer Museum
Church Street, NR27 9HB (01263 513543, www.museums.norfolk.gov.uk). Open Mar-Oct. Admission £4.40; free-£4.20 reductions. The museum was closed at the time of going to press; opening times to be confirmed, check website.

If you're visiting Cromer Church, it's worth popping next door into this small local history museum, housed in a Victorian fisherman's cottage. There are plenty of old photos, fossils and other items to gawp at, and plenty of themed events and dressing-up days for children in the summer holidays. There is also a display celebrating the life and work of pioneering Norfolk photographer Olive Edis.

RNLI Henry Blogg Museum
The Rocket House, The Gangway, NR27 9ET (01263 511294, www.rnli.org.uk). Open Wed-Sun 10am-5pm. Admission free.

Named after coxswain Henry Blogg, the RNLI's most decorated lifeboater and a man who helped to save 873 lives around the Cromer coast, this little museum about the town's lifeboat crews is a particular hit with kids, who can dress up, practise Morse code and play with model boats.

Places to visit

INLAND TO AYLSHAM

Blickling Hall 💜
www.nationaltrust.org.uk/blicklingestate. Open Hall 11am-3pm daily; Garden summer 10am-5pm; winter 10am-4pm; Park dawn-dusk. Admission Hall & Gardens £10, free-£5 reductions. Park free. Advance booking recommended at busy times, including for parking.

Beautifully laid out to present a stunning aspect and approach from the moment it comes into view, this magnificent Jacobean red-brick mansion has many pleasures, from the Long Gallery to the glorious plasterwork ceilings and excellent collections of furniture, pictures, tapestries and books – the servants' library is a real eye-opener. Outside, there are superb formal gardens, including an orangery, and a huge park that features meadows, woods and an artificial lake surrounding the house. At one time the place belonged to the Boleyn family; look out for the ghost (headless, of course) of Anne Boleyn. There are bicycles available to hire at the cycle hub (01263 733708), including electric bikes, tagalongs and balance bikes. And with over 4,600 acres to explore, you can decide your own route or follow the four-mile off-road multi-use trail.

Felbrigg Hall 💜
Felbrigg, nr Cromer, NR11 8PR (01263 833444, www.nationaltrust.org.uk). Open House spring noon-4pm Mon-Wed, Sat & Sun; summer noon-4pm daily; winter closed. Garden Easter-Oct 10am-4pm daily. Park 9.30am-4pm daily. Admission £8, free-£4 reductions. Advance booking recommended at busy times.

An impressive and fascinating mix of 17th-century architecture with 18th-century furniture and pictures and interior remodelling makes this elegant, good-sized country house a real pleasure to explore. The Chinese bedroom with its hand-painted 18th-century wallpaper is particularly fine. Outside, a walled garden, orangery and extensive park and woodland ensure plenty of photo-taking opportunities.

Mannington Estate
Mannington Hall, NR11 7BB (01263 584175, www.manningtongardens.co.uk). Mannington Gardens Open June-Sept 11am-5pm Thur, Fri & Sun; Park dawn-dusk daily; Hall by appointment only. At the time of going to press, only the park was open; gardens are set to open once government restrictions have been lifted. For admission please check the website.

Mannington, the estate of Lord and Lady Walpole, is a medieval moated manor with a stunning landscaped garden, a superb collection of roses and a sensory garden with water feature and plants selected for touch, sound and taste, scent and colour. There's also a lakeside walk and a tea room. The park provides miles of waymarked footpaths through wildflower meadows and ancient woodland.

St Michael & All Angels
Church Road, Booton, NR10 4NZ (www.visitchurches.org.uk). Admission free.

This eccentric, late 19th-century Gothic-style folly is the work of one Reverend Whitwell Elwin (a descendent of Pocahontas, no less), who cherry-picked all his favourite bits of churches around the country and, with no architectural input, constructed a structure that incorporates a minaret-like pinnacle and two skinny, soaring twin towers. Edwin Lutyens described it as 'very naughty but built in the right spirit'. The wooden angels were carved by James Minns, more famous for creating the bull's head that still features on Colman's Mustard packaging.

Fellbrigg Hall

Sheringham *see p69*

75

high tide. The rock beds that form the cliffs along this stretch of coast are almost two million years old in parts, and a haven for fossil hunters (evidence of rhinos, hyenas and, most famously, a 16-foot-high mammoth have been found here).

West Runton has a decent pint-and-grub stop in the form of the pretty

Four Norfolk art galleries

Bircham Gallery
Holt's best art gallery stocks the work of more than 200 artists and craftspeople, including a wide range of very affordable prints. See p60.

Cat Pottery
Offering a mad mix of wild- and wide-eyed china cats sitting on every conceivable surface, and old railway memorabilia, this pottery-cum-shop in North Walsham is a photographer's dream. See p104.

Norwich Castle Museum & Art Gallery
From horses and bucolic countryside scenes by local old boy Alfred Munnings to contemporary works by photographer Richard Billingham and YBA Abigail Lane, the Castle's permanent collection and temporary exhibitions are always worth a look. See p92.

Sainsbury Centre
Norwich's major art gallery, housed in an award-winning Norman Foster building. Ancient figurative pieces that are teeny-tiny in size but huge in importance sit alongside paintings by Francis Bacon in an occasionally changing but always fascinating juxtaposition. See p93.

Bircham Gallery

Village Inn, while the **Hillside Animal & Shire Horse Sanctuary** (*see p72*) will entertain children for a couple of hours. Nearby, **Beeston Regis** village is the centre of 30 acres of heath and woodland for walkers who prefer solitude to the seaside screams of seagulls and overexcited children. Next to St Mary's, a ruined Augustinian priory, is **Priory Maze** (*see p72*), combining gardens with a hedge maze, plant centre and tearoom.

East Runton is larger and has more facilities, including a village shop that stays open until 9pm (a rarity in these parts). A duck pond and large green with a play area add to the child-friendly appeal, and a chip shop and the **Fishing Boat** pub, on the High Street, should ensure a happy day for the grown-ups too.

Where to eat & drink

There's plenty of choice in Sheringham, though no outstanding pub. Of the numerous cafés, try **Roy Boys** (37 Station Road, 01263 822960, www.royboys.co.uk, closed Sun) for a decent bacon sarnie or cooked breakfast. On the High Street, **Ellie's Sweet Shop** has a great range of Ronaldo's ice-cream (*see p43*) – and often a queue – while **Pungleperrys** is a coffee shop and ice-cream parlour, and **Joyful West's Shellfish Bar** (01263 825444) serves the best crab sandwiches in Norfolk. The Wests, one of Sheringham's oldest fishing families, make the sandwiches to order from freshly boiled crustaceans. For fish and chips, **Daves** (7-11 Co-operative Street, 01263 823830, www.davesofsheringham.com) is recommended.

East and West Runton offer good beach-based options, from takeaway chips to tasty sandwiches and full-blown pub meals.

Sheringham *see p69*

setting that's the main draw; the large bay windows offer great sea views. The six guest rooms are comfortable and welcoming, and some have great sea views (£135-£140 double incl breakfast).

Where to stay

There are no boutique hotel options in this area, so the choice lies between cosy B&Bs or rather old-fashioned hotels. Sheringham's plethora of B&Bs means finding a decent, well-priced room shouldn't be hard; there are plenty of options on the Rise and Holway Road. Our favourites offer something a little special, whether it's as simple as a fridge with fresh milk or views that are as expansive as the never-ending horizons.

At the other end of the scale, the **Links Country Park Hotel** (01263 838383, www.links-hotel.co.uk, £190-£235 double incl breakfast; online discounts available) in West Runton won't win any architecture or fashion awards, but it does have 35 acres of lightly wooded coastal parkland, a nine-hole golf course, a tennis courst, an indoor swimming pool and a gym.

The Dales ♥

Lodge Hill, Sheringham, NR26 8TJ (01263 824555, www.dalescountryhouse. co.uk). Rates £210-£255 double incl breakfast (online discounts available).

Spacious rooms – 23 in total , including seven suites – stuffed with sumptuous fabrics and impressive oak furniture, alongside stained-glass windows and big open fireplaces, make the interior of this Grade II-listed Victorian rectory cosy and luxurious. Outside, in the four acres of gardens, you can take a turn round the Norfolk-shaped pond or indulge in country pursuits such as tennis and croquet.

Manor Farm Camping & Caravan Site

Mill Lane, East Runton, NR27 9PR (01263 512858, www.manorfarmcaravansite. co.uk). Open Easter-Sept. Camping £20-£26 per pitch for 2 people.

Constantia Cottage Restaurant

High Street, East Runton, NR27 9NX (01263 512017, www. constantiarestaurant.co.uk). Dinner served 7-10pm Mon-Sat.

Mostly Greek food – accompanied by live Greek music, of course – is served at this small restaurant housed in a charming flint cottage. The lengthy menu covers all the standards as well as the likes of steak and chicken chasseur. Note that it's only open in the evening.

No.10 ♥

10 Augusta Street, Sheringham, NR26 8LA (01263 824400, www. no10sheringham.com). Dinner served 6.30-9pm Wed-Sun.

A husband-and-wife team run this attractive restaurant in the centre of town. The menu changes every few weeks, but has a Mediterranean slant: fish soup with gruyère, followed by tallegio and roast vegetable tart with avocado and tomato salad, for example.

Two Lifeboats

2 High Street, Sheringham, NR26 8JR (01263 822401). Open 11am-10.30pm daily. Food served 11am-8.30pm.

Good pub grub and a Sunday roast make this a decent inn for food, but it's the

This campsite spreads across 18 acres of peaceful countryside on a working farm, but the rural setting doesn't mean roughing it; three fields share six amenity blocks with power showers, and two laundry rooms (hair dryer and razor points provided). Many of the pitches have sea views.

CROMER

Four short miles connect Sheringham with Cromer, but the two have distinctly different characters. While Sheringham's growth from a fishing port to a tourist resort was slow, small-scale and late, Cromer – the self-styled 'gem of the north Norfolk coast' – became popular with visiting gentry in the late 1700s; nowadays, it's a splendidly old-fashioned seaside resort that's gradually being gentrified.

The beach, sandy then pebbly and backed by rows of brightly coloured beach huts, is the town's highlight.

The pretty and popular pier, featuring the long-running **Pavilion Theatre** (*see p79*), a children's funfair, a modern café, a fishing area and a lifeboat station, adds hugely to its appeal, but away from the sea there are plenty of other attractions, among them a model-boating lake in **North Lodge Park**, a crazy golf course, an amusement arcade, the **RNLI Henry Blogg Museum** (*see p73*) and **Cromer Church** (*see p73*) with its impressively tall tower.

As with most seaside towns, Cromer is easily navigable and enjoyably explored in an afternoon, with plenty of shops offering poke-around pleasures. New Street, the tiny alley behind the front, is home to a wonderful second-hand bookshop, **Bookworms** (01263 515078, 10am-5pm Mon-Sat, 2-5pm Sun). Around the corner on Church Street, more second-hand books and

Pavilion Theatre *see p79*

Things to do

SHERINGHAM & THE RUNTONS

Poppy Line (North Norfolk Railway)💜
Sheringham station, Sheringham, NR26 8RA (01263 820800, talking timetable 01263 820800, www.nnrailway.co.uk). Open days vary; phone for details. Tickets £40 return for compartment for 4 people; up to 2 additional adults £5 each; additional children £2.50 each.

The utterly enchanting, predominantly steam-driven Poppy Line takes passengers on a 20-minute trip between Sheringham and Holt, with a proper stop at Weybourne and a halt at Kelling Heath. It's a scenic route, hugging the coast and golf course before heading inland. The vintage carriages and genial staff in spick-and-span uniforms add to the charm. Also available are on-board 'dining experiences', from sedate Sunday lunch or romantic evening dinner trains, to sociable fish & chip trains or even a murder mystery train. Sheringham station is close to the town centre (and near the national network station on the Norwich to Cromer line). Holt station is about a mile outside the town, though the Holt Flyer, a vintage Routemaster bus, will (for an extra charge) take passengers into the centre.

Sheringham Little Theatre
2 Station Road, Sheringham, NR26 8RE (01263 822347, www. sheringhamlittletheatre.com). Box office open 9.30am-4pm Mon-Sat. Tickets £8-£15.

The delightfully tiny Little Theatre hosts a wide range of activities, including music, theatre, films, children's events and exhibitions, with highlights being a ten-week professional repertory season in summer and pantomime in winter. The friendly Hub café serves scones and snacks.

CROMER

Pavilion Theatre
Cromer Pier, Cromer, NR27 9HE (01263 512495, www.cromerpier.co.uk). Box office 6-8pm Tue-Sat. Tickets £10-£30.

Home of the famous 'Seaside Special' summer show, the theatre also hosts a season of celebrity concerts and performances, with tribute bands, themed songbook shows and local talent all firm favourites.

Sticky Earth Café
15 Church Street, Cromer, NR27 9ES (01263 519642, www.stickyearthcafe.co.uk). Open 9am-4pm Mon-Fri; Sat by appointment only.

This well-equipped café and ceramics studio has friendly staff on hand to help children paint their own mugs, jugs, plates and animals.

INLAND TO AYLSHAM

Bure Valley Railway
Aylsham station, Norwich Road, Aylsham, NR11 6BW (01263 733858, www.bvr.co.uk). Open days vary; phone for details. Tickets £15 return; free-£7.50 reductions; £40 family.

The 18-mile round trip from Aylsham to Wroxham in the Broads on this narrow-gauge railway is a steamy adventure. Trains barrel alongside the River Bure through wood, pasture and heath, taking in mills, villages and pretty hump-backed bridges. There's a café and model train shop at Aylsham station.

Keys Auctioneers
Keys Aylsham Salerooms, off Palmers Lane, Aylsham NR11 6JA (01263 733195, www. keysauctions.co.uk). Open 9am-4pm Mon-Fri; Sat by appointment only.

General and specialist auctions are held regularly, and they're huge fun to attend, even if you have no intention of buying. Novices will find a useful beginner's guide on the website, but generally it's pretty straightforward: register for a bidding card, view the items, head for the auction room and see what happens. You might pick up an oak dining table for a bargain £18, a bag of vintage tennis racquets or a cricket bat for a fiver, or more specialist items such as books and paintings.

antiques are available at the charmingly named **Much Binding Antiquarian Booksellers** (seasonal opening only). In addition to books, it deals in all manner of fascinating bits and pieces. The **Crossways** tobacconist on Chapel Street is another oddity, a lovely old-fashioned shop that still sells snuff and all sorts of pipe and tobacco paraphernalia (as well as the evil weed in hundreds of forms, of course).

But it's not all old junk and used books; Garden Street, adjoining New Street, is rather swish these days, with old-timers such as **Richard and Julie Davies' crab shack** (01263 512727) joined by the likes of the **Garden House Gallery** (01263 511234, www. gardenhousegallery.co.uk), which stocks a winning mix of painting and photography by local artists, as well as home accessories.

More arts and crafts are available on Church Street: ceramics, wood sculptures, glass and limited edition prints at **The Gallery Norfolk** (01263 515745, www.thegallerynorfolk.co.uk), and Danish jewellery, Venetian carnival masks and Russian hand-painted brooches at **Artyfax** (01263 512233, www.artyfax.com). The increasing number of such lively independent shops suggests a growth in wealth and tone that's long overdue for this once-grand and rather special resort – after all, where else in Britain can you see the sun both rise and set over the sea?

Where to eat & drink

It's de rigeur to eat fish and chips on the seafront (**Mary Jane's** on Garden Street or **No 1** on New Street) or buy dressed crabs to take home (from **JWH Jonas** or **J Lee's**, both on New Street), but more refined alternatives do exist, and their numbers are growing. For smarter crab dishes, try **Bolton's Bistro** at the Cliftonville Hotel (*see p81*), or enjoy lunchtime sophistication at the curvy chrome and blue **Rocket House Café** above the RNLI Henry Blogg Museum (*see p73*), with sterling sea views.

Garden Street Grill
16 Garden Street, NR27 9HN (01263 515110, www.gardenstreetgrill.co.uk). Food served noon-8pm Mon-Sat; noon-4pm Sun.

Truly trad and sporting wood as far as the eye can see, the Garden Street Grill is a haven for those who crave nothing more than a pile of peas, some grilled mushrooms and a dollop of mash next to a large portion of meat. Desperate Dans will love it.

Peggotty's Café
6 Hamilton Road, NR27 9HL (01263 511876). Open 9am-3pm daily.

As authentic as they come, this gorgeous little café serves just what you'd expect:

Virginia Court Hotel see p81

steak and kidney pudding, liver and bacon casserole and mac 'n' cheese.

Tides
Cromer Pier, NR27 9HE (01263 511236, www.cromer-pier.com). Open 10am-4pm (8pm on show days) daily.

Situated at the land end of the pier, Tides offers Cromer delicacies such as crab salad and crab linguine, or you can choose fish and chips or pizza. The setting is atmospheric, particularly when the rolling seas are crashing outside and the slate grey sky seems endless.

Where to stay
As befits its retro feel, Cromer still boasts guesthouses of blessed cheesiness: flock wallpaper, candlewick bedspreads and tinned tomatoes with your egg and bacon. Look along Alfred Road and Cadogan Road (both off the A149) for some likely contenders.

Cliftonville Hotel
29 Runton Road, Cromer, NR27 9AS (01263 512543, www.cliftonvillehotel. co.uk). Rates £240-£290 double incl breakfast.

Edwardian splendour on the seafront, with stonkingly good views of both sea and town, make this independent hotel a great choice for fans of expansive vistas and old-fashioned design. There are 30 rooms, and lots of original features give the place real character (act out your *Gone with the Wind* fantasies in the main lobby). The elegant Bolton's Bistro serves a good range of seafood and big steaks.

Hotel de Paris
High Street, Cromer, NR27 9HG (01263 513141, www.leisureplex.co.uk). Rates £112 double incl breakfast.

One for romantics and lovers of faded Victorian grandeur, the imposing Hotel de Paris could do with a brush-up, but has a terrific seafront location, rooms (63 in all) with tantalising views, some beautiful original features (particularly in the public spaces) and the kind of ambience that harks back to a more genteel age of tourism.

Link
The Lighthouse, Overstrand Road, Cromer, NR27 0JH (01386 701177, www. ruralretreats.co.uk). Rates from £723 per week.

Book the children in at grandma's – babies and children aren't allowed at this former lighthouse keeper's cottage. Set in the base of the white octagonal tower of the working Cromer Lighthouse, it's a ten-minute walk from town via the coast path (a mile by road) and adjacent to the highly rated Royal Cromer golf course (*see p83*). There's room for just one couple.

Red Lion Hotel
Brook Street, Cromer, NR27 9HD (01263 514964, www.redlion-cromer.co.uk). Rates £125-£170 double.

The clifftop location makes the Red Lion a good bet. The 14 rooms are individually decorated, while the decor retains some original features. Some rooms have cosy little bay nooks in which you can sit and gaze out to sea. Others have wrought-iron beds, or balconies, but nearly all have sea views, and are warm, modern and comfortable. Dogs are welcome.

Virginia Court Hotel ♥
Cliff Avenue, Cromer, NR27 0AN (01263 512398, www.virginiacourt.co.uk). Rates £140-£195 double incl breakfast.

Just three minutes' walk from the seafront and pier, the rather grand Virginia Court was built at the end of the 19th century as a gentlemen's club for Edward VII. The independent hotel has been lovingly refurbished by its owners, who have turned the 23 rooms into clean-lined, contemporary spaces. The restaurant is open to non-residents.

INLAND TO AYLSHAM
South of Cromer and Sheringham, simple seaside pleasures give way to grander attractions in the shape of imposing houses and gardens: privately owned Mannington Estate (*see p74*) and two wonderful

Ten Norfolk golf courses

Norfolk is blessed with more than 30 golf courses, many of them excellent, and a few among the best in the UK. Check each course's website for playing restrictions and prices.

five for experienced golfers...

Hunstanton

Golf Course Road, Old Hunstanton, PE36 6JQ (01485 532811, www.hunstantongolfclub. com).

Hunstanton is very welcoming to visitors. It's a great course for winter golf as the greens are renowned for being fast and true all year round. Three- and four-balls have very limited availability, so check before travelling.

King's Lynn

Castle Rising, King's Lynn, PE31 6BD (01553 631654, www.kingslynngolfclub.co.uk).

A friendly club a few miles outside King's Lynn, with an attractive tree-lined course built on a seam of sand that makes for excellent, year-long playing conditions.

Royal West Norfolk

Brancaster, PE31 8AX (01485 210087, www. rwngc.org).

A lovely links course, with the sea on one side and the saltmarsh on the other, but attitudes here are 'old-school' and only the most persistent visiting golfers will manage to book a round. If you're able to reach the first tee, then a delightful experience awaits, especially if you're fortunate enough to catch the tide just right – it creates some interesting water hazards.

Sheringham

Sheringham, NR26 8HG (01263 823488, www.sheringhamgolfclub.co.uk).

Another links course with beautiful views from a clifftop position, where the welcome extended to non-members is similar to Hunstanton. The Sheringham-to-Holt steam railway runs the length of the course.

Thetford

Brandon Road, Thetford, IP24 3NE (01842 752169, www.thetfordgolfclub.co.uk).

A fabulous heathland course on the edge of the Breckland forest, on the county border with Suffolk. It's one of the best courses of its type, and something of a hidden gem. A warm welcome is guaranteed.

properties now owned by the National Trust, **Felbrigg Hall** (*see p74*) and **Blickling Hall** (*see p74*).

Pretty villages lay claim to a clutch of churches with unusual features. **St Peter's** in the tiny village of **Brampton**, for example, is notable for its brick-crowned round tower; **St Andrew's** in **Little Barningham** is famed for its 17th-century wooden skeleton; **St John the Baptist** in **Aylmerton** boasts a round tower and some notable early 18th-century gravestones, including one decorated with a coffin, a skull and a snake devouring its own tail (symbolising eternity); and the Anglo-Saxon round tower of **St Mary's** in **Bessingham** is unique in being built of local carrstone rather than the more common flint or medieval brick.

Walkers and drinkers will appreciate the area's excellent trails and paths, and refreshment stops, in picture-perfect villages such as **Erpingham**, **Heydon** and **Wolterton**, and there's even good shopping to be had. For instance, the farm buildings at **Alby Crafts** (01263 761590, www.albycrafts. co.uk), located on the main A140 between Cromer and Aylsham, are home to a handful of craftsmakers, creating everything from wildlife habitats to ceramic wall plates, as well as a gallery, gift shop, furniture showroom and café.

And then there's the market town of **Aylsham**. Located about ten miles south of Cromer, halfway to Norwich, this compact and attractive settlement is proud of its medieval heritage and long-held position as a thriving market town for the surrounding agricultural communities. The general market on Friday, and farmers' market on the first Saturday morning of the month, are very popular.

Good links – via roads, numerous paths, the lovely Bure Valley Railway (*see p79*) and a cycle path that links it to Wroxham in the heart of the

Broads – have helped ensure it's a vibrant destination with plenty to offer visitors, including a couple of excellent places to stay.

Where to eat & drink

Pubs and tearooms are the norm in this area, which caters largely to walkers and families. The former will find much to enjoy at Aylsham's **Black Boys Hotel & Restaurant** and Wolterton's **Saracen's Head** (for both, *see p84*), both of which also offer quality accommodation. The **Buckinghamshire Arms** (01263 732133, www.bucksarms.co.uk), a Jacobean coaching inn just outside the gates of Blickling Hall, is a foodie pub with four bedrooms.

For families, the tearoom at **Mannington Hall** (*see p74*) offers a surprisingly wide range of locally sourced food; and youngsters can run around in the garden of Aylsham's **Old Tea Rooms** (18A Red Lion Street, 01263 732112, closed Wed and Sun).

Walpole Arms

The Common, Itteringham, NR11 7AR (01263 587258, www.thewalpolearms. co.uk). Open noon-3pm, 5.30-11pm Mon-Sat; noon-5pm Sun.

The authentic menu of Spanish tapas is prepared using locally sourced, seasonal ingredients. Expect the likes of *bomba de pescado* (haddock croquettes) or *chistorro al vino tinto* (Spanish pork sausage in Riojan red wine) and a paella Sunday special (there are also a few Modern British dishes). The two-acre landscaped garden and vine-clad terrace make it particularly lovely.

Where to stay

Of the many pubs in the area that offer accommodation, the **Buckinghamshire Arms** (*see above*) is a fine choice – though it's only got four rooms. It's worth looking into self-catering options too, via websites such as www.norfolkcottages.co.uk;

... and five for less experienced golfers

Barnham Broom

Honingham Road, Barnham Broom, NR9 4DD (01603 334157, www.barnham-broom. co.uk). Open summer 6.30am-7pm; winter 7.30am-4pm.

On the outer edge of Norwich, these two 18-hole courses are attached to a four-star hotel and spa complex. It's an easy-going environment for visiting golfers; you can just turn up and play without being interrogated by a retired colonel.

Norwich Golf Course

Drayton High Road, Hellesdon, Norwich NR6 5AH (01603 429928, www.royalnorwichgolf. co.uk).

Situated on the north edge of Norwich, this well-established club offers an interesting layout either side of the Drayton High Road. Non-members are welcome.

Royal Cromer

145 Overstrand Road, Cromer, NR27 0JH (01263 512884, www.royalcromergolfclub. com).

Quality links more than 300ft above the beach, Royal Cromer is good at making visitors feel cherished. The course plays more parkland than links, but is almost always in excellent condition. If you have a good card in your hand, beware holes 14 and 15 by the lighthouse – they bite.

Royal Norwich

Weston Longville, NR9 5JZ (01603 429928, www.royalnorwichgolf.co.uk).

Based around an old country estate nine miles from Norwich, Weston is set in beautiful parkland. The 18-hole course and six-hole academy course feature state-of-the-art facilities including practice bunkers and practice putting green.

Sprowston Manor

Sprowston Park, Wroxham Road, Norwich, NR7 8RP (01603 254290, www. britanniahotels.com/hotels/sprowston-manor-hotel-country-club).

Part of a Britannia hotel complex – so again, not fusty – this course is created around a manor house and grounds. The 18-hole course features USGA specification greens and over 70 strategically placed bunkers. Its proximity to Norwich may also be advantageous for non-golfers.

many places offer short and weekend stays at heavily discounted prices outside peak season.

Black Boys Hotel & Restaurant

Market Place, Aylsham, NR11 6EH (01263 732122, www.blackboyshotel.co.uk). Rates £80-£200 double incl breakfast.

Eight characterful and comfortable rooms (one of them a family room) in warm colours make the Black Boys one of the nicest places to stay in the area. Traditionalists will like the period pieces in the bedrooms as well as the resolutely English menu – generous portions of steak and ale pie, lamb shank, and fish and chips – on offer in the bar/restaurant downstairs.

Saracen's Head

Wall Road, Wolterton, NR11 7LZ (01263 768909, www.saracenshead-norfolk. co.uk). Rates £120 double incl breakfast.

Isolated, ivy-clad and instantly appealing from the outside, this former coaching inn (built to serve neighbouring Wolterton Hall) is just as attractive inside. The six rooms (five double and one family room) are bright and contemporary. The Modern British cuisine is equally original and tempting, with dishes such as roast cod (long shoreline caught from Lowestoft) with creamy mustard sauce and spinach, or trio of best-end lamb chops with a herb crust, from animals reared and grazed at Hevingham.

Sheringham cliffs see p69

Norwich

Despite good links via road and rail, Norwich feels slightly removed from the rest of Britain, and can often give the impression of being somewhere far away, rather than a city less than two hours from London by rail. This sense of isolation gives it a more individual character than many of England's homogenised civic centres, and means that the inhabitants make much of what they have here, rather than looking to London for entertainment.

The lovely city centre is compact enough for you to really get to know it in a couple of days, though there's so much packed in that you could easily stay for a week and not run out of things to do. There's an impressive clutch of historical and cultural attractions, a dizzying array of good pubs and decent eating options, and some very nice places to stay. Shopping is fun here too – there are many interesting independents – and best of all, there's no need for a car in the centre of town.

Rural escape is also hassle-free; there are a number of enjoyable villages and market towns within reach, and fast access to the natural wonders of the Norfolk Broads (see p115) to the east and the Norfolk coast to the north (see p27).

The centre

It's easy to orientate yourself: the cathedral, castle, market square, railway station and even the football ground on Carrow Road are an easy stroll away. In the very heart of Norwich is **Michael Hopkins's Forum** (Millennium Plain, 01603 727950, www.theforumnorwich. co.uk), a millennium project built after the Central Library was destroyed by fire in 1994. It's home to a variety of organisations including the Millennium Library, the BBC, Café Bar Marzano and Pizza Express. (Sadly, the excellent tourist information centre has now closed.) The broad façade of this airy and transparent building acts as a useful meeting and orientation point. Opposite is the largest medieval church in the city, **St Peter Mancroft** (The Chantry, 01603 610443, www. stpetermancroft.org.uk).

Centuries overlap everywhere in Norwich, which is hardly surprising given its age. By 1004 the city's meandering River Wensum had helped turn it into a thriving centre for trade and commerce in the east of England. Nowadays, remains of this past can be seen wherever you look: along the riverside path, home to the **Cow Tower** medieval brick lookout and the stone arch of **Pull's Ferry** (once a 15th-century water gate); and on **Chapelfield**, where the 14th-century city walls stand. Beneath a Georgian façade you're quite likely to find a Norman building; medieval beauties include the **Guildhall**, **Dragon Hall** (see p92) and the **Norwich Castle Museum & Art Gallery** (see p92). Tudor relics are evident at **Armada House** on St Andrew's Plain, supposedly built with timber from Spanish Armada ships wrecked on the East Anglia shore, and

Norwich Cathedral *see p93*

throughout the delightful, cobbled area of **Elm Hill**.

More modern architectural attractions include local hero George Skipper's breathtaking art nouveau **Royal Arcade** shopping centre (*see p91*); the impressive art deco **City Hall & Clock Tower** (*see p92*) that Hitler vowed – but failed – to destroy; and the city's two stunning cathedrals: the **Cathedral Church of St John the Baptist** (*see p92*) designed by George Gilbert Scott, and **Norwich Cathedral** (*see p93*), one of 32 pre-Reformation churches in the city.

Shopping

Norwich has a large number of deconsecrated churches, and on Saturdays many of them open their doors to stallholders of all hues, transforming the city into a vast flea market. You can certainly expect a tea and cake stall, and you'll often find a minstrel strumming a guitar in the nave.

At the other extreme, in the sparkling, modern **Chantry Place** (www.chantryplace.co.uk), there's the usual range of high-street shops, including an Apple store. Close by is the superbly stocked independent **Jarrold's** department store (01603 660661, www. jarrold.co.uk); the picturesque **Norwich Lanes** (*see p91*); quaint **Elm Hill** (check out the **Jade Tree** – 15 Elm Hill, 01603 664615, www.thejadetree.co.uk – for classy crafts); more big-name high-street shops along the length of **Gentleman's Walk** and **London Street**; heaps of charity shops; and a great **market** (*see p91*) six days a week. One fine addition to London Street is **Book Hive** (no.53, 01603 219268, www.thebookhive.co.uk) – an independent bookseller stuffed with the kind of stock you'd be hard-pressed to find in most cities these days. Nearby is the **Anteros Arts Foundation** on Fye Bridge Street.

Elm Hill see p88

Culture

Nowadays, a visiting Steve Coogan will find a city that's a far cry from the cultural backwater so mercilessly lampooned by Alan Partridge. The independent **Cinema City** (St Andrew's Street, 0871 902 5724, www. picturehouses.co.uk) screens a wide variety of films, including children's movies on Saturday mornings. The **Theatre Royal** (Theatre Street, 01603 630000, www.norwichtheatre.org) shows opera and ballet as well as plays; there's also the smaller **Maddermarket Theatre** (St John's Alley, 01603 620917, www.madder market.co.uk), and the **Playhouse** (42-58 St George's Street, 01603 630000, www.norwichtheatre.org), which hosts regular comedy nights. Children will love **Norwich Puppet Theatre** (*see p95*). And then there are the many and varied options provided by the University of East

Maddermarket Theatre see p89

Anglia, not only art exhibitions at the **Sainsbury Centre** (*see p93*), but also concerts, readings and other cultural activities – have a look at their very useful website, www.ueaticketbookings.co.uk.

Golden Triangle

A good area to base yourself in if you want to be outside the centre of town, the Golden Triangle is the area between the interestingly named Unthank Road, and the Ipswich and Newmarket roads. It's home to galleries, cafés, bars, pubs, restaurants and a mixed bag of independent hotels and guesthouses. On seemingly every corner there's a pub with a resolutely trendified sign. The leafy streets are home to middle-class young families, professionals and students.

Where to eat & drink

Norwich folk are proud of the fact that they reputedly have a pub for every day of the year and a church for every week of the year, but they're also gladdened by the city's increasingly impressive restaurant scene. Most well-regarded chains have outlets in Norwich, but they are just part of a scene that includes an array of lively independents.

International cuisine is well covered. You can eat Mexican at **Mambo Jambo** (14-16 Lower Goat Lane, 01603 666802, www.mambojambo restaurant.co.uk), Belgian at the **Waffle House** (39 St Giles High Street, 01603 612790, www.wafflehouse norwich.co.uk) and Italian at **Pinocchio's** (11 St Benedicts Street, 01603 613318, www.pinocchios restaurant.net). All are buzzy and rammed at weekends.

The trendy Golden Triangle area groans with good gastropubs and bars too, including the **Fat Cat** (*see p97*).

But the big daddy when it comes to eating out is undoubtedly the **Tombland/Queen Street area**, aka **Restaurant Row**, where many of the city's best restaurants are located.

Norwich Market

Three places to shop

Norwich Lanes
www.norwichlanes.co.uk.
A vibrant independent retail scene spread over several streets, with the best shops not actually on the picturesque lanes, but the larger cross-streets they link: St Benedicts Street, St Giles Street and Pottergate. You'll find music, vintage and contemporary fashion, and homewares. Upper St Giles Street is a highlight.

Norwich Market ♥
01603 213537, www.norwich-market.co.uk.
Open 9am-4pm Mon-Sat.
This is a lovely traditional market (with more than 190 stalls), the like of which it's hard to find these days. Wristwatch straps? Check. Wincyette pyjamas for a fiver? Check. Big jars of boiled sweeties and chocolate mice? Check. Plus bacon butties, dress fabrics, used books, CDs and fruit and veg, alongside organic produce, a groceries stall, a great cheese stall, local Aldous ice-cream and sparkling shellfish.

Royal Arcade ♥
www.royalarcadenorwich.co.uk. Open Arcade 9am-6pm daily; shops vary.
This 1899 art nouveau shopping arcade opposite the market, designed by local star George Skipper, is a real beauty, with Doulton tiles, Italian terrazzo stone flooring, decorative pillars and stained glass. And that's before you check out Langleys toy shop (01603 621959); Artisan Chocolates by Saffire (01603 616815); or blow the budget on a piece of jewellery at Sonkai or Juels' Limited.

Places to visit

Cathedral Church of St John the Baptist

Cathedral House, Unthank Road, NR2 2PA (01603 624615, www.sjbcathedral.org. uk). Open 7.30am-6.30pm daily. Admission free. Tower tours Sat 1.30pm (summer only). Admission £5; children over 8 (or at least 130 cm tall) £3.50.

George Gilbert Scott's 20th-century Gothic Revival building – the city's Roman Catholic cathedral – stands imposingly at the top of Grapes Hill. Stunningly decorated, elegant, cruciform in shape, it's breathtaking both outside and in, particularly if you stand at the junction of the north and south transepts and gaze at the soaring space above. On summer Saturdays tower tours offer marvellous views of the city.

City Hall & Clock Tower

St Peter's Street, NR2 1NH (01603 213999, www.visitnorwich.co.uk). Open City Hall 8.45am-5pm Mon-Fri. Clock Tower by arrangement. Admission free.

While it's easy to admire the imposing exterior of Norwich's 1938 City Hall, it's worth taking a guided tour of the building, when you can explore the art deco interior and timber-panelled rooms. If you can't manage that, sneak a peak into the ground-floor entrance hall and first-floor landing, both lined with Italian marble.

Dragon Hall

115-123 King Street, NR1 1QE (01603 877177, www.dragonhallnorwich.org.uk. Tours Dragon Hall Heritage Volunteers run guided tours of the building on the 1st & 3rd Mon of each month at 2pm. Admission free, suggested donation £5.

Discovered in the 1970s, this medieval merchant's trading hall raises some interesting questions about history and its preservation, having been stripped of centuries of partitioning and conversions to create two halls topped with a timber crown post roof and intricately carved and painted dragon. It's spectacular and well worth a visit, but is only open two Mondays per month as it is now home of the National Centre for Writing.

Eaton Park

South Park Avenue, NR4 7EH (www. visitnorwich.co.uk). Open 24hrs daily.

Opened in 1928 by the then Prince of Wales, this pretty park – the city's biggest – would probably mightily please the current Prince of Wales, with its classical features, ornamental gardens, lily and model boating ponds, and domed mosaic fountain. He might be less enamoured of the miniature train, skate park and sports facilities, which include tennis, bowls and crazy golf.

Norwich Castle Museum & Art Gallery

Castle Meadow, NR1 3JU (01603 495897, www.museums.norfolk.gov.uk). At time of going to press the castle was closed but is set to reopen as soon as government guidelines permit. For up-to-date opening hours and admission fees check the website.

From pretty much anywhere in central Norwich you'll catch beguiling glimpses of the 900-year-old castle keep that's now the centrepiece of this excellent museum and art gallery. The squat but elegant Norman structure, built of dazzling Caen limestone (and refaced with Bath stone in the 1830s), is equally arresting inside. You'll find the likes of Snap the Dragon, the centuries-old star of Norwich's mayoral processions, plenty of gibbets, torture instruments and other ghoulish exhibits that will appeal to kids, and various interactive displays – plus a chilling well that descends more than 120ft. Next door are a dizzying array of galleries

covering everything from Egyptian and Viking history to decorative arts and fashion. You really need more than one visit to take it all in; if time is limited, aim for the ceramics collections, the paintings by equestrian artist Alfred Munnings, and the wonderful display of teapots in the Twining Teapot gallery.

Norwich Cathedral 💜
12 The Close, NR1 4DH (01603 218300, www.cathedral.org.uk). Open 7.30am-6.30pm daily. Admission free.

Founded in 1096 and constructed of Caen stone, this stunning Romanesque cathedral has a number of standout features, including the fan-vaulted roof, the transepts, Thomas Gooding's skeleton tomb, the monastic cloister, the presbytery and the surprisingly contemporary decoration on the spire, England's second highest. The Cathedral Close and grounds are worth exploring too. Look out for the statue of Nelson gazing at the school he attended; the memorial to local hero Edith Cavell, who was executed by the Germans in World War I and is buried in the cathedral; and the saint-studded Erpingham Gate. On the north side of the cathedral, on Bishopgate, is the **Bishop's Garden**, a walled gem open to the public on certain days in summer.

Plantation Garden 💜
4 Earlham Road, NR2 3DB (01603 219630, www.plantationgarden.co.uk). Open 9am-6pm daily; 9am-dusk in winter. Admission £2.

Known locally as the 'Secret Garden', these three acres of glorious gardens, in a medieval chalk quarry next to the Roman Catholic cathedral, are a fantastic place to spend an hour or two. Gothic fountains, an Italianate terrace, a summer house, a sculptured terrace wall and numerous walkways link imaginatively planted flower beds, ensuring a visual natural feast that's unrivalled in the city.

Sainsbury Centre 💜
University of East Anglia, Earlham Road, NR4 7TJ (01603 593199, www.sainsburycentre. ac.uk). Open 9am-6pm Tue-Fri; 10am-5pm Sat & Sun. Admission free.

Sir Norman Foster's elegiac building may look like an aircraft hangar dropped into the middle of a rural university campus, but there's no doubting that it works brilliantly in presenting a collection that resembles a mini version of the British Museum with a bit of Tate thrown in. The focus is very much on the educational, but it's done in an understated and visually compelling manner. Imaginative, beautifully designed temporary exhibitions are held in a basement space that draws the eye to the parkland vistas in unexpected ways.

Strangers Hall
Charing Cross, Norwich NR2 4AL (01603 667229, www.museums.norfolk.gov.uk). At time of going to press the museum was closed but is set to reopen as soon as government guidelines permit. For up-to-date opening hours check the website. Admission £4.50; free-£5.15 reductions; £19 family.

One of Norwich's oldest buildings (dating from 1320) houses a range of historical displays in a series of interlinked rooms decorated with textiles and period pieces. Costumed invigilators provide plenty of fascinating detail about daily life in Tudor and Stuart England.

Sainsbury Centre

Assembly House

Assembly House, Theatre Street, NR2 1RQ (01603 626402, www. assemblyhousenorwich.co.uk). Open 9am-4.30pm daily.

The gorgeous interiors of this Georgian mansion are best enjoyed over an hour or two in the stunning restaurant, which serves breakfast, morning coffee, high tea and brasserie staples for lunch and early suppers. There are 11 sumptuous rooms (£190-£220), some with their own private courtyard, and three more to come. The Richard Hughes Cookery School is based here too.

Cinema City Dining Rooms♥

Cinema City, St Andrews Street, NR2 4AD (07504 356378, www.picturehouses. co.uk). At time of going to press the restaurant was closed but set to reopen as soon as government guidelines permit.

Three gorgeous medieval spaces paved with huge flagstones make this a great place to eat, and that's before tasting the excellent Modern British and European food served in the bar and restaurant. The sandwiches (salt beef, watercress and mustard) and salads (warm butterbean and chorizo, cherry tomatoes and parsley) are winners at lunch, but make the most of it by visiting for dinner when dishes such as Norfolk estate venison with hazelnut crumb, spiced red wine poached pear and buttered greens appear.

Delia's Restaurant & Bar/Yellows

Norwich City Football Ground, Carrow Road, NR1 1JE (01603 218705, www. deliascanarycatering.com). Open from 5.30pm Fri & Sat only.

With limited opening hours (following government restrictions) and serious competition in the city centre, it's hard to imagine why you'd make the trek to Carrow Road until you taste Delia's no-nonsense but delicately prepared classics served in an elegant white space decked out with crisp linen and the kind of comfortable touches you'd expect from the everywoman chef. Currently on offer is a three-course dinner menu (with canapés and coffee) for £39.95 per person.

The Last

70-76 St George's St, NR3 1AB (01603 626626, www.lastwinebar.co.uk). Lunch served noon-3pm, dinner served 6-9.30pm Mon-Sat.

Sited in a former Victorian shoe factory, this swish restaurant serves tempting Modern British and French dishes – such as pan-fried hake with hay-smoked celeriac, mussels, lyonnaise potato and warm tartare dressing – in an airy and elegant space that still manages to feel intimate and personal.

Fika

25 Wensum Street, Norwich, NR3 1LA (www.fikanorwich.co.uk). Open 8am-2pm Mon-Fri. No credit cards.

This coffee shop has a Swedish focus on friendship and taking time out for a proper cup of coffee (or tea) and a pastry.

Red Lion

52 Eaton Street, Eaton, NR4 7LD (01603 454787, www.redlion-eaton.co.uk). Breakfast served 8-10am daily; lunch served noon-2.15pm; dinner served 6.30-9pm Mon-Sat; food served noon-5pm, 6-8.30pm Sun. (Reduced hours and simplified menu while government restrictions are in place.)

The bygone decor – Dutch gables, beams, panelled walls and inglenook fireplaces – and Modern British cuisine make this 17th-century pub and hotel worth leaving the city for – it's on the outskirts of Norwich. Expect local ingredients such as Cromer crab, a good range of steaks and a daily specials board featuring big meat favourites such as steak and kidney suet pudding and Norfolk lamb's liver. Six comfortable rooms upstairs and in a stable annex make this a popular B&B option too (from £70 double excl breakfast)).

Roger Hickman's♥

79 Upper St Giles Street, Norwich, NR2 1AB (01603 633522, www. rogerhickmansrestaurant.com). Lunch served noon-2pm Mon-Sat; dinner served 7-10pm Mon-Thur, 5.45-10pm Sat & Sun.

Roger Hickman has brought his imaginative take on Modern British food

Things to do

Bittern Line
www.bitternline.com (National Rail enquiries 03457 484950; tickets www.nationalrail. co.uk).

This 30-mile scenic railway connects Norwich with Cromer and Sheringham via the Norfolk Broads at Salhouse, Hoveton and Wroxham. If you're bringing a bicycle, arrive early: trains can take only four bikes.

Norwich City FC
Carrow Road, NR1 1JE (01603 721902, tickets 01603 721902, www.canaries.co.uk).

The home ground of Norwich's popular Canaries (named after the singing canaries introduced by 16th-century Dutch weavers to keep them entertained as they worked at their looms) shouldn't be missed. Buy a ticket to a match here and join some of the country's most loyal fans.

Norwich Puppet Theatre
St James, Whitefriars, NR3 1TN (01603 629921, www.puppettheatre.co.uk). Open varies; check website for details. Admission £9; £32 family (4 people). Currently closed; set to reopen Oct 21.

This lovely theatre is housed in a medieval church. Both in-house productions and touring puppet companies offer a wide range of shows for kids and adults, as well as an imaginative programme of craft-based workshops for all ages.

Paul Dickson Walking Tours
www.pauldicksontours.co.uk. Tours last between 90 mins and half a day. Cost from £7.

Local historian Paul Dickson conducts a number of regular themed walks around the city, covering general history (Norwich, an Introduction, for example) to the more specific, such as Norwich: a Black History or The City of Stories, and the downright spine-tingling (Norwich on the Dark Side).

Sportspark
University of East Anglia, Earlham Road, NR4 7TJ (01603 592398, www.sportspark. co.uk). Open 6.30am-10.20pm Mon-Sat; 8am-3.45pm Sun. Admission varies; check website for details.

Follow a visit to the Sainsbury Centre with a workout: facilities include an Olympic-sized swimming pool, astro pitches, squash and tennis courts and a climbing wall.

Norwich City FC

Fat Cat see p97

to this classically elegant, warm space. Add gorgeous little pre-starters and amuse bouches to superbly cooked dishes such as pork fillet, sweet potato, savoy cabbage, coppa ham and squid, or mushroom ravioli, fermented beetroot and dill, and you've got a dining experience par excellence. The taster menus – vegetarian (£60) and non-vegetarian (£70) – are a real treat.

Tatlers
21 Tombland, NR1 3RF (01603 858070, www.tatlersnorwich.co.uk). Lunch and dinner served (check website for opening days and times).

With burgandy walls, simple wooden tables and chairs and ingredients sourced from Norwich Market, this laid-back bistro is a great Tombland feature. The Modern European cooking – seafood and tapas dishes predominate – is very popular, so booking is recommended.

Where to stay
The compact nature of Norwich's city centre means that hotels are usually within easy range of almost everything you'd want to visit, and plenty of competition ensures keen pricing. Further afield, on the south-west edge of the city, the **Red Lion** (*see p94*) also has rooms.

Dunston Hall
Ipswich Road, NR14 8PQ (01508 470444, www.qhotels.co.uk). Rates £129-£144 double incl breakfast.

Pretend you're one of the country set at this Elizabethan-style red-brick mansion, built in 1859 and now run by the upmarket QHotels chain. Facilities include an indoor swimming pool, sauna, steam room and fitness suite, an 18-hole golf course and acres of parkland. The rooms are as plush and comfortable as you'd expect.

Georgian House Hotel
30-34 Unthank Road, NR2 2RB (01603 615655, www. thegeorgiantownhousenorwich.com). Rates £138-168 double incl breakfast.

This pretty three-star hotel, set in landscaped gardens, and with a large, free car park (a rarity in central Norwich) has 36 comfortable en-suite bedrooms in styles ranging from traditional to contemporary. The garden setting, library-lounge and conservatory create the feel of a country hotel. The restaurant serves lunch and dinner daily.

Gothic House
King's Head Yard, Magdalen Street, NR3 1JE (01603 631879, www.gothic-house-norwich.com). Rates £125 double incl breakfast. No credit cards.

This beautiful Grade II-listed Regency house in the heart of the city is a real treat, but it has only two rooms (one double, one twin), so you'll need to book well in advance. Each room has its own private bathroom, with Molton Brown toiletries, bathrobes and fluffy white towels.

Maids Head Hotel
Tombland, NR3 1LB (01603 209955, www.maidsheadhotel.co.uk). Rates £155-£230 double incl breakfast.

The 13th-century Maids Head Hotel is Britain's oldest hotel, apparently; Elizabeth I was once a guest. With 84 vastly differing rooms and suites (including the one Bess is reputed to have stayed in), it should have something to suit most tastes.

Sprowston Manor Hotel

Wroxham Road, NR7 8RP (www. britanniahotels.com). Rates from £105-£165 double incl breakfast.

This Britannia Hotel Golf & Country Club on the outskirts of town (thus great for exploring both the city and the Broads) comes with 170 acres of mature parkland to wander around, a health and beauty spa, indoor pools for children and grown-ups, and one of Norfolk's best golf courses.

St Giles House Hotel♥

41-45 St Giles Street, NR2 1JR (01603 275180, www.stgileshousehotel.com). Rates £155-£365 double incl breakfast.

Gorgeous hotel, cool bar, spa and top-class restaurant... you could stay here and never get out to explore the classy boutiques on this happening street. Designed by renowned local architect George Skipper in 1906, the building is now a striking mash-up of old and new, with 24 individually designed rooms. Disabled and pet friendly rooms are available.

38 St Giles

38 St Giles Street, NR2 1LL (01603 662944, www.38stgiles.co.uk). Rates £140-£160 double incl breakfast.

This stylish Georgian house has just six rooms and two suites (an eclectic mix of traditional and contemporary), so reserve early if you want to sample the own-made cakes, friendly service and excellent facilities. The location is ideal, in the centre of town near the Market and the Lanes.

Wedgewood House

42 St Stephens Road, NR1 3RE (01603 625730, www.wedgewoodhouse.co.uk). Rates £85-£95 double incl breakfast.

This small, friendly B&B is a five-minute walk from the centre and the same from Chapelfield, which means a peaceful night's sleep and easy access to buses for the Sainsbury Centre. The three rooms are comfortable and cosy, and all have Wi-Fi. Owners Elspeth and Nigel Evans will happily point you in the direction of good food and attractions nearby.

Three Norwich pubs

Adam & Eve
Bishopgate, NR3 1RZ (01603 667423). Open noon-7pm Mon & Tue; noon-8pm Wed & Thur; noon-9pm Fri & Sat; noon-6pm Sun.

Norwich's oldest pub is proud of its 800-year history, and equally proud of its fine range of beers and annual listing in the *Good Pub Guide*.

Eagle
33 Newmarket Road, NR2 2HN (01603 624173, www.theeaglepub.co.uk). Open noon-11pm Mon-Sat; noon-9pm Sun. Food served noon-3pm Mon-Fri; noon-9pm Sat; noon-6pm Sun.

An oldie in the Golden Triangle area, this friendly Georgian pub also offers excellent, reasonably priced food (slow roast pork belly, beer-battered fish and chips or chargrilled aubergine). Summer barbecues are served on the terrace, and it's very child-friendly for a city boozer.

Fat Cat Pub
49 West End Street, NR2 4NA (01603 624364, www.fatcatpub.co.uk). Open noon-11pm Mon-Wed, Sun; noon-midnight Thur, Fri; 11am-midnight Sat. No credit cards.

The winner of the *Good Pub Guide*'s Beer Pub of the Year on ten different occasions (and every year from 2016-2020) may not look like much from the outside, but it's heartily recommended for its excellent drinks list (including its own brews, numerous guest ales on tap and 50 bottled beers from around the world) and friendly punters.

and 700 more...
Norwich once had more than 700 pubs, a figure that has dwindled considerably in the last couple of decades. The **Historic Pubs** walking tour starts from the 16th-century Maids Head Hotel bar on Wensum Street. Amongst other things, you'll see where Paul Simon once sang solo and visit Alan Partridge's favourite Norfolk bar. There are stories of gruesome murders, sixties music heroes and more. No beer stops en route, unfortunately, but you'll be invited to sample the Maids Head Ale at the end of the 1½-hour tour (www.pauldicksontours.co.uk).

North-east Norfolk

Normally sleepy Norfolk is positively in a coma in this isolated part of the county, which isn't to say there's nothing here – though if coastal erosion continues unchecked, there will be considerably less than there is today. Here, erosion not only means the washing away of cliffs but also whole communities, particularly in fast-disappearing Happisburgh and some of the villages around it.

Star attractions in the area include huge sandy beaches at Waxham, Horsey and Winterton-on-Sea, stretching for mile after empty mile and more than a match for the famed beaches of the north Norfolk coast. Handsome (currently) inland villages, such as Trunch and Knapton, and borderline Broads villages such as East Ruston, offer the timeless pleasures of flint cottages, pretty pubs and singular medieval churches. They act as delightful counterpoints to the kiss-me-quick charms of the seaside towns and the isolated beauty of the vast beaches nearby.

OVERSTRAND TO HEMSBY

Overstrand

If you judged Norfolk's coastline by the reams of tourist pamphlets, accommodation guides and tourist board-sanctioned attractions available, you'd be forgiven for thinking the coast ended at Cromer. Consequently, most people make it as far east as Cromer and then turn inland to head towards Norwich and civilisation. But just two miles further east is the wonderful village of Overstrand, home to three Edwin Lutyens buildings (**Overstrand Hall**, the **Methodist Church** and the **Pleasaunce**), lovely **St Martin's Church**, the terrific **Clifftop Café** (see p105) overlooking a glorious beach, some great places to stay, a decent pub with rooms (the **White Horse**, see p106) and an excellent range of walks – whether coastal, rural or a combination of the two.

The village was a fashionable, upmarket holiday destination by the late 19th century – Winston Churchill holidayed here just days before the outbreak of World War I – and was dubbed Poppy-land owing to the profusion of poppies growing in the area. The nearby villages of Sidestrand and Trimingham are equally underrated pleasure spots offering expansive and empty beaches – plus, of course, chips or sand-speckled sandwiches to go with them.

Mundesley & Bacton

A few miles further east, **Mundesley** steps things up a gear. This sizeable village is something of an oddity, exhibiting as it does the vestiges of a once illustrious past in a handful of fading Victorian hotels with an attractive promenade and gardens, and a crazy golf course (Adventure Island, see p112). The North Norfolk Railway used to serve the village, bringing holidaymakers in their thousands to explore the town and its pretty millpond, but mostly to enjoy the sea air and the excellent beach (a

Happisburgh Lighthouse *see p104*

regular Blue Flag winner). The branch line was axed in 1964, though part of the old railway track is still visible inland near North Walsham, at Pigneys Wood local nature reserve (www.norfolkwildlifetrust.org.uk).

The lack of easy public transport has resulted in Mundesley being a quiet and appealing village with more amenities than most. There's the **Maritime Museum** (Beach Road, 01263 722068; open June-Sept), surely the world's smallest, housed in a coastal lookout station, and some interesting buildings – notably the unusual **Coronation Hall**, home to the Mundesley Players (www. mundesley.org), who stage regular shows and musicals. There are a couple of cafés (including the Corner House, Cromer Road, 01263 720509),

and clifftop pub the **Ship** (Beach Road, 01263 722671, www.mundesley ship.co.uk), which claims to have 'probably the best beer garden in Norfolk'.

Gather picnic ingredients at **Country Pickings** delicatessen (19 High Street, 01263 720054, closed Sun) and the **Lobster Pot** seafood stall in the village car park (fresh and smoked fish and seafood) and make the most of the coast; with its eye-catching if dilapidated groynes, gaily painted beach huts and wide sandy beach, it's a real winner. Just beyond the village, on the coast road, are the four white sails of **Stow Mill**, an 1820s corn mill that continued operating until 1930.

Thanks to the plethora of caravan parks along this stretch of coast, there's no shortage of pubs, cafés and

Winterton-on-Sea *see p103*

Winterton-on-Sea *see p103*

fish and chip shops heading out of Mundesley, but because of the sheer length of that coastline – just over 35 miles from Sheringham to Great Yarmouth – it's easy to escape the crowds once you get past frankly horrible Bacton (surely the reason the coastline beyond has remained such a secret).

Lacking Mundesley's Victorian charm, **Bacton** is resolutely 20th century, a shambolic string of tawdry-looking B&Bs and guesthouses. It's best avoided by heading inland to North Walsham and returning to the coast at Happisburgh (pronounced, in typical Norfolk fashion, 'Haisbro').

Happisburgh to Hemsby

Visible for miles, red and white striped Happisburgh Lighthouse (*see p104*) is just one reason to stop at this lovely village; a great pub, fine church, sweet tearooms, well-stocked wet fish and shellfish shop, and exhilarating walks along the crumbling clifftop or beach below are the others. Erosion is a major problem here, as is evident from the wooden sea defence barriers stretching the length of the beach.

Expansive beaches are the norm for the next 20 miles, some the focus for miniscule Blackpool-esque resorts (Sea Palling and Hemsby), others glorious expanses of nothing but clean sand, big blue skies and seemingly endless sea (Waxham, Horsey and Winterton-on-Sea). All have something to recommend them; **Sea Palling**, in particular, is great for families who want an understated mini-resort with child-friendly facilities such as ice-cream stands and doughnut parlours, a good café and a tiny amusement arcade, while the stretch between **Waxham** and Winterton-on-Sea is a birdwatching hotspot. Twitchers shelter in the beach cuttings and hunker down in the dunes to catch sight of chiff-chaff,

stonechat, cranes and red-throated and black-throated divers.

Around the old smugglers' village of **Horsey** – worth a look for the thatched, round-towered **All Saints' Church** and a pint and a pie at the **Nelson Head** (*see p106*) – the beach is particularly quiet, visited only by birdwatchers, dog walkers and the colony of grey seals who come every year to bask on the beach. Sitting on the sea defence wall with no other soul around, just watching the 100 or so new pups born each winter is a real joy (and beats a packed boat at Blakeney into a cocked hat). But keep your distance. Volunteer wardens from **Friends of Horsey Seals** (www.friendsofhorseyseals.co.uk) patrol the beaches to protect the grey seals from disturbance by the public. This is particularly important during the late autumn and winter, when they come ashore to give birth and mate.

The pleasures (and seals) continue south at **Winterton-on-Sea** ♥. Backed by the pastel-painted **Hermanus roundhouses** (*see p107*), Winterton-on-Sea has one of the area's best beaches. The water is deep enough to attract windsurfers from around the country and the extensive dunes provide a great habitat for all manner of wildlife, including terns, natterjack toads and the odd adder. The attractive streets, filled with neatly thatched cottages and white picket-fenced gardens, a cute village store, a good fish and chip shop and a picturesque 300-year-old pub, make it one of the prettiest villages, too.

Make the most of it; south of here, 'lively' **Hemsby**, all fast-food joints, amusement arcades, discos and seaside tat shops, is something of a culture shock after the quiet emptiness of the rest of east Norfolk's breathtaking coastline... but a very good introduction to the charms of Great Yarmouth (*see p133*).

Places to visit

OVERSTRAND TO HEMSBY

Happisburgh Lighthouse

Happisburgh, NR12 (www.happisburgh.org/ lighthouse). Open Easter-Aug days vary; check website. Admission £5; free-£1 reductions. No children under 1m. No credit cards.

East Anglia's oldest working lighthouse, dating from 1790, is also Britain's only independently run one. There are regular open days in summer, a gift shop and a starring role in the occasional TV drama (anyone remember Stephen Fry's *Kingdom?*) The 112-step climb to the lantern room is definitely not for vertigo sufferers; indeed, the spiral stone staircase is hair-raising for anyone. Views from the top are as far-reaching and glorious as you'd expect – on a clear day you can see for about 13 miles.

Horsey Windpump & Mere

Horsey, NR29 4EF (01263 740241, www. nationaltrust.org.uk). Open 10am-4pm daily. Admission £6.50; £3.50 reductions; £16.50 family.

Just south of Horsey, the elegant five-storey Horsey drainage windpump hoves into view on the land side of the beach road, and offers a great couple of hours' entertainment that could stretch into a whole day if the weather is good. The mill itself is fun to explore, and there's a lovely three-mile circular walk that skirts part of Horsey Mere on the easternmost fringes of the Broads, before cutting through flat Norfolk fields to emerge at the Nelson Head pub (see p106).

Waxham Great Barn

Waxham Road, Sea Palling, NR12 0DY (01692 598824).

This impressive, Grade I-listed 180ft long barn (Norfolk's biggest, built around 1570) is constructed from the remains of several dissolved monasteries. The barn is currently used as a wedding venue, although it was closed at time of going to press and its future opening hours were uncertain. However, the popular café, housed in the converted cow shed, continues to serve delicious crab sandwiches and pastries (9am-5pm daily).

NORTH WALSHAM & AROUND

Cat Pottery

1 Grammar School Road, North Walsham, NR28 9JH (01692 402962). Open 9am-4pm Mon-Fri.

Down a wee cobbled lane, what were tinsmiths' workshops are now filled with old railway and transport paraphernalia and hundreds of wide-eyed ceramic cats (and the odd dog) created by the late Jenny Winstanley and continued by her family. The felines look down from battered display cases, peek from old fire hydrants, and sit like ranks of soldiers on rickety shelves, creating one of the maddest little museums (and shops – most of the pottery is for sale) you're ever likely to visit.

East Ruston Old Vicarage Gardens ♥

East Ruston Old Vicarage, East Ruston, NR12 9HN (01692 650432, www.e-ruston-oldvicaragegardens.co.uk). Open Mar-Oct noon-5.30pm Wed-Sun. Admission £11; free-£2 reductions.

The 30 acres of coastal garden here are utterly magical, largely due to the sheer horticultural exuberance created by owners and designers Alan Gray and Graham Robeson. The duo bought the house in the mid 1990s, inheriting what they call a 'blank canvas', and have turned it into an imaginative extravaganza taking in everything from a wildflower meadow to formal Dutch gardens and towering ferns to a Californian border of explosive colour. It's all the more impressive considering the exposed nature of the site. Clever peepholes and topiary bring views of the surrounding area, and a pretty tearoom completes what is surely Norfolk's best garden. (Check out the fabulous new brochure on their website.) No dogs allowed.

Norfolk Motorcycle Museum

Railway Yard, North Walsham, NR28 0DS (01692 1-2 Norwich Road, North Walsham, NR28 9JP (01692 406266, https://norfolk-motorcycle-museum.business.site). Open June-Sept 10am-4.30pm daily; Oct-May 10am-4.30pm Mon-Fri. No credit cards.

Strictly one for two-wheel enthusiasts, this unlikely-looking museum has a collection of more than 100 vehicles from the 1920s to the 60s, as well as old die-cast toys.

Where to eat & drink

This section of coast may be quieter than elsewhere in Norfolk, but it's still the seaside, so there are traditional caffs, greasy spoons and chippies galore. **Poppylands Café** at Delph Farm (01493 393393; 10am-3.30pm daily), a converted barn on the coast road between Sea Palling and Waxham, is worth a weekend stop if you don't fancy pub grub or caff staples. On the B1159 near Walcott, the **Lighthouse Inn** (01692 650371, www.lighthouseinn.co.uk) is a sprawling, popular pub.

East Ruston Old Vicarage Gardens

Clifftop Café 💙

22 Cliff Road, Overstrand, NR27 0PP (01263 579319, www.clifftopholidays. co.uk). Open 8am-4pm daily. No credit cards.

There's been a café on this spot since 1925, though probably not always painted powder blue and furnished with pretty pine tables and striped tablecloths. The current incarnation does great full English breakfasts, homely cooked lunches and cakes. Dogs are welcome.

Fishermans Return

The Lane, Winterton-on-Sea, NR29 4BN (01493 393305, www.fishermansreturn. com). Open Summer 11am-10.30pm daily. Winter 11am-3pm, 5-10.30pm daily. Lunch served noon-2pm, dinner served 6-9pm daily.

This deservedly popular pub specialises, as you might guess from the name, in fish dishes – the fish pie, and seafood omelette with prawns and smoked salmon are both terrific. Bar food snacks and five real ales are available, and there are also six comfortable B&B rooms (£110 double incl breakfast). A lodge sleeping up to six is also available.

Hill House Inn 💙

The Hill, Happisburgh, NR12 0PW (01692 650004, www.hillhouseinn.co.uk). Open noon-3pm, 5pm-close Mon-Fri; noon-close Sat & Sun.

Located on a small hill, the Hill House is a Grade II-listed, 16th-century inn rightly lauded for its well-kept ales and good pub food, and famous for its one-time guest, Arthur Conan Doyle. The menu includes ploughman's, local crab and fish dishes, and pile-'em-high meat and three veg options on Sundays, and there's normally an annual Solstice Beer Festival in June. Two rooms (£75 double incl breakfast) are available, one of them housed in a converted 1901 signal box overlooking the sea.

Nelson Head
The Street, Horsey, NR29 4AD (01493 393378, www.thenelsonhead.com).
At time of going to press the pub was closed but set to reopen in the summer in accordance with government guidelines.

A very welcome sight after a fine circular walk from Horsey Windpump (*see p104*) to the beach, the Nelson Head offers real ale and excellent roasts and pies in front of a roaring log fire – perfect on a winter's day. Dogs are welcome too.

Smallsticks Barn Café
Cart Gap Road, Happisburgh, NR12 0QL (01692 583368, www.smallstickscafe. co.uk) Open 10am-4pm Thur-Sun).

This delightful little café is a godsend for walkers enjoying the isolated stretch of beach between Happisburgh and Lessingham. Located in a converted barn some 100 yards from the Cart Gap lifeboat station, it's open for all-day breakfast, lunchtime snacks, cakes and cream teas, and offers expansive views from its enclosed terrace.

White Horse Overstrand
34 High Street, Overstrand, NR27 0AB (01263 579237, www.whitehorseoverstrand. co.uk). Open 8am-11pm daily. Lunch served noon-2.30pm, dinner served 6-9pm daily.

The chefs at the White Horse keep winning awards for their consistently reliable British menu and use of local produce, including lobsters from Overstrand, local marsh samphire and crabs, of course, from Cromer. They smoke their own fish, churn their own ice-cream and all the bread, preserves and even the tomato sauce are made in-house. There are also eight guest rooms (from £99 double incl breakfast).

Nine Norfolk Gardens

East Ruston Old Vicarage Gardens
A 30-acre gem packed with colour and interest, plus a pretty tearoom. If you only have time to visit one garden, make it this one. See p104.

Gooderstone Water Gardens
Waterlogged grazing ground transformed into a six-acre water garden. A charming tearoom completes the idyll. See p174.

Hoveton Hall Gardens
Imaginative planting makes the woodland and lakeside walks a treat; kingfishers are often seen by the lake. See p123.

Plantation Garden
Near the centre of Norwich, but hidden away in a medieval chalk quarry, this 'secret' garden features Gothic fountains, an Italianate terrace, a summer house and numerous walkways. See p93.

Priory Maze & Gardens
Formal gardens, woodlands and meadows, plus a hedge maze based on the footprint of nearby ruined Beeston Priory. There's a tearoom too. See p72.

Raveningham Gardens
A set of gardens that includes huge herbaceous borders, an Edwardian rose garden, a lake and an 18th-century walled kitchen garden. See p143.

Sheringham Park
A vast, Humphry Repton-designed park, where the displays of rhododendrons and azaleas (from mid May to June) are stunning. See p72.

Walsingham Abbey Grounds
Snowdrop walks in early spring are just one of the highlights of these 20 acres of woodland, parkland and gardens. See p53.

West Acre Gardens
A garden centre unlike any other, set in the walled garden of a manor house. The display gardens are hugely inspirational. See p175.

Beechwood Hotel *see p111*

Where to stay

The coast road (B1159) from Cromer to Great Yarmouth has a range of accommodation options with great locations and views. Most of the village pubs dotted along the coast have B&B rooms too, including **Hill House Inn** in Happisburgh (*see p105*) and **Fishermans Return** in Winterton-on-Sea (*see p105*).

If you're looking to self-cater, **Shoal Cottage** (01263 579319, www.clifftopholidays.co.uk), which sits next to the **Clifftop Café** in Overstrand, has expansive sea views and sleeps eight.

Hermanus Holiday Camp💜

The Holway, Winterton-on-Sea, NR29 4BP (01493 393216, www. hermanusholidays.com). Rates £595 single roundhouse per week.

The story goes that the owner of this terrifically located holiday camp (overlooking the dunes and a golden beach) constructed the fairytale-like thatched roundhouses after seeing similar ones on a visit to Hermanus Bay in South Africa. Although quite basic (think cute caravans), the pastel-painted cottages are well equipped. As well as the roundhouses, there are bungalows, chalets and apartments. In addition, there's an outdoor heated pool from late May to mid September, lovely gardens, family entertainment, games and an on-site restaurant and bar.

Sea Marge Hotel💜

High Street, Overstrand, NR27 0AB (01263 579579, www.seamargehotel. co.uk). Rates £200-£260 double incl breakfast.

A clifftop location and four acres of gardens and terraced lawns leading down to the foreshore make this elegant

Ten Norfolk delicacies

Booja-Booja chocolates
www.boojabooja.com.

Let's face it, if you think of posh chocolates, you don't immediately think of down-to-earth Norfolk. And yet the Booja-Booja Company has won more than 25 awards for its small range of organic, vegan chocolate truffles and ice-cream, possibly because they are dairy-free, gluten-free, soya-free, made without refined sugar and... delicious.

Bray's Cottage pork pies ♥
www.perfectpie.co.uk.

Outdoor-reared rare-breed pigs, a dash of onion marmalade and seasoning are all you need to create the perfect pork pie, according to Bray's Cottage proprietors. Test their theory with the ready-cooked version on a picnic, or take home the frozen variety.

Breckland Orchard soft drinks
www.brecklandorchard.co.uk.

Claire Martinsen's old-fashioned sodas have been garnering praise from all quarters: the ginger beer with chilli was highly rated by *Observer Food Monthly*. If ginger beer's not your thing, the cloudy lemonade or strawberry and rhubarb will tumble you into Enid Blyton territory faster than you can say 'those pesky kids'.

Chillis Galore sauces
www.chillisgalore.co.uk.

Richard and Kathy have been growing chillis in Norfolk since 1990, bottling them as own-made jellies, sauces and relishes with some tantalising and original flavours – among them jalapeño, lime and coriander chilli jelly, and Caribbean chilli sauce.

Cley Smokehouse
www.cleysmokehouse.com.

Smoked prawns, eels, kippers, haddock, potted shrimp, pickled herrings, cured meats, smoked cheese... they smoke a lot of stuff at Cley Smokehouse (*see p50*), and have been doing so for more than 30 years, trying as much as possible to use locally sourced ingredients. There's a great range of own-made pâtés too.

Edwardian building a beauty. The 25 bedrooms (all en suite) include original features in contemporary settings. Food is served in the bar and two restaurants; non-residents are welcome. There's also a lounge with games. Guests have free use of leisure facilities at the Links Country Park Hotel, five miles up the coast (tennis court, indoor heated swimming pool and gym), and a nine-hole round of golf for a tenner.

Stow Mill
Stow Hill, Paston, NR28 9TG (01263 720298, www.stowmill.co.uk). £1,035–£1,340 per week; 3-night minimum.

Built as a flour mill by James Gaze in the 1820s, this traditional Norfolk windmill has been converted into a stunning one-bedroom living space on three floors, with no expense spared.

NORTH WALSHAM & AROUND

No village in east Norfolk rivals the likes of Burnham Market on the north Norfolk coast – but given the sheer abundance of them (there's a village or hamlet every mile or so), it's easy to find a sizeable number that have a notable attraction, whether it's a stunning church, a great pub, a particularly harmonious aspect or a picture-perfect village pond. And there are signs that the Farrow & Ball effect is gathering pace: Northrepps, for example, a typical flint cottage-heavy village just inland from Overstrand, has **Northrepps Cottage** (*see p112*), a boutique country hotel and restaurant.

The busy market town of **North Walsham** is the heart of this area (known as 'Griffon Country' after the arms of the Paston family, who once owned most of it) and has a number of decent accommodation options, as well as a handsome market square, a 14th-century wool church, a tiny row of shops that began life as medieval stalls (in Pope's Passage, on the north side of the churchyard), and Paston

College, now a sixth-form college but in the 1760s the school attended by Horatio Nelson. The shopping is forgettable, but it's a pleasant place with some attractive streets and houses, and a **Cat Pottery** (*see p104*) that's a real one-off.

The noted **Paston Way** starts out here too; beginning in the Market Place, the 20-mile waymarked trail takes in 15 churches and villages en route to Cromer, through quiet lanes, along high cliffs and across arable fields and grazing pastures. There's more good walking (and cycling) on the **Weavers' Way**, a 60-mile trail between Cromer and Great Yarmouth, which also passes through the town.

North Walsham is also not a bad base for exploring the surrounding villages of **Trunch**, **Knapton** and **Worstead**, each of which makes for a good half-day excursion. Trunch stands out for its thatched 17th-century manor house and late 14th-century **St Botolph's Church**. The latter is notable for a highly carved wooden font canopy (one of only four in England) and an impressive angel hammerbeam roof, only outdone in the area by the church of **St Peter & St Paul** in Knapton, which has an even more beautiful double-hammerbeam roof with 138 angels. And if you like a good round tower, don't miss **St Mary's Church** in Roughton, which boasts a particularly lovely one, built partly of ironstone.

Nearby, in the extensive grounds of **Gunton Park**, the hard-to-find church of **St Andrew** is definitely worth visiting. This Palladian, chapel-like building is the only church designed by the great Robert Adam, and the hunt for it, through a large wooded estate with a deer park, fishing lake, an observatory tower, the shell of the original Gunton Hall (gutted by fire in 1882) and an occupied hall of private apartments, makes for a great walk, particularly

Houghton Hall venison
Largesse from the Marquess of Cholomondley, whose Norfolk estate supplies selected local butchers with the meat of the unusual white fallow deer that roam the 450 acres of parkland surrounding the hall (see p41).

Mrs Temple's Cheese ♥
Catherine Temple produces a number of Norfolk cheeses, the most famous of which is probably binham blue, a subtle, soft-veined blue cheese, but there's also crumbly walsingham, gouda-style warhans and even a melton mozarella. All the cheeses are handmade from the family's own dairy cow herd and widely available at farmers' markets, delis and farm shops.

Norfolk Lavender shortbread
www.norfolk-lavender.co.uk.
You'll find lavender shortbread in many of Norfolk's tearooms, where it's worth trying for its wonderfully delicate flavour. Buy some of the ingredients at Norfolk Lavender (see p20) if you're smitten, or bags of the ready-made variety at various farm shops.

Samphire sausages
www.samphireshop.co.uk.
Made from outdoor-reared rare-breed pigs and subtly flavoured with nutmeg, sage, coriander and ginger, Samphire's sizzling range of sausages were once described by the late Gary Rhodes as the best he'd ever tasted. Buy them at local markets and fairs.

Stoneground flour & bread
Letheringsett Watermill (see p52) near Holt produces a range of stoneground wheat, including whole wheat and spelt, that's available across Norfolk, both as flour and in pastries, loaves and cakes.

when you eventually spy the light, beautifully proportioned church in its perfect setting. It's now cared for by the Churches Conservation Trust (www.visitchurches.org.uk).

Heading south, the village of **Worstead** – heart of the area's 14th-century weaving trade and the origin of the word 'worsted' – is another good halting point, not least for the impressive scale of its 14th-century wool church, **St Mary's**. The convivial village pub, the **White Lady** (*see p111*), is, in normal years, at the heart of the three-day **Worstead Festival** (www.worsteadfestival.org) in July, which bills itself as the largest village festival in Norfolk and offers an intriguing mix of terrier racing, sheep shearing, folk music and ceilidhs.

A few miles east, the Broads/Griffon borders hold a few more pleasant sights: in the village of East Ruston, **St Mary's Church** lies in a great open-fields setting and the **Old Vicarage Gardens** (*see p104*) offer one of Norfolk's best attractions, while the tiny traditional hamlets of **Ingham** and **Lessingham** are home to a lovely church apiece and two good pubs with rooms: the **Swan Inn** (*see right*) and the **Star** (*see p111*). Both of them make good bases for exploring the coast and the Broads.

Where to eat & drink

North Walsham is the best bet for lunch, with coffee shops, cafés and, most popular of all, **Kelly's Plaice** fish and chip shop on the market square.

There's still a pub in most villages, many offering a good selection of real ales and pub grub. For Modern British food in a grander setting, country hotels **Beechwood** (*see p111*) and **Northrepps Cottage** (*see p112*) won't disappoint.

Chubby Panda
22 Market Street, North Walsham, NR28 9BZ (01692 500920). Open currently for dinner only 5-10.30pm Tue-Thur, Sun; 5-11pm Fri & Sat.

Above-average international food is rare in small towns, so all hail the Chubby Panda, which serves decent Thai and Chinese food in an understated, elegant space with leather armchairs and damask tablecloths.

Crown Inn
Smallburgh, NR12 9AD (01692 536314, www.smallburghcrown.co.uk). Open 11am-11pm daily. Lunch served noon-2pm Mon-Sat; noon-2.30pm Sun. Dinner served 7-9pm Tue-Sat.

The Crown is a sprawling, 15th-century thatched coaching inn with a pretty dining room and classic beer garden. There are real ales and homely food, plus two guest bedrooms (£95 double incl breakfast).

Ingham Swan
Sea Palling Road, Ingham, NR12 9AB (01692 581099, www.theinghamswan. co.uk). Lunch served noon-2pm Mon-Sat; noon-3pm Sun. Dinner served 6pm-8.30pm daily.

Dating back to the 14th century when it was part of the Ingham Priory, this well-sited restaurant next to a fine church serves an exciting menu of seasonal dishes using locally sourced ingredients. There's a three-course lunch and dinner set menu (£28) and a seven-course taster menu (£65) as well as à la carte. Expect the likes of yeast-glazed beef fillet, salmon en papillote or barbecued lamb rump. Seven en-suite rooms are also available, set in a converted barn and three in a cottage just down the road (£145-£195 double incl breakfast).

Shambles
6 Market Street, North Walsham, NR28 9BZ (01692 405282, www. shamblescafenorfolk.co.uk). Open bar 10am-9.30pm Wed, Thur; 10am-10pm Fri. Sat; noon-4pm Sun. Food served 11am-2pm, 5.30-8pm Wed-Fri; 11am-3pm, 5.30-8pm Sat; noon-3pm Sun.

Mediterranean/Middle Eastern-inspired food (smokey meatballs or felafel salad) is on the menu at this welcoming and award-winning bistro with a café and bar and a courtyard with outside seating.

Star
School Road, Lessingham, NR12 0DN (01692 580510, www.thestarlessingham. co.uk). Open noon-3pm, 6-11pm Tue-Sun.

This cosy village inn serves a small range of well-kept Norfolk ales and changing guest ones (they even won the CAMRA Rural Pub of the Year award a few years ago), and a daily specials menu that often includes locally caught fish and shellfish, as well as rib-eye steak or Norfolk sausages with gravy and mash and, on Sundays, excellent roasts with all the trimmings. Eat in the small restaurant or better still, nab the table next to the giant inglenook fireplace in the lounge.

Vernon Arms💜
2 Church Street, Southrepps, NR11 8NP (01263 833355, www.vernonarms.com). At time of going to press the pub opening hours were not available but they are set to reopen as soon as government guidelines permit.

A charming, ultra-friendly pub, which serves good food cooked entirely on the premises. Straightforward lunchtime grub includes hot baguettes, jacket potatoes, ploughman's and salads; come the evening, dishes range from pork with red onion marmalade, melted stilton and mash to the pub's signature dish, the Vernon Arms Black and Tan – a beef, Guinness and ale pie with gravy, proper chips and mushy peas. There's a good collection of beers too.

White Lady
Front Street, Worstead, NR28 9RW (01692 535391, www.thewhitelady. co.uk). At time of going to press the pub was closed but set to reopen as soon as government guidelines permit.

This handsome pub looks after its real ales and visitors in equally good measure.

Daily blackboard specials are offered in a pleasant space that includes a small bar with a big fire, two lounges, a summer garden and a cosy dining area. There are five guest rooms available (£85-£95 double incl breakfast) and six self-catering options, each sleeping six to eight people.

Where to stay
There are plenty of B&Bs, inns and hotels in this area. Self-catering places are often available for as few as one or two nights out of season.

Beechwood Hotel💜
Cromer Road, North Walsham, NR28 0HD (01692 403231, www.beechwood-hotel.co.uk). Rates £110-£249 double incl breakfast.

The rooms in this smart country hotel are vibrantly decorated and feature numerous welcome touches, among them bathrobes and free-standing bathtubs. The two luxurious garden spa rooms are a recent addition. The restaurant is equally appealing, as is the Modern British food – locally sourced, of course: wood pigeon, compressed pear, marinated blackberry and red wine syrup to start, for example. Agatha Christie stayed here many times in the 1930s, when the house was owned by close friends.

Deers Glade Caravan & Camping Park
White Post Road, Hanworth, NR11 7HN (01263 768633, www.deersglade.co.uk). Open All year. Pitch £17.50-£25 for 2 people.

A great family-friendly campsite and caravan park in a woodland setting. There's a natural play area for children, a fishing lake, two large, clean shower/toilet blocks, a shop and even Wi-Fi access from your tent. In August, tent-only Muntjac Meadow opens for campers wanting a more low-tech, back-to-nature vibe; at night there's a communal campfire to gather round. There are also bell tents, pods and a shepherd's hut to rent.

Things to do

OVERSTRAND TO HEMSBY

Adventure Island
Beach Road, Mundesley, NR11 8BG (no phone). Open summer from 10am (closing time varies). Admission £5; £4 reductions.

A great, old-fashioned 12-hole themed crazy golf course, with lakes and waterfalls, pirates, monsters of the deep and all manner of inventive papier mâché. Floodlit too, should you fancy an after-dark round.

NORTH WALSHAM & AROUND

Bittern Line
www.bitternline.com (National Rail enquiries 08457 484950).

The Bittern Line may not have cute steam engines, but this 30-mile railway linking Cromer with Norwich is well worth taking if you want to get a real sense of rural Norfolk and a land's view of the Broads villages. Stops at North Walsham, Gunton and Worstead make the line great for exploring this area, bikes are welcome (though it's essential to book ahead in summer) and a 20p through ticket enables you to use the area's buses too.

Gunton Arms💚
Cromer Road, Thorpe Market, NR11 8TZ (01263 832010, www.theguntonarms.co.uk). Rates £99-£320 double incl breakfast.

This gorgeous house set in a deer park has been refurbished by art dealer Ivor Braka and his artist wife Sarah Graham to offer 12 rooms that are a real treat. Forget soulless 'boutique-style' hotels; here, you'll find warmth and character, thanks to the confident use of lovely antiques, textiles and furnishings. Boldly coloured public spaces include the welcoming restaurant. Even if you don't stay, come for the food; head chef Stuart Tattersall has worked with restaurateur Mark Hix in London, so you're guaranteed the best use of local, seasonal produce, and great service.

Northrepps Cottage💚
Nut Lane, Northrepps, NR27 0JN (01263 579202, www.northreppscottagehotel. co.uk). At time of going to press the hotel was closed but set to reopen as soon as government guidelines permit.

A small, luxurious country house hotel and restaurant, where eight smart en-suite rooms feature underfloor heating, power showers, flatscreen TVs and ultra-fluffy towels. The setting and extensive gardens are gorgeous, and the restaurant serves imaginative Modern British food: wild boar, Norfolk pork and pistachio terrine with rhubarb chutney is a typical dish.

Scarborough Hill Country Inn
Old Yarmouth Road, North Walsham, NR28 9NA (01692 402151, www. scarboroughhill.co.uk). At time of going to press the hotel was closed but set to reopen as soon as government guidelines permit.

Nine individually decorated bedrooms make up this country house hotel; some border on the OTT, but all are well appointed and very comfortable. There are also two self-contained apartments for families. The restaurant, set in a twinkling glass conservatory, serves an extensive menu, often using local fish and game.

Waxham *see p103*

Northern Broads

If there's one Norfolk attraction most people have heard of, it's the Norfolk Broads, the sprawling network of seven rivers (the Ant, Bure and Thurne in the north and the Yare, Wensum, Waveney and Chet in the south) and 63 shallow inland lakes fringed by reeds, marshland and woodland on which water-bound holidaymakers spend happy weeks. These ancient flooded pits, ranging in width from a few feet to several miles, were created by the large-scale excavation of peat, an important and valuable fuel – first by the Romans, then by local monasteries in the Middle Ages. Over the centuries, rising sea levels and newly formed channels created 117 square miles of wetland that, since their discovery by Victorian sailing enthusiasts looking for the latest thrill, have become one of England's most popular 'natural' wonders.

This is a landscape that feels a long way from civilisation and its manifold distractions. Walking gingerly through the wetlands or sitting on a boat travelling at four miles an hour slows the world right down, enabling water, trees, marsh, sky and wildlife to create a very special landscape. Add in the sound of rustling reeds, soft breezes in the trees and water sucking against the banks of 125 miles of tranquil rivers, tributaries and lakes, and you're bound to feel at peace. On land you'll find medieval stone bridges, picturesque drainage windpumps, beautifully proportioned flint churches and a wealth of other man-made but naturally harmonious structures. You don't have to sleep aboard a boat to appreciate the beauty, tranquillity and leisurely pace of life of the Broads, but if you only explore the area by car, bike or foot, you'll definitely miss out – so at the very least hire a day-boat and take to the water.

HICKLING & BARTON BROADS

Hickling Broad
If you only have time to get out on one Broad, make it the biggest, Hickling, which covers more than 320 acres. This serene stretch of water is magical, and the surroundings quieter than the area around Hoveton and Ranworth Broads further west.

The starting point, the Broads Haven marina at **Potter Heigham** (pronounced 'Potter Ham') has a well-stocked information centre, a couple of decent places to eat and its very own department store, Lathams. Although a key Broads hub, it's surprisingly quiet, thanks to the **Potter Heigham Old Bridge**, a medieval hump-backed bridge whose six-foot eight-inch headroom makes it impassable by big boats, thus keeping the stretch of the River Thurne between here and Hickling (and further to Horsey Mere) as peaceful as possible. Swirling currents beneath the bridge make navigating it a little tricky, but the fearless day-boater is rewarded with the sight of pretty fretworked wooden cottages topped with the reed thatch and sedge that are cut back regularly from the waterways, to keep them open for both man and beast. Downstream of the bridge, keep an eye out for the **Dutch Tutch**, a 12-sided black and white house and adjacent shed made up of two sections of a 19th-century helter-skelter from Great Yarmouth.

Once the houses have vanished, a deep tranquility descends, broken only by the sound of ducks, geese and swans on the river and, further back from the reed and sedge banks, numerous other species; kingfishers, kestrels, tits, warblers and bittern all live in this rich landscape of marsh, wood and water. The names of the areas they inhabit are just as lyrical and lovely as the birds themselves: **Sound Plantation**, **Whispering Reeds**, **Deep-Go Dyke**, **Candle Dyke** and **Hundred Acre Marsh**. Many have little moorings, where you can stop to listen and look; a motor boat travelling at just four miles an hour creates enough noise to frighten off wildlife. At Candle Dyke junction, turn left for **Hickling Broad**. (If you turn right, there's an enjoyable diversion to **Horsey Mere** for some great walking and a look around the National Trust windpump – see p104.)

The wide expanse of water can be unnerving after the restraining riverbanks, but follow the marked channels and you'll be fine, soon arriving at the far end of the broad, at the **Pleasure Boat Inn** (www.thepleasureboatinn.com), where you can stop for some landside exploration. A 20-minute walk past the thatched boathouses at Hickling Staithe will bring you to the **Hickling Broad National Nature Reserve** (see p122). Hickling village, split between waterside Hickling Heath and Hickling Green inland, has little of note beyond the **Greyhound Pub** (see p117) and **Whispering Reeds boatyard** (if you're hiring a boat here,

Thurne Dyke Mill see p130

it's useful to know that they're all able to pass under Potter Heigham Bridge).

An alternative option is to continue straight on at the Candle Dyke junction, rather than turning left. This leads to **Martham Broad National Nature Reserve**, a hotspot for swallowtail butterflies. Adjacent is **West Somerton**, a lovely village with some fine riverside walks and a beautiful 900-year-old church, **St Mary**. Perched on a hill, it provides great views over the countryside and towards **Winterton-on-Sea**. Martham village has various shops and a decent pub set around a green, and a wonderfully eccentric **scarecrow festival** every May.

Barton Broad

Back on dry land, the roads radiating from Potter Heigham offer a number of different Broads experiences. Head west on the A1062 or north-west on the A149 to the area around Barton Broad. The villages of **Irstead** and **Barton Turf** offer something special in their churches, both called St Michael (including a glorious, brightly coloured rood screen at Barton Turf), but have few other enticements. Nearby **Neatishead** is bigger; it's a lovely Georgian village with a shop, a decent restaurant, a homely pub and a comfortable guesthouse. The spectacular waterside homes north of the village are known locally as Millionaires' Row. Thanks to their waterside but slightly off-the-beaten-track settings, all three villages are pretty and unspoilt. At **Gays Staithe** (between Neatishead and Irstead), you can follow the **Barton Broad Boardwalk** for sweeping views across the broad, or take a boat trip on the solar-powered *Ra* (*see p126*).

Travelling north from Barton Broad on the River Ant brings you to **Stalham Staithe**, home to the award-winning **Museum of the Broads** (*see p122*), and pretty **Sutton Staithe**. Tiny Sutton village has a church and a (non-working) cornmill built in 1789. A whopping nine storeys high, it's the tallest windmill in England. The market town of **Stalham** is rather rundown, but useful if you need food supplies, or want to stock up on wet-weather gear and all manner of other items at the **Original Factory Shop** (129 High Street, 01692 580882). The **Swan Inn** (*see right*) is a good lunch stop, and the town hall hosts a farmers' market and an enjoyable bric-a-brac market on alternate Saturdays.

If you're travelling by road, the A149 runs past Sutton and Stalham, and on to upmarket hotel/restaurant **Wayford Bridge Inn** (*see p118*), before heading south (as the A1151) to decidedly more upbeat and bustling Wroxham.

Where to eat & drink

This region is a long way from the foodie mecca of the north Norfolk coast, but there are plenty of picturesque pubs, often by the water, serving hearty and reliable food. Try the popular **Falgate Inn** (Ludham Road, 01692 670003) in Potter Heigham; the **Greyhound** (The Green, 01692 598306, www.greyhoundinn.com) in Hickling Green, which has a beautiful garden; or the **White Horse** (The Street, 01692 630828) in Neatishead, where huge portions are served in a handful of tiny slate-floored bars or a nice dining room.

For more special occasions, there are upmarket restaurants in the **Wayford Bridge Inn** and the **Sutton Staithe Hotel** (for both, *see p118*). If you just want good fish and chips, try **Harry's** (Bridge Road, 01692 670415) in Potter Heigham, or **Broadland Fish & Chips** ♥ (27 High Street, 01692 580247, closed Sun) in Stalham.

Swan Inn
90 High Street, Stalham, NR12 9AU (01692 582829). At time of going to press the Swan was opening noon-6.30pm Sun-Thur; noon-8.30pm Fri & Sat; longer opening hours will return.

Luckily, one of the only pubs in Stalham serving food does a good job of it, offering the likes of toasted sandwiches, beer-battered cod and chips, and burgers. You can eat in the spacious, modern lounge bar, a small, summery restaurant or on the back patio. There's free Wi-Fi too for email fiends.

Where to stay

You'll find a decent number of B&Bs – generally of the chintz-and-pine variety. The 18th-century **Regency Guest House** (The Street, 01692 630233, www.regencyguesthouse.com) in Neatishead is a standout. For campers, the tiny **Causeway Cottage Caravan Park** (Bridge Road, 01692

670238, closed Nov-Mar) in Potter Heigham is close to the water and shops, and has good amenities and friendly staff.

Sutton Staithe Hotel
Sutton, NR12 9QS (01692 580244, www. suttonstaithehotel.co.uk). Rates £85 double incl breakfast.

This largeish hotel next to the River Ant (with 11 rooms, ranging from single to family in size) won't win any design prizes for its decor, but it's comfortable and well located. Food is dependable and recommended by Broads regulars.

Wayford Bridge Inn♥
Off A149, nr Stalham, NR12 9LL (01603 363677, www.wayfordbridge.co.uk). Rates £120-£140 double incl breakfast.

Twenty-nine comfortable, contemporary-styled rooms (some facing the river), a restaurant serving a traditional menu of burgers, seafood and steaks, and a peaceful but handy location make this a good alternative to a B&B. In summer, the large waterside terrace is a great spot for dinner or a drink.

RANWORTH BROAD & AROUND

Wroxham & around
Wroxham, the so-called capital of the Broads, thanks to its location near the head of the navigable River Bure (the westernmost of the region's four rivers and thus the 'beginning' of the Broads), is the antithesis of the region in general. Where the waterways can be placid and relaxing, the town – actually two towns, Wroxham and Hoveton, linked by a hump-backed bridge – is heaving, especially in the summer holidays. It's also on both the **Bure Valley** (*see p79*) and **Bittern Line** (*see p112*) railways, which brings in more visitors. Fortunately, there's little to reason to linger here once you've poked your head into Roy's department store, had a pleasant stroll around the bridge area and

along the river, and sampled a lovely ice-cream from **Wroxham Ices** in the precinct on the riverside, or fish and chips from Ken's takeaway/restaurant next to the bridge. Better to head out of town, west towards Coltishall or east towards Ranworth (via the delightful villages of Salhouse and Woodbastwick on the B1140 or Horning on the A1062 – or all of them if you're on the river).

Coltishall, set on the Bure at the far western tip of the Broads, and the starting point for most cruises, is large, pretty and distinctly upmarket, with lots of elegant Dutch-gabled houses and a thatched church. There's plenty to explore here, including two thriving riverside pubs, a chippie, tearooms, an antiques outlet and various independent shops. It's also a halt on the Bure Valley Railway.

Salhouse has its fair share of 18th-century thatched cottages. You pass some of them on the ten-minute walk from the village car park to Salhouse Broad, where the (unusual) sandy shoreline is backed by bluebell woods. You can hire canoes here or catch the summer water taxi to reach the nature trail around **Great Hoveton Broad**.

A couple of miles further on is the village of **Woodbastwick♥**, where stern notices warn of private roads barred to 'anglers and scouts', the village blacksmith watches strangers with a beady eye, and you suspect the gunsmith does a roaring trade. Woodforde's brewery, maker of the highly praised *Wherry* and *Sundew* bitters, certainly does; it's located behind the popular **Fur & Feather pub** (*see p126*) and scents the air with a delicious heady hit of malt. The visitor centre and shop are open daily and brewery tours are available on selected days; call 01603 720353 or check www.woodfordes.com for details. The village is picture-postcard pretty: a glorious array of thatched cottages, almshouses and a large flint church are grouped around a triangular green that contains a canopied well; away from the green, the houses get even grander. Covered with a generous dollop of snow, the whole scene would resemble something out of a Richard Curtis film.

From Woodbastwick, it's just a couple of miles by road to the beautiful village of **Ranworth**, which sits next to Malthouse Broad (a popular sailing spot) and is a short distance from **Ranworth Broad** – now a NWT nature reserve (see p123) and closed to boats. The other main attraction here is obvious: imposing **St Helen's Church** (see p123) dominates the skyline, and provides an unmissable bird's-eye view of the Broads region from its tower. A mile further on, **Fairhaven Woodland & Water Garden** (see p122) in South Walsham normally offers boat trips to the **St Benet Abbey** ruins that are otherwise only really visible from the River Bure (these boat trips have been suspended until further notice).

Horning & around
On the other (north) side of the River Bure, **Horning** ♥ is one of the Broads' most attractive villages, with a positive panoply of reed-thatched cottages (with cutely matching boat houses) and half-timbered Edwardian buildings lining the banks of the Bure. With assorted restaurants and riverside pubs, an art gallery, a delicatessen and a clutch of little shops and tearooms, the village is a terrific base, perfect for rural or river forays, or visits to nearby attractions such as the **RAF Air Defence Radar Museum** (see p123) and **Bewilderwood** (see p122). There's even a colourful paddle-steamer, *Southern Comfort* (01692 630262, www.southern-comfort.co.uk), which runs regular cruises along the Bure.

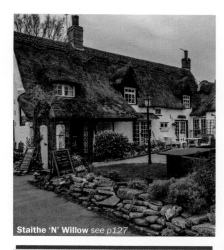
Staithe 'N' Willow see p127

Three pick-your-own farms

Fairgreen Farms
Hill Road, Middleton, nr King's Lynn, PE32 1RN (07761 285864, www.blueberrypicking.co.uk). Open mid July-Sept 9am-5.30pm Mon-Sat.

They scorn such humdrum soft fruits as strawberries and raspberries at Fairgreen, opting instead for big, delicious blueberries, available as PYO in summer or frozen all year round.

Grange
Fleggburgh Road, Rollesby, NR29 5AJ (01493 740236). Open mid June-Sept 10am-5.30pm daily.

Next to the A149 in the northern Broads, the Grange has a wide range of vegetables, including asparagus, beetroot, sweetcorn, courgettes, cucumbers, onions, tomatoes and potatoes in its farm shop, as well as blackberries, raspberries, strawberries and gooseberries available for PYO.

Leith House Plum Orchard
Leith House Farm, nr Burnham Overy, PE31 8JL (07881 378900, www.leithorchards.com). Open mid July-mid Sept 10am-4.30pm daily.

A lovely plum orchard in north Norfolk containing 3,000 plum trees and more than 35 varieties, both ready-picked and PYO. Apple juice and jams are also for sale and they are now licensed so you can sip a glass of wine or a beer in the orchard when you've finished picking.

Hickling Broad *see p115*

Places to visit

HICKLING & BARTON BROADS

Museum of the Broads 💜
The Staithe, Stalham, NR12 9DA (01692 581681, www.museumofthebroads.org.uk). Open 11am-2pm Tues, Thur, Sun. Admission £6; free-£2 reductions.

This award-winning museum, telling the human history of the Broads, from medieval peat diggers to 21st-century holidaymakers via reedcutters, boat builders, thatchers and sailors, manages to engage the imaginations of both children and adults. There's an excellent programme of activities (among them painting, quizzes and playboat events) and a permanent display that evokes the history of the Broads meticulously and entertainingly.

NWT Hickling Broad National Nature Reserve
Hickling, NR12 0BW (01692 598276, www. norfolkwildlifetrust.org.uk). Open Reserve dawn-dusk daily. Visitor centre summer 10am-5pm daily; winter 10am-4pm Fri-Sun. Admission £4.50; children free. Boat trip £8.50; £6 reductions. Additional trips are available. Booking advised.

Being on the water is great, but an equally terrific way to explore the marshland of the Broads is via this wonderful nature reserve, run by the Norfolk Wildlife Trust. A range of short trails and boardwalks gives you close-up access to all sorts of wildlife, including wading birds, otters and lizards. For a final sense of how amazing this area is, take the two-hour Water Trail boat trip through the backwaters of the Broad (not navigable any other way) and climb the galvanised steel staircase up to the tree tower. The opening of the Hickling boat hides will be reviewed in-line with government measures.

RANWORTH BROAD & AROUND

Bewilderwood 💜
Horning Road, nr Horning, NR12 8JW (01603 783900, www.bewilderwood.co.uk). Open Feb half-term, end Mar-Oct 10am-5pm daily. Closed some weekdays Feb-April and Sept-Oct, so phone in advance to check. Admission £19.50; free-£17.50 reductions.

Every child we know who's been here has loved every minute spent clambering around Bewilderwood's beautiful, magical

treehouses, following its imaginative and inventive trails and marsh walk, crossing its jungle bridges and aerial ropewalks and whizzing down its zipwires. Parents are encouraged to get down and dirty with their offspring, and there are lots of special events throughout the year, making this one of the best days out for families in Norfolk. Even the food is great. Don't miss it.

Fairhaven Woodland & Water Garden
School Road, South Walsham, NR13 6DZ (01603 270449, www.fairhavengarden.co.uk). Open 10am-5pm daily. Admission £7.95, free-£6.95 reductions.

A great place for nature lovers, with 131 acres of ancient woodland, water gardens and a private broad. Gnarled ancient oaks – including a 950-year-old king oak – feature on a three-and-a-half-mile woodland walk, and from everywhere you get superb views across South Walsham Inner Broad. The 50-minute boat trip on the private broad to the ruins of St Benet's Abbey is suspended until further notice. But there are other activities to enjoy, such as wildlife canoe trails, stand-up paddle

NWT Upton Broad & Marshes Nature Reserve

boarding, wildlife photography workshops and wildlife warden walks (see website for details).

Hoveton Hall Gardens
Hoveton, NR12 8RJ (01603 784297, www. hovetonhallestate.co.uk/gardens). Open Apr-Aug 10.30am-5pm Sun-Fri. Times vary, check website for details. Admission £8; free-£7 reductions.

An ornamental wrought-iron Spider's Web gate leads to 15 acres of woodland and lakeside walks, plus a 1920s water garden and lake (a great place to spot kingfishers). The imaginative formal and informal planting dates from the early 20th century.

NWT Ranworth Broad Nature Reserve
Ranworth, NR13 6HY (01603 270479. www. norfolkwildlifetrust.org.uk). Open Reserve dawn-dusk daily. Visitor centre Apr-Oct 10am-5pm daily. Admission free.

A pretty boardwalk trail that meanders through oak and carr woodland and reedbeds, studded with information and interpretation boards, makes this reserve a particularly good option for children. At the end of the boardwalk, the floating

visitor centre – topped with reeds and very picturesque – offers plenty of hand-on learning opportunities for the kids and expansive views across the tranquil water (no boats are allowed) for the grown-ups.

RAF Air Defence Radar Museum
Royal Air Force Neatishead, nr Horning, Norwich, NR12 8YB (01692 631485, www. radarmuseum.co.uk). Open 10am-5pm Tue-Sat (and bank holiday Mon). Admission £12; free-£10 reductions.

An engaging and lucid collection that uses a range of imaginative displays – among them an original Cold War operations room (used until 1993), a nuclear bunker and a Night Blitz room – to show the history and development of radar from the 1930s to the present. There's also a gift shop and a café.

St Helen's Church 💜
Ranworth, NR13 6HT (01603 270769, www. ranworth.churchnorfolk.com). Open summer 9.30am-5.30pm; winter 9.30am-dusk. Admission free.

The entrance to the tower of 14th-century St Helen's Church, aka the Cathedral of the Broads, warns that it contains '89 uneven steps, 2 ladders, 1 trapdoor'. And as you'd hope in a church, they don't lie. The stairs are dark, narrow and irregular, the ladders are unnerving and the final trapdoor is likely to hit you on the top of your head as you emerge blinking into the light – but boy, is it worth it. The views are terrific and as far-reaching as you'd expect; five broads are visible from the top, and on a clear day you can see the spire of Norwich Cathedral. Don't miss the church itself, which houses what many experts say is England's finest painted chancel screen, dating from 1419, and a 15th-century illuminated service book.

Wroxham Barns Craft Centre
Tunstead Road, Hoveton, NR12 8QU (01603 783762, www.wroxhambarns.co.uk). Open Barns 10am-5pm daily; Junior Farm & Fun Park 10am-5pm Sat, Sun and daily during school holidays. Admission Barn free; Junior Farm & Fun Park term time £8.99; school holidays £12.99.

This curious crafts-themed amusement park has a large number of family-focused activities, enabling adults and children to learn about, watch and even occasionally

Places to visit

have a go at activities such as apple-pressing, wood-turning, pottery, quilting and jewellery-making. If the little ones tire of crafts, there's a funfair, animal farm, picnic area, mini golf and even weekend camping experiences. There's lots of country fayre on sale in the various food shops and cafés.

TRINITY BROADS

Caister Castle & Car Collection

Castle Lane, Caister-on-Sea, NR30 5SN (01664 567707, www.caistercastle.co.uk). Open mid May-Sept 10am-4.30pm Mon-Fri, Sun. Admission £17, free-£15 reductions; £45 family.

The atmospheric ruins of this 15th-century castle, built by Sir John Fastolf (supposedly the inspiration for Shakespeare's Falstaff) provide a pleasing backdrop to the biggest private car collection in Britain. You can climb the 90ft castle tower for great views before gawping at the rare veteran, vintage, classic and sports automobiles and motorcycles, from the likes of Lotus, Bugatti, Ford and Harley-Davidson. The French-made Panhard et Levassor from 1893 is claimed to be the world's first 'real' car. A woodland walk, café and picnic area provide respite from all the machinery.

NWT Upton Broad & Marshes Nature Reserve

Low Road, Upton, NR13 6EQ (01603 625540, www.norfolkwildlifetrust.org.uk). Open Reserve dawn-dusk daily. Admission free.

Windpump remains, a medieval broad and primeval-looking alders make this reserve of open water, fen, reedbed, woodland and marsh a pleasure to wander round, via a series of waymarked trails and boardwalks. The reserve is one of the UK's top ten sites for dragonflies.

Thrigby Hall Wildlife Gardens

Thrigby Road, nr Filby, NR29 3DR (01493 369477, www.thrigbyhall.co.uk). Open 10am-5pm daily (last entry 4pm). Admission £15.50; free-£14.50 reductions.

A curious selection of animals – from big cats to cockatoos and red pandas to monkeys – can be found in the pleasant gardens here, making it an enjoyable half-day attraction for both grown-ups and kids. The latter will love the swamp house crocs and snakes. Most of the paths and wooden walkways around the park are pushchair and wheelchair friendly. There's a café and play areas with tree ropes and two mazes.

For a lovely walk beside the Bure, follow Lower Street out of the village for about a mile towards **Horning Ferry** (a seasonal foot ferry across to Woodbastwick Staithe), and on to the impressive village church of **St Benedict**, dating from around 1220. From here you'll have a clear view of splendid St Helen's Church on Ranworth Broad.

If you're planning to visit Horning in June, you'll need to book well ahead; the village is the starting point for the famous **Three Rivers Race** (www.3rr.uk), a gruelling 45-mile test along the Ant, Bure and Thurne.

Four miles east of Horning is **Ludham**, the last village of note in the Wroxham/Ranworth ring. After the perfection of Woodbastwick and Horning, it might disappoint at first, but its church, **St Catherine**, houses two excellent restored 15th- and 16th-century painted screens, and what the village lacks for in charm it makes up for in amenities. There are a couple of good pubs, as well as the friendly **Wayfarers Café** (01692 630238) and shop.

Nearby, **How Hill House** (01692 678555, https://howhilltrust.org.uk) is a grand Edwardian house that operates as a privately owned study centre. On certain days, the public can visit the estate, which is home to **Toad Hole cottage**, a traditional 19th-century marshman's home, as well as a nature trail and riverside walks. You can also explore the tiny hidden dykes of adjacent **How Hill Nature Reserve** on the *Electric Eel*, a six-seater, Edwardian-style boat (01692 678763, www.broads-authority.gov.uk, closed Nov-Mar). A two-mile walk across the grazing marshes on the outskirts of Ludham will bring you to the isolated and atmospheric ruins of **St Benet's Abbey**, on the north bank of the Bure. From Ludham, it's just over a mile to Potter Heigham.

New Inn, Horning *see p126*

Where to eat & drink

The year-round appeal of gorgeous villages such as Horning and Woodbastwick ensures a wide variety of food along this stretch of the Bure. You'll find everything from posh nosh at proper hotels – including the **Norfolk Mead Hotel** and **Wroxham Hotel** (for both, *see p129*) – to adventurous dishes in lovely little restaurants, as well a vast range of pubs serving reasonably priced, own-cooked food.

In Coltishall, the **Rising Sun** (28 Wroxham Road, 01603 737440, www.risingsuncoltishall.co.uk) has a lovely riverside garden. Next door but not next to the river, the **Kings Head**♥

125

Nine ways to explore the Broads

BOAT HIRE

Canoe

Explore the tiny tranquil channels off the main waterways (and see more wildlife than you ever would on a larger craft) with the help of the **Canoe Man** (07873 748408, www.thecanoeman.com). You can just hire a canoe for a day, take a weekend camping and canoeing trip or embark on longer guided and unguided B&B canoe holidays. Gear is supplied and food can be arranged en route. They also run bushcraft courses and fungi foraging.

Motor boat

Norfolk Broads Direct (01603 782207, www.broads.co.uk), operating out of Wroxham, has everything from small motor boats that can be hired by the hour through to luxury holiday cruisers. The day-boats are easy to manage and enable you to get very close to the water, with easy mooring at pubs and along the rivers and broads, but you'll have to trade up a bit if you want to make a cup of tea.

Yacht

If you want to get out on the water, but would rather sail than motor along, do it in style on a beautiful 1930s wooden yacht, bookable from a half day to a week at historic **Hunter's Yard** (01692 678263, www.huntersyard.co.uk, closed in winter) in Ludham. With no engine or electricity on board, this is a low-tech, eco-friendly way to explore the broads.

BOAT TOURS

Barton Broad

Climb aboard the unusual-looking, solar-powered catamaran *Ra* (named after the Egyptian sun god) for a 75-minute trip around Barton Broad. Trips leave from **Gay's Staithe** at Neatishead, and run from April to October. Book ahead on 01603 782281.

Horsey Mere

Take a one-hour guided cruise on the tranquil waters of Horsey Mere with **Ross's Wildlife Boat Trips** (07791 526440; text before 9.30am on the day of travel or book at the departure point) on the *Lady Ann*,

(26 Wroxham Road, 01603 737426, www.kingsheadcoltishall.co.uk) makes up in decor for what it lacks in watery delights. The raised wooden deck is a great spot from which to enjoy some of the best pub food in the area, and the four smart bedrooms are a good place to recover from a gastronomic blowout.

In Horning, the friendly **New Inn** (Lower Street, 01692 631101) offers free moorings and a riverside garden with play area; and the distinctive **Swan Inn** ♥ (01692 630316, www.vintageinn.co.uk/restaurants/east/theswaninnhorning) dishes out standard pub grub in a terrific setting on a sharp bend in the river. It also has B&B rooms.

The **Kings Head** (Station Road, 01603 782429) in Hoveton is highly rated by Broads aficionados and it too has rooms; the **Fur & Feather** (Slad Lane, 01603 720003, www.woodfordes.com/the-fur-feather-restaurant-brewery-tap) in Woodbastwick is next door to Woodforde's brewery, so ideal for real ale fans and it does good food too; the **Ship Inn** (18 The Street, 01603 270049, www.shipsouthwalsham.co.uk) in South Walsham has a decked terrace and a varied menu; the **King's Arms** (High Street, 01692 678386, www.kingsarmsludham.co.uk) in Ludham is great for children, with a playground and beer garden, as well as a model train running around the beamed ceiling inside; and the **Maltsters** (01603 270900, www.themaltsters.com) in Ranworth has a good beer garden.

Bure River Cottage Restaurant

27 Lower Street, Horning, NR12 8AA (01692 631421, www.burerivercottagerestaurant.co.uk). Dinner served 6.30-9.30pm Tue-Sat.

A fine Modern European restaurant, specialising in fish and seafood dishes, with many ingredients locally sourced. Service is excellent, and the the quality of the cooking sings out. The glass frontage provides good views of the hustle and bustle on the river and of this lovely village.

Old Mill Restaurant
8 The Old Mill, Wroxham, NR12 8DA (01603 783744). Food served Summer 9am-7pm daily. Winter 9am-4pm daily.

The riverside terrace makes the Old Mill a pukka lunchtime choice for well-made traditional English food, but hungry boat folk also come here for breakfast (served (9-11.30am), tea and takeway dishes.

Recruiting Sergeant
Norwich Road, Horstead, NR12 7EE (01603 737077, www.recruitingsergeant. co.uk). Open 10.30am-10.30pm daily; food served noon-8.30pm Mon-Sat; noon-8pm Sun.

This large and lovely whitewashed pub near Coltishall is one of the best in the area for gastropub fare that makes the most of local produce. The variety of daily specials (around 20 a day) makes choosing fiendishly hard. And the shaded back terrace, leafy garden and indoor dining room are all so well designed you'll have a hard time deciding where to sit.

Staithe 'N' Willow ♥
16 Lower Street, Horning, NR12 8AA (01692 630915). Open varies; phone for details.

With its riverside location and lovely garden, this thatched cottage would make a great lunch spot even if the food wasn't good. Fortunately, it is, thanks to an enterprising use of local produce to create a menu that ranges from breakfast dishes to sandwiches, cakes and full-blown meals.

Where to stay
If you plan to spend a lot of time on the water, Wroxham isn't a bad base. Reliable B&B options include the **Coach House** (96 Norwich Road, 01603 784376, www.coachhousewroxham.com)

a pretty wooden boat that seats a dozen passengers. You can then stretch your legs on the three-mile nature trail around the mere. Trips run several times a day from April to October; well-behaved dogs are allowed.

ON FOOT & BICYCLE
Bike hire
You can hire bikes for adults (£18 a day) and children (£7-£15), as well as tagalongs, baby seats and trailers, from **Broadland Cycle Hire** (07747 483154, www.norfolkbroadscycling. co.uk), based at Bewilderwood (see p122). The comprehensive 'Broads by Bike' – available to download from www.thebroadsbybike. org.uk – details 16 circular routes, with information on cafés, pubs, attractions and sites of interest.

Boardwalk trails
For a close-up look at the vegetation, insects, birds and other wildlife on the edge of the water, follow the boardwalk nature trails set up at many of the key broads, including Barton, Ranworth, Hickling and Upton – all managed by the Norfolk Wildlife Trust (01603 270479, www. norfolkwildlifetrust.org.uk).

Weavers' Way
This long-distance path runs between Cromer and Great Yarmouth, taking in part of the northern broads. From Stalham it loops around Hickling Broad to Potter Heigham, then follows the River Thurne to the waterside hamlet of Thurne and further south to Acle. You can download maps and details from www.norfolk.gov.uk/out-and-about-in-norfolk/norfolk-trails.

Wherryman's Way
The Wherryman's Way follows the River Yare for 35 miles from Great Yarmouth to Norwich, running through various southern broads villages, nature reserves and landmarks such as eerie Breydon Water, the pretty village of Reedham and isolated Berney Arms Mill. Download a brochure showing the whole trail plus 12 smaller circular routes from www.norfolk.gov.uk/out-and-about-in-norfolk/norfolk-trails.

Hickling Broad *see p115*

and **Wroxham Park Lodge** (142 Norwich Road, 01603 782991, www. wroxhamparklodge.com) – though the decor in the latter might be a bit flouncy for some tastes – while the smart, modern **Wroxham Hotel** (The Bridge, 01603 782061, www. hotelwroxham.co.uk) has 18 rooms, some with riverside balconies, plus a bar and restaurant.

Otherwise, Hoveton is a good bet, thanks to the **Kings Head** pub (*see p126*) and, down the road in Coltishall, **Bridge House** (1 High Street, 01603 737323, www.bridgehouse-coltishall. co.uk) offers fine B&B rooms in a 300-year-old ex-coaching inn and converted barns.

Norfolk Mead Hotel♥

Coltishall, NR12 7DN (01603 737531, www.norfolkmead.co.uk). Rates £135-£220 double incl breakfast.

An elegant, creeper-covered Georgian country mansion set in extensive, relaxing grounds on a quiet stretch of the Bure (with moorings available for boaters). The decor is different in each of the 14 rooms and two cottages (sleeping four and six people), but all the bedrooms have a pretty, homely vibe. The restaurant is recommended for its classy Modern European cooking and imaginative use of local seasonal ingredients.

Seven Acres House

Seven Acres Lane, Great Hautbois, NR12 7JZ (01603 736737, www.norfolk broadsbandb.com). Rates £400-£680 per week.

This cute single-storey self-catering cottage sleeps three. French windows lead onto a private patio, but it's the seven acres of grounds surrounding the handsome late Edwardian house near Coltishall that are so enticing: the rolling green lawns seem to stretch for ever.

TRINITY BROADS

Acle

Heading east from South Walsham brings you inexorably towards Acle, where the road forks: east towards Great Yarmouth, and north towards Thurne and three more broads – **Ormesby**, **Rollesby** and **Filby**, collectively known as the Trinity Broads. At first sight, the large village of Acle isn't much to look at – but it grows on you. Its position close to the River Bure and its railway station (on the Norwich to Great Yarmouth line) combine to make it a key centre for boaters, cyclists, and walkers, but it's always been important – 1,000 years ago it was a wealthy fishing and trading port on a sandbank surrounded by sea and estuary, and in the 19th century was the heart of a thriving boatbuilding trade.

The village centre – a huddle of shops, cafés and pubs around a green – is worth exploring. The Thursday market dates back to the 13th century, and the splendid Norman church, **St Edmund's**, is one of the best in the area, with a turreted round Saxon tower and a 15th-century belfry topped with eight figures looking down on the nave's thatched roof. **Horners** (0800 9754416, www. horners.co.uk) holds a household and general goods auction every other Thursday and an antiques auction every sixth Saturday, and there's a farmers market in the church every second Saturday. The little painted **June's Café,** adjacent to the bridge over the Bure just north of the village, is one of the Broads' sweetest sights.

There are pleasant walks in the various woods around Acle (detailed on boards around the village or you can download a **Burlingham Woodland Walks** guide from www. countrysideaccess.norfolk.gov.uk). Alternatively, stroll to nearby Upton for a pint in the **White Horse** pub (see below) or to spot dragonflies at **Upton Broad & Marshes Nature Reserve** (see p124).

Thurne to Caister-on-Sea
Five miles north of Acle, the peaceful waterside hamlet of **Thurne** and its staithe are home to a striking whitewashed drainage mill (**Thurne Dyke Mill**, www.thurnewindmill. co.uk), pretty cottages, a little gift shop with work by local artists, and a pub, **The Lion** (see below), that doubles as the village shop. The long-distance **Weavers Way** footpath runs through the village; while its 56 miles may be a step too far for most, the three-mile riverside stretch to Potter Heigham is lovely.

From Thurne the obvious route is east towards the final group of northern broads, the Trinity Broads (officially five broads: Ormesby, Rollesby, Filby and the much smaller Ormesby Little and Lily). The **Muck Fleet Dyke** links them with the River Bure, but is not navigable by boat – resulting in a tranquility that's hard to find on the other waterways. Most of the surrounding villages are unremarkable, though **Stokesby** is sweet and has two waterside eating and drinking options. Five miles further east, elegant **Ormesby St Margaret**, centred around a green, offers some relief from quaint thatched cottages with some distinctly modernist-looking 1960s buildings.

Eastwards, as the Broads give way to the coast, big holiday parks begin to blight the landscape, stretching the length of the coast from Hemsby to Caister-on-Sea. **Caister** is a modern residential town that's largely indistinguishable from Great Yarmouth to the south – the racecourse is all that separates the two towns. A few attractions are worth seeking out: to the north, just off the A149, the foundations of a **Roman fort** (now run by English Heritage)

might interest history buffs. The **Caister Castle & Car Collection** (see p124) is a must for petrolheads, and the ruined medieval castle to which it's attached is impressive. A few miles inland, **Thrigby Hall Wildlife Gardens** (see p124) near Filby has an impressive array of primates, big cats and reptiles, as well as fine views over the most remote northern broads.

Where to eat & drink
Pubs offer the best food in this rural area. They mostly come frills-free, but are usually cheap, cheerful and very careful with their cask- and bottle-conditioned ales.

Next to Acle Bridge, the **Bridge Inn** (Old Road, 01493 750288, www. aclebridge.co.uk) is a popular lunch venue thanks to its extensive riverside seating (and plenty of moorings if you're arriving by boat), **The Lion** (The Street, 01692 671806, www. thelionatthurne.com), in Thurne, serves pizzas, burgers, fish and chips and so on as well as a more exciting three-course set menu at £34.95 per head; while the **Ferry Inn** (The Green, 01493 751096, www.theferryinnstokesby.co.uk) in Stokesby occupies an idyllic riverside setting, and serves a pleasing array of dishes from king prawn and chorizo linguine to ham, egg and chips.

Places worth a pint stop include **The Boathouse** (Eels Foot Road, 01493 730342, www.theboathouse ormesbybroad.co.uk) on the banks of Ormesby Broad, and the **White Horse** (17 Chapel Road, 01493 750696, www.whitehorseupton.com) in Upton. Smokers get sofas and wicker armchairs in a covered barn outside the pub. Non-smokers will enjoy the snug interior and well-kept beers.

The Hermitage

64 Old Road, Acle, NR13 3PQ (07826 757733, www.piehousehermitage.co.uk). Open noon-11.30pm daily; Food served noon-2.30pm, 5-9pm Mon-Sat; noon-4pm Sun.

A brand new pie and ale house in this classic Norfolk Broads pub is dishing up a rotating selection of traditional home-made pies served with mash or chips, and gravy.

Kings Head Inn

The Street, Acle, NR13 3DY (01493 717892, www.kingsheadinnacle.co.uk). At time of going to press the pub was closed but set to reopen later in the year (check website).

This 16th-century coaching inn in the middle of Acle is a good choice for walkers and cyclists. Food is pub standards done well. There's a leafy garden and six bedrooms.

Waterside 💜

Main Road, Rollesby, NR29 5EF (01493 740531, www.thewatersiderollesby. co.uk). Café open summer 9am-5pm; winter 10am-3pm. Brunch served until noon; lunch served from noon.

A good eating option in this rural area, not least for its stunning waterside location and huge decked terrace overlooking Rollesby Broad. Even on dull, cold days the floor-to-ceiling picture windows offer a lovely view over rushes and reeds to the water beyond. Food consists of good-quality roasts, fish dishes, and good-looking desserts. Service is cheerful and efficient.

Where to stay

The remote setting of the Trinity Broads means options are less varied than elsewhere, but comfortable B&Bs are plentiful.

Clippesby Hall 💜

Clippesby, NR29 3BL (01493 367800, www.clippesby.com). Rates Camping £44 per pitch in peak season. Cottages & lodges £1,315-£1,685 per week.

A range of accommodation, including camping, cottages and wooden lodges, in an excellent location three miles north of Acle. The tent and caravan pitches are spread over eight areas, and the facilities are comprehensive, with tennis, mini-golf, cycle hire and a brand new Base Camp, which has tourist information, café, bar and shop. The self-catering buildings are varied in style, set in glades and furnished to a high standard.

Thurne Dyke

Great Yarmouth & Southern Broads

For many people, the Norfolk Broads end at the A47, the horizontal slash of dual-carriageway that bisects the county from Great Yarmouth in the east to King's Lynn in the west. Virtually the whole of Norfolk's coastline and all its most popular broads lie north of this road. The handful of broads south of it – Surlingham and Rockland on the western stretch of the River Yare, the villages that line the banks of its eastern stretch and the Chet tributary, and those that border the Waveney into Suffolk's Oulton Broad – tend to be forgotten, like embarrassing hicksville relatives of the city boy made good. For this reason, the waterways of the southern broads tend to be more tranquil and less touristy than their northern counterparts. Alternatively, for old-fashioned bucket-and-spade fun, and some surprising pockets of historical character, there's the brash seaside resort of Great Yarmouth.

GREAT YARMOUTH

Like Blackpool without the roving gangs of drunken lads and hen parties, Great Yarmouth offers seaside tat all the way from the pier along the length of Regent Road and up to the shopping precinct. And yet, you can't help but like this town. It's partly to do with the down-at-heel but not down-on-its-luck feel of the place – the sense that people flock here not because they can't afford anything else, but because they like paddling in the sea, building sandcastles, eating familiar food and taking in the seaside air, just as holidaymakers have done since the town's late-Victorian rise as a popular seaside resort.

Great Yarmouth's prosperity and importance stretches back much further, however. The settlement developed in the tenth century around herring (known as 'silver darlings') fishing, expanding through the Middle Ages to become England's fifth richest town; as recently as 1913, it still supported more than 1,000 herring fishing boats. And it retains an impressive architectural history that's still evident – if you can find it. Mid 20th-century urban planning has not been kind to the town's heritage quarter, with uninviting alleyways (some of them remainders of the 145 medieval 'rows' that formed the east/west links with the north/south main streets) that are more Thatcher's Britain than thatched Britain, leading to grim council estates. But it's worth making the effort to seek out attractions, such as one of the most complete **medieval town walls** in England (seen at its best in the north-west tower at North Quay); the 12th-century **St Nicholas's Church** (England's largest parish church); a 300-year-old **smokehouse**; and a heritage quarter containing **merchant houses** that are more than 400 years old. Fortunately, navigation is easy thanks to the town's compact size and a rectangular street grid that has drawn comparisons with Manhattan.

Heritage quarter
It's tempting to see the seafront as the focus of Great Yarmouth, but most of the old town was built not facing the sea, but looking inland towards the River Yare – specifically the channel parallel to the coastline that has for centuries provided a safe harbour and lucrative port. It's in this sliver of land between the river's banks on the west and the sea to the east that the handful of period properties and museums that make up the heritage quarter lie; most are on or near South Quay. The best are the **Time & Tide Museum** and the **Elizabethan House Museum** (for both, *see p142*).

Other places are worth visiting too, including the Great Yarmouth **Row Houses** and nearby remains of a 13th-century Franciscan friary (South Quay, www.english-heritage. org.uk, 10am-5pm Fri-Sun; closed Oct-Mar). **The Tolhouse** (Tollhouse Street, 01493 858900, www.museums. norfolk.gov.uk), located in one of the oldest (12th-century) buildings in East Anglia, has some imaginative interpretive ways of looking at the history of crime and punishment in Great Yarmouth over the centuries.

To find out about the various buildings and their accessibility – some are open only by appointment or on a guided tour – visit the **tourist information centre** on the seafront (25 Marine Parade, 01493 846346). You can also join in a historical tour with **Heritage Guided Walks** (details on 01493 846346). The tourist office will also be able to direct you to such sights as the timber-cottage birthplace of *Black Beauty* author Anna Sewell; the 18th-century **St George's Church**, now a theatre and arts centre (www. stgeorgestheatre.com); and the 1930 *Lydia Eva* steam drifter, the last vessel built at the King's Lynn shipyard.

For refreshments, **Quayside Plaza** (9 South Quay, 07500 740827) is a pleasant little Portuguese-inspired bistro.

The seafront
Heading from South Quay towards the sea, the streets broaden out to create the more familiar look of a genteel English seaside resort, with grand Victorian and Edwardian houses (now gaily painted B&Bs) leading to masses of interchangeable restaurants and greasy spoons, pound-shops, fast-food outlets and the occasional oddity. Take **Regent Road**, the street leading directly to the pier. Traditional grill restaurants and souvenir shops are interspersed with shops selling mock Crocs, air rifles, goth gear and personalised everything. You can also buy cowboy gear at Klobbers Western Wear. There are even a few modern-looking cafés.

Pockets of more innovative and inventive commerce are close at hand, however. The **Victoria Arcade** houses a number of indie boutiques, while **Market Row** and neighbouring rows are reminiscent of Brighton's Lanes and filled with eminently browsable shops; the stalls at the Wednesday and Saturday market are worth a look too.

But no one comes to Great Yarmouth for its shopping, and all the resort clichés and tat are quickly forgotten once you reach the front and its glorious expanse of sand and sea. Donkey rides under the Britannia Pier and strongman photo-ops on top of it will send older folk down memory lane, while younger visitors will enjoy the funfair rides and amusement arcades. The beach is terrific: miles of golden sand broken by two piers. At the northern end, fun-filled **Britannia Pier** (www.britannia-pier.co.uk) has been rebuilt a number of times in its 160-year history (twice after being cut in two by ships). At the southern end, the 1854 **Wellington Pier** (www.

Great Yarmouth Beach

wellington-pier.co.uk) is the older of the two. A third pier, the quiet Jetty, a popular fishing spot said to have been where Horatio Nelson landed on his return from Copenhagen in 1801, was demolished in 2012.

Marine Parade, the wide seafront promenade, is home to a dizzying range of attractions, including the **Pleasure Beach amusement park** (South Beach Parade, 01493 844585, www.pleasure-beach.co.uk, closed Nov-Feb) – featuring 70 rides and attractions (including the scenic roller-coaster); the **Castaway Island** 18-hole adventure golf course and sister course **Pirate Cove** (www. castaway-island.co.uk); the **Sea Life Centre** (*see p142*); and the wonderful **Merrivale Model Village** (*see p142*). There are also horse-drawn carriage rides, boat trips to the grey seal colony and wind farm at **Scroby Sands** and, of course, plenty of perfect spots to paddle, scoff fish and chips, or soak up the sun in a deckchair while gazing beyond the wind farms to the horizon.

Look inland too; a scan of the front reveals some fine architectural constructs, such as the grand 1911 **Empire Cinema** (sadly closed), and towering **Nelson's Monument**. The latter's grim setting belies its splendour: more than 144 feet tall, it was erected in 1819, predating Nelson's Column in Trafalgar Square by 24 years, as perhaps befits his status as a Norfolk hero. Oddly, it's not topped by the local boy himself, but by the figure of Britannia.

Near Great Yarmouth

When you tire of sand in your sandwiches, the incessant noise of amusement arcade automata and the smell of fried food, there are a clutch of attractions just outside town. North of town, on the way to Caister, is **Great Yarmouth Racecourse♥** (Jellicoe Road, 01493 842527, www.

Great Yarmouth seafront see p134

greatyarmouth-racecourse.co.uk). Time your visit to coincide with one of the popular flat race meetings (April to October) – hugely exciting and a great way to spend a day. Greyhound and motor racing fans should head to nearby **Yarmouth Stadium** (Yarmouth Road, 01493 720343, www.yarmouthstadium. co.uk), which looks like something you'd find in the Midwest. Keep an eye out en route to it for the lovely bus station, its art deco façade decorated with large tile-mosaics of modes of transport through the ages, including a penny farthing.

Alternatively, head south across the River Yare towards the sweetly old-fashioned town of **Gorleston**, where you'll find part of a medieval priory, a serene yacht pond, an Edwardian music hall, a traditional seaside theatre, gently clambering cliffs and even a small-scale version of Liverpool Cathedral. It's a laid-back, genteel resort and a perfect transition from the brashness of Great Yarmouth to the gentle waterways of the southern broads and Suffolk.

Where to eat & drink

You'll be hard-pressed to find outstanding cooking in Great Yarmouth, with the notable exceptions of **Andover House** (*see p140*) and the **White Swan seafood restaurant** (1 North Quay, 01493 858041). Otherwise, carefully peruse greasy-spoon menus and choose one you like, or opt for standard pub food.

Olive Garden 💚

68 High St, Gorleston-on-Sea, NR31 6RQ (01493 444779, www. olivegardengorleston.co.uk). Lunch served noon-2pm Tue-Thur. Dinner served 6-9pm Mon-Thur; 6-10pm Fri, Sat.

Looking bright and contemporary, the Olive Garden draws in eager punters with a varied menu that uses locally sourced produce whenever possible. Specialising in Greek and Cypriot food, the dishes here all have a Mediterranean influence, such as beef stifado or seafood risotto. They also offer a takeaway and delivery service (4.30-8.30pm Tue-Thu; 4.30-9pm Fri, Sat).

Pirate Cove mini-putting course

Nine Norfolk Churches (and one Abbey)

Churches of the Fens ♥
A triumphant triumvirate of goodies in adjoining villages. St Mary the Virgin, in Wiggenhall St Mary, has the best 15th- and 16th-century carved benches in Norfolk, if not England. In Walpole, St Peter (the biggest of the three churches) has the most impressive features, including fine medieval bosses, a spectacular nave and medieval paintings of saints, while St Andrew has unusual octagonal turrets. See pp165-166.

Norwich Cathedral ♥
One of Britain's most stunning cathedrals. The interior of this Romanesque structure (founded 1096) is dominated by a gorgeously ornate and beautifully proportioned fan-vaulted roof. The monastic cloister is beautiful and there's some surprisingly contemporary spiral stone decoration on the spire, England's second highest. Don't miss the quirky, spooky-looking skeleton tomb of Thomas Gooding. See p93.

St Helen's, Ranworth
Spacious St Helen's, aka the Cathedral of the Broads, has a 14th-century tower that provides amazing views of five broads and, on a clear day, the spire of Norwich Cathedral. The downside, especially for those with no head for heights, is the 89 uneven steps, two ladders and one trapdoor you'll have to negotiate to get to the top. See p123.

St Margaret, Hales
Located in the middle of open countryside, with a thatched roof and an impossibly cute round tower, this Grade I-listed Norman church will knock your socks off. Little has changed since it was built in the 12th century. Highlights include the magnificent carved and columned Norman doorway, an octagonal 15th-century font and the wall paintings. See p146.

St Mary, Barton Bendish ♥
Tiny St Mary's, with its thatched roof and delicate simplicity, is a real delight. Inside is an ethereal, spare space, decorated only with a 14th-century wall painting and some carved pieces, all bathed in pure white light.

Where to stay
The streets leading off the front are packed with B&Bs; Trafalgar Road has some particularly spick-and-span ones painted in gay mixes of white and pink, white and yellow, and white and blue, their gardens tumbling with hanging baskets and pansies.

Classic Lodge (13 Euston Road, 01493 852851, www.classiclodge. com) has rich fabrics and original Victorian features in good-sized rooms. **Barnard House B&B** (2 Barnard Crescent, 01493 855139, www.barnardhouse.com) is more stylish and modern, with three well-appointed rooms (two double, one twin) that come with bottled mineral water and Wi-Fi. There's also a self-catering cottage in the garden that sleeps two.

Andover House
28-30 Camperdown, NR30 3JB (01493 843490, www.andoverhouse.co.uk). Rates £111-£137 double incl breakfast. No children under 13.

The 27 comfortable rooms with neutral decor have welcome splashes of colour in the paintings or throws. Funky design and attitude (steel and leather bar stools, black wallpaper, stripped wooden floors and young friendly staff) make this place a rare treat in Great Yarmouth. The restaurant serves very good Modern British food, such as ham hock scotch egg or spiced cauliflower with lime mayonnaise and coriander, followed by sirloin of beef, baby hasselback potatoes, root vegetables and cavolo nero with crispy shallots and bacon jus.

Kensington
29 North Drive, NR30 4EW (01493 844145, www.kensington-hotel.co.uk). Rates £158-£190 double incl breakfast.

Looking out over the sea-facing landscaped gardens of North Drive to the water beyond, the detached Kensington has 26 rooms, with contemporary furnishings, that are comfortable and bright. There's a bar, several lounge areas one with a big screen TV, a restaurant serving bistro-type food and a terrace with sea view.

AROUND BREYDON WATER

Just to the west of Great Yarmouth lies the natural wonder that's responsible for keeping the southern broads as quiet as the grave: the vast Breydon Water – the tidal confluence of the Rivers Yare, Waveney and Bure. Tricky channels, shallow water and tides make this four-mile-long, one-mile-wide body of water difficult to navigate, which effectively turns it into a barrier between the northern and southern broads, but it is passable at the right times.

Berney Arms & Burgh Castle

If you're on the water, the tiny settlement of Berney Arms, in the middle of the windswept Halvergate Marshes, at Breydon Water's western end, is an ideal place to moor. Its 19th-century windmill is the tallest in Norfolk, standing nearly 70 feet high. It normally houses a small museum,

Andover House See p140

The key is available from the big house opposite the church's entrance. *See p172.*

St Mary, Haddiscoe

Dating from around 1100, and containing both Saxon and Norman elements in its structure, this round-towered church stands out for its notably tall tower. The tower's distinctive crenallated top, with a chequerboard pattern in flint, is from the 15th century. Inside, the space is simple and elegant. *See p144.*

St Michael & All Angels, Booton

A Gothic fantasy designed and built in the 19th century by Reverend Whitwell Elwin, who took elements of all his favourite churches and put them together to construct a building that's mad but also glorious and gorgeous. Traditionalists might prefer the distinctly more restrained churches at nearby Cawston and Salle. *See p74.*

St Nicholas's Chapel, King's Lynn

This chapel was founded in 1146, although most of the existing building dates from the early 15th century. The structure is breathtaking: look out for the carvings and star-vaulted ceiling in the porch, and the wooden ceiling decorated with angels playing musical instruments. There's an interesting collection of 17th- and 18th-century monuments and memorials, as well as George Gilbert Scott's 19th-century spire. *See p18.*

St Peter, Forncett St Peter

A typical round-towered flint Norfolk church, set in a tiny village. The exterior is particularly lovely, especially the Saxon tower – possibly the finest example in England. To get inside, you'll need to get the key from the churchwarden. *See p154.*

Wymondham Abbey ♥

The torrid history of this huge and splendid Norman abbey, founded in 1107, includes a centuries-long dispute between parishioners and monks and the grisly death of William Kett on the walls of the western tower. *See p157.*

Places to visit

GREAT YARMOUTH

Elizabethan House Museum
4 South Quay, NR30 2QH (01493 855746, www.museums.norfolk.gov.uk, www.national trust.org.uk). At time of going to press the museum was closed; check the website for opening times and entry fees.

This well-crafted National Trust museum convincingly evokes different aspects of domesticity in the 16th century with a series of period rooms that illustrate life both above and below stairs. It also houses the Haddiscoe Hoard, a collection of more than 300 silver coins that form part of a display on life in Great Yarmouth during the Civil War.

Merrivale Model Village
Wellington Pier Gardens, Marine Parade, NR30 3JG (01493 842097, www. merrivalemodelvillage.co.uk). Open late Mar-Oct daily; times vary. Nov-early Dec weekends only. Christmas Wonderland & Santa's Grotto booking essential. Check website for all details. Admission £9.99 (includes crazy golf).

With more than 200 miniature shops, houses and buildings set in sweet landscaped gardens, Merrivale is an utter delight, particularly when it's lit up by the tiny street lights at dusk. Play areas, crazy golf, rides, a shop and a café ensure fun for all ages.

Sea Life Centre
Marine Parade, NR30 3AH (01493 330631, www.sealife.co.uk). Open summer 10am-4pm (9.30am-4pm in school holidays); winter 11am-3pm. Admission £18.95; £15.95 reductions (cheaper online in advance).

A terrific aquarium that has an underwater tunnel for viewing sharks and sea turtles, a pirate cove, coral reef inhabitants, rock pool, jellyfish tank, crocodiles, rays, seahorses, and – of course – a shop and café. There's even a colony of Humboldt penguins.

Time & Tide Museum
Blackfriars Road, NR30 3BX (01493 743930, www.museums.norfolk.gov.uk). At time of going to press the house was closed but set to reopen as soon as government guidelines permit.

This award-winning museum, housed in a restored Victorian herring curing works, features some excellent re-creations of bygone days. There's a Victorian terrace and fisherman's home, a 1950s quayside and a seaside holidays gallery that will have older visitors tripping happily down memory lane. The interactive displays will keep children amused, and the Silver Darlings café (open to all, not just museum-goers) serves a selection of good snacks, including the fishy kind such as kipper paté and marinated herrings, alongside the more usual sandwiches, soups and cakes.

AROUND BREYDON WATER

Pettitts Adventure Park

Church Road, Reedham, NR13 3UA (01493 700094, www.pettittsadventurepark.co.uk). Open Apr-Oct 10am-5pm daily. Admission £16.50; free-£15.50 reductions; £59 family.

Children and adults will fall in love with the tiny African pygmy goats and miniature horses here, but the rabbits, owls, raccoons, pigs and lemurs will elicit lots of 'aahs' too. And when you're done with feeding and petting, there's a half-mile-long miniature railway, heaps of rides and numerous activities and playgrounds.

WEST OF REEDHAM

Raveningham Gardens

Raveningham, NR14 6NS (01508 548152, www.raveningham.com). Open At time of going to press the gardens were open 11am-4pm Wed-Fri; their future timetable will be decided once government restrictions have been lifted. Admission £5; free-£4.50 reductions.

Priscilla Bacon lived at Raveningham for 50 years and in that time developed a garden that's a joy to visit, from its impressive borders to its rose beds and Edwardian summerhouse. Sympathetic contemporary touches include a herb garden, lake and sculptures.

RSPB Strumpshaw Fen

Low Road, Strumpshaw, NR13 4HS (01603 715191, www.rspb.org.uk). Open Reserve dawn-dusk daily. Visitor Centre Summer 9am-5pm daily. Winter 9am-4pm daily. Admission £4.50; free-£3 reductions. Visitor Centre and hides currently closed in accordance with government guidelines.

A wonderful habitat of reedbeds, woodland and meadows, plus a good range of walks, as well as three hides from which to spy the likes of marsh harriers, bitterns and kingfishers. There's plenty here for kids and non-twitchers too, with activity rucksacks available for the former and a range of guided walks for birdwatching beginners.

RSPB Strumpshaw Fen

work at the time of writing. The hamlet is more than two miles from a road and can only be reached by boat, on foot, or – incredibly – by rail. The station is Norfolk's remotest, part of the wonderfully atmospheric **Wherry Lines railway**♥ (www.wherrylines. org.uk) that runs from Norwich and Acle, with trains stopping at Berney Arms on request. (Sadly, the Berney Arms Inn, Norfolk's most remote pub, has closed.)

Paths around the area, including the **RSPB's Breydon Water & Berney Marshes reserve** (01493 700645, www.rspb.org.uk), are numerous. Railway, river and footpath also take you quite close to the stumpish yet evocative remains of the third-century Roman fort of **Gariannonum**, at the village of Burgh Castle on the southern side of the River Waveney. Civilisation encroaches here, not only with roads but with two good pubs, as well as a pretty campsite and marina. All have great views over Breydon Water and across the marshes to

Halvergate. This magical area offers a sense of peace and wonder; you'll feel a long, long way from the hurly-burly of Great Yarmouth, just a few miles to the east.

Haddiscoe & Reedham

From Burgh Castle, the Waveney and Yare take off in different directions across the county. The Waveney heads southward, flowing through some nice villages and attractions as it heads to Beccles, Bungay and beyond. For much of its length, it forms the boundary between Norfolk and Suffolk.

In **Haddiscoe**, a few miles south of Burgh Castle, the **church of St Mary** ★ has an intriguing round tower. Dating from around 1100, the church has both Saxon and Norman elements. The telescope-like banded tower is four storeys high; its crenallated 15th-century top features a distinctive knapped flint and stone chequerboard pattern. The spare simplicity of the interior reflects the elegance of the exterior,

Reedham see p145

and the checked, tiled floor echoes the banding on the tower. From here, it's a short walk to **Herringfleet Marshmill** – the last full-size working windmill in the country – on the far bank of the Waveney, or you can wend your way the three miles to Reedham beside the River Yare.

Reedham ♥ is a great place to spend a few hours. It's a substantial village, and a sprawling one: the four-mile circular walk around it takes in a train station; the **Humpty Dumpty Brewery** (Church Road, 01493 701818, www.humptydumptybrewery.com; open noon-5pm daily); and **Pettitts Adventure Park** (*see p143*). There's also the chain ferry: the Broads' last remaining ferry (6.30am-8pm Mon-Fri; 8am-8pm Sat, Sun) and, at £4.50 for a car crossing of some 20 feet, surely the most expensive way to travel in Britain. The village's three pubs – the **Ferry Inn** (*see below*), **The Ship** (*see right*) and the **Nelson Head** (www.lordnelsonpub.com) – all have lovely riverside settings.

Where to eat & drink

You'll find good food here. **The Queens Head** (High Road, 01493 780363, www.queenshead.co.uk) is a decent pie or pizza lunch stop if you're in the Burgh Castle area, while the **Red Lion** at Halvergate (Marsh Road, 01493 700317) is a great choice if you're doing the circular walk to Berney Arms. At St Olaves, the 16th-century **Bell** (Beccles Road, 01493 488249, www.bellinn-stolaves. co.uk) offers hearty pub grub and a grand riverside garden in which to enjoy it.

Ferry Inn
Ferry Road, Reedham, NR13 3HA (01493 700429). At time of going to press the pub was closed but set to reopen as soon as government guidelines permit.

High-quality pub standards – bangers and mash, fish and chips – join the likes of fish stew and Brancaster mussels on the menu at this characterful pub.

Priory Farm Restaurant
Beccles Road, St Olaves, NR3 9HE (01493 488432, www.prioryfarmrestaurant. co.uk). Lunch served noon-2pm, dinner served 6-8.30pm daily.

The charming location makes Priory Farm a nice lunch stop, especially if you have kids, who'll love tearing around the priory ruins. The vast selection on the standard menu will ensure something for everyone, whether it's stir-fry, vegetable moussaka ot steak and kidney pie.

Ship
Riverside, Reedham, NR13 3TQ (01493 700287). Food served noon-2pm Mon-Thu; noon-2pm, 6-9pm Fri; noon-3pm, 6-9pm Sat; noon-4pm Sun.

A terrific riverside setting, next to the swing railway bridge, and a huge beer garden make this a top pick for summer evenings, and there's a nice play area too. Food, served in the bar and a separate restaurant space, consists of good own-cooked seasonal dishes alongside pub standards such as steak pies, roasts and pizza.

Where to stay

Accommodation can be sparse once you get outside Great Yarmouth, so it's a good idea to book ahead. The **Queens Head** (*see left*) in Burgh Castle offers rooms.

Reedham Ferry Touring Park & Campsite
Reedham Ferry, NR13 3HA (01493 700999, www.archerstouringpark. co.uk). Rates £16 per night.

Set over four acres bordering the Yare, this is a campsite for those who like their home comforts. Top-notch facilities, including electric hook-ups, laundry room, bar, restaurant, barbecue area and a private fishing lake, mean it's very popular. There are just 20 pitches, so it's a good idea to book ahead. Proximity to the **Ferry Inn** (*see p145*) is another draw.

WEST OF REEDHAM

Loddon & around

From Reedham, it's a few short miles north-west to the Norwich broads of Surlingham and Rockland, but it's well worth making a short detour south-west to the lively Chet riverside villages of **Loddon**♥ and **Chedgrave**. Loddon, a popular boating centre for the southern broads, is an attractive small market town, with a good chippie, a community shop, a lovely weatherboard watermill spanning the river, a waterside picnic area and – standing high over the town – the impressive 15th-century **Holy Trinity Church**, a great example of the Gothic Perpendicular style. Good examples of Georgian and Victorian buildings abound, but Loddon offers a rare modern treat for architecture fans in a sweet collection of 1960s housing by Lowestoft architects Tayler and Green, whose delicate, well-proportioned bungalows between the Low and High Bungay Roads are standout examples of post-war public housing.

It's well worth hiring a day-boat here to follow the enchanting three-and-a-half-mile stretch of the River Chet to **Hardley Cross**, the 1556 boundary marker between the city of Norwich and the borough of Great Yarmouth. The route takes in pretty wooded riverbanks before turning into a canal bordered by expansive views of grazing marshes. If you prefer to stay on dry land, a number of **Wherryman's Way** circular walks (*see p127*) at Loddon and Chedgrave follow the Chet footpath past the Hardley Flood, fantastic for spotting water birds and wildlife – including otters.

The village of **Hales**, just to the south, is unremarkable but for one

feature: the tiny Norman church of **St Margaret**♥. The building, along with St Gregory in neighbouring Heckingham, is a glorious example of East Anglian Norman church architecture, with classic round towers, thatched roofs, magnificent Norman doorways and idyllic open field settings. Garden fans will want to continue along the B1136 to Raveningham, famous for the lovely **Raveningham Gardens** (*see p143*).

Surlingham, Lingwood & around

Heading north-west towards Norwich, the villages of **Surlingham** and **Lingwood** – both around six miles from Loddon, on different sides of the Yare – are worth a stop. Each has thatched cottages and a riverside pub; the former has a farm shop (with a fish van 10am-4pm on Thu), and there are grander 17th- and 18th-century houses in the latter. Either is a good base for botany and wildlife fans, given their proximity to **Surlingham Church Marsh** (01603 715191, www.rspb.org.uk), with its lovely short trail through a former grazing marsh, with pools and dykes to explore. For others, Surlingham's picture-perfect location on a horseshoe bend of the Yare and range of good pubs gives it the edge; it's also closer to **Wheatfen Nature Reserve** (The Covey, 01508 538036, www.wheatfen.org), which has a great two-mile walk over the fenland tidal marshes and carrs on the Yare.

More excellent nature trails lie near **Buckenham**, just a mile or so south of Lingwood and notable for its church, **St Nicholas**, which is one of only five churches in Suffolk with a hexagonal church tower. Attractions here include two RSPB reserves at **Buckenham Marshes** and **Strumpshaw Fen** (*see p143*), **Strumpshaw Steam Museum** (01603 714535, www. strumpshawsteammuseum.co.uk, open daily July-Sept, check for other times) and the little village of **Strumpshaw**.

The nearby riverside village of **Brundall** is well worth a stop. There are several places to hire boats – Silverline Marine (01603 712247, www.silverlinemarine.co.uk) or Buccaneer Boats (01603 712057, www. buccaneerboatsmarina.co.uk) – and a high street with a pub, small shops and a post office. After looking round the village, a gently meandering boat trip up the Yare to the outskirts of Norwich seems the perfect way to end any exploration of this region's quiet charms.

Where to eat & drink

Pubs serving good traditional British dishes are the best options for food in this part of the world. Standouts include the refurbished **Coldham Hall Tavern** in Surlingham (Coldham Hall Carnser, 01508 538366, www. coldhamhall.com), which occupies a terrific riverside spot on the Yare; **Ferry House**, also in Surlingham (Ferry Road, 01508 538659, www. surlinghamferry.co.uk), which

provides fresh, resolutely traditional dishes such as liver and bacon, beer-battered cod and Sunday roasts; and the **New Inn** in Rockland St Mary (12 New Inn Hill, 01508 538211), which does much the same fare.

Where to stay

The two rooms at **Pottles Barn** (Ferry Road, Surlingham, 538823, www.pottlesbarn.co.uk) occupy a comfortable barn conversion in a half-acre garden. There's also a self-contained annexe sleeping two adults and two children.

For some peace and quiet in a rural setting, **Little Willows** (Nursery Road, Chedgrave, 01508 528525, www. littlewillows.co.uk) is a delightful self-catering cottage sleeping four. Raveningham's **Orchards** (Beccles Road, 01508 548322) is a former rectory set in three lovely acres, while Lingwood's **Station House** (Station Road, 01603 715872, www. stationhouselingwood.co.uk) is one for railway fans: its three rooms are in a restored Victorian station house on the Wherry Lines railway.

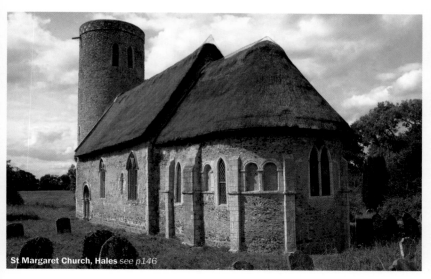

St Margaret Church, Hales *see p.146*

South Norfolk

Norfolk's undisputed architectural wealth lies in its 800-plus churches, some 700 of them medieval and 124 with round towers; the best examples are found in the southern half of the county, a 50-mile-long swathe of land running the length of the A47 and stretching 20 miles south to the Suffolk border. But there are other pleasures here too. Market towns and villages such as Diss, Harleston, Attleborough, Wymondham and Hingham are some of the oldest and most charming in Norfolk. The terrain of South Norfolk is varied too, from marshy fens and scrubland in the far west to the broads in the east, in between encompassing river valleys, woodland, forest and grazing meadows, sometimes dotted with Roman remains. It makes for a rich mix of attractions for all manner of visitors, including walkers, fishing fans, church buffs and amateur historians – just don't expect most children to go crazy for it.

HARLESTON & AROUND

Villages & churches

Day-trippers from Norwich rarely head south, opting instead for the Broads to the east or the coast to the north, but for those who do venture here, immediate reward lies in the privately owned village of **Framingham Pigot**, just off the A146. It retains the kind of traditional village appeal that makes it a total charmer, from the Dickensian shopfronts to **St Andrew's**, a church that's a fine example of rural Victorian architecture.

Signs directing you to nearby **Caistor St Edmund's** Roman town (Venta Icenorum; www.norfarchtrust. org.uk) promise a bit more than the remains actually deliver: a large field with some information panels showing the layout of the town that once stood here. You can download a guided walk to your mobile phone – details are on the noticeboard at the entrance – which allows a decent reconstruction of the town, if you're imaginatively inclined. If not, best

head instead for **Poringland**, a mile and a half away, to see the village sign that depicts Norfolk artist John Crome working on *The Poringland Oak* (the painting is on display at Tate Britain). Three miles west is **Stoke Holy Cross**, an impressive village with some fine examples of grand English village architecture, including Gothic Revival and mock Tudor mansions near the church. The huge white weatherboard mill is where Colman's Mustard was first produced. It's now a restaurant, but food lovers should head for the local pub, the **Wildebeest Arms** (*see p151*).

This area is stuffed with attractive villages and impressive churches. At **Shotesham**, a clutch of lovely thatched cottages and houses are overlooked by the 16th-century **All Saints' Church**. Peek inside to view the wall paintings (including a red naked woman burning in the flames of hell, two eerie-looking heads and a delicate tree of life fragment), as well as some geometric-patterned stained glass. **Saxlingham Nethergate** is equally picturesque, with more

Waveney Valley

thatched dwellings, another church, **St Mary** – famous for its 13th-century stained glass, some of the oldest and best in East Anglia – and a parsonage built in 1784 by Sir John Soane. The church buff should continue south to **Shelton**, where **St Mary's** is regarded as one of the best examples of Perpendicular architecture in Norfolk. The banded red-brick porch is arresting, and the stained glass in the soaring east window is particularly fine.

Four miles south, **Pulham Market** is worth a visit if you like quintessentially English conservation villages: pretty thatched cottages, church, shop and post office are set around a village green, where you'll also find the whitewashed **Crown Inn** (*see p151*). **St Mary's Church** in the next-door village of **Pulham St Mary** is definitely worth a stop for its stonework; check out the trumpet-blowing angels on the 15th-century porch and the story of local king and saint St Edmund carved in the parapets.

Harleston

From Pulham Market it's a ten-minute drive to the area's hub and the heart of the Waveney Valley, the market town of Harleston, admired by Pevsner for its excellent timbered and Georgian architecture. The focus of the town is the elegant market square (still home to a weekly Wednesday market), but the streets radiating from it deliver treats too – Old Market Place, in particular, has some fine houses. The shops aren't quite as impressive, though a wander will reveal a few gems, such as traditional butcher's **Frank Spurgeon** (29 The Thoroughfare, 01379 852230); and the **Adnams Cellar & Kitchen Store** (23A The Thoroughfare, 01379 854788, www.adnams.co.uk). **Diminutive Harleston Museum** (Broad Street, 01379 854423, closed Oct-Apr) is worth a look if it's open (10am-noon, 2-4pm Wed, 10am-noon Sat); if not, you could go for fish and chips at one of the town's chippies – **Norman's** (12 London Road, 01379 852242) is the best, and offers a pretty space if you want to eat in.

Pick up a leaflet featuring three local walks (available in most pubs and hotels) and take a stroll through the **Waveney Valley**, much loved by Edwardian painter Alfred Munnings, born just across the border in Suffolk. The walks take in scenes that would have been very familiar to the artist, including the 17th-century Needham Mill, Cuckoo Hill (offering terrific views up and down the valley) and Munnings's birthplace, the quaint village of Mendham.

West from Harleston, **Waveney and Blyth Arts** (www.waveneyand blytharts.com), in Diss, host occasional art events and organised trails; while Scole is notable for the 17th-century **Diss by Verve** (formerly the Scole Inn)(*see p152*), an imposing red-brick monolith with high gables and squat chimney stacks. The nearby **Crossways Inn** (*see below*) might be a cosier bet.

Where to eat & drink

If you're staying in Harleston, **JD Young** (*see p152*) offers gastropub standards at very good prices in a genial, comfortable space. In Framingham Pigot, **Brasted's** (Manor Farm Barns, 01508 491112, www.brasteds.co.uk, open Thur-Sat only) has an inventive menu, and uses plenty of local produce. In Pulham Market, the **Crown Inn** (Harleston Road, 01379 676184, www.thecrowninn-pulham.co.uk) is perfect if you crave trad pub food in a proper thatched village pub on a green.

Crossways Inn
Bridge Road, Scole, IP21 4DP (01379 742547). Open noon-11pm daily. Lunch served 12.30-2.30pm, dinner served 6.30-8.30pm daily.

This beamed building is a delight inside and out, with dark nooks and crannies, leather armchairs and big hearths and

fireplaces combining to create the kind of village pub that townies dream of. Decent pub food and a great atmosphere put it firmly at the heart of village life.

Wildebeest Arms ♥
82-86 Norwich Road, Stoke Holy Cross, NR14 8QJ (01508 492497, www. thewildebeest.co.uk). Open daily for lunch and dinner, although with shorter 'alfresco dining times' until government guidelines permit.

Chef Patron Daniel Smith takes local, seasonal ingredients 'using all that is great and good from Norfolk' to create an imaginative range of elaborate Modern European dishes, such as warm ham hock terrine, burnt apple purée, pickled red onions and pork puff for starter, followed by beetroot glazed Gressingham duck breast, pressed potato terrine, charred spring onions, glazed Roscoff onion, sauté beetroot and jus.

Where to stay

Rural accommodation close to Norwich is plentiful, ranging from B&Bs to traditional market town hotels, such as the **Swan Inn** in Harleston (01379 852221, www. harlestonswanhotel.co.uk; £60-£135 double room incl breakfast) at the

Things to do

HARLESTON & AROUND

Playbarn
West Green Farm, Shotesham Road, Poringland, NR14 7LP (01508 495526, www.theplaybarn.co.uk). Open Playbarn 9.30am-4pm (9.30am-5pm school holidays) Tue-Sun; 10am-5pm Sun. Children's farm 10am-4pm daily. Admission Adults £3 with a hot drink included; under 8s £5; crawling children £4; babies free.

A rainy-day saviour in the form of an indoor and outdoor playcentre for young children, with pedal tractors, climbing apparatus, sandpit, ball pool and soft play inside, and a small farm, pony rides, tractor rides, and picnic and play areas outside.

Wildebeest Arms *see p151*

heart of the Waveney Valley. Then there are the corporate country houses such as **Caistor Hall** in Caistor St Edmund (01508 494998, www.caistorhall.com), which has 20 large luxurious bedrooms. You'll need to book well ahead for **Hillside Farm** in Bergh Apton (Welbeck Road, 01508 550260, www.hillside-farm.com), a gorgeous 16th-century thatched farmhouse with just two rooms.

Diss By Verve

Ipswich Road, Scole, IP21 4DR (01379 740481, www.vervediss.co.uk). Rates £85-£120 double incl breakfast.

A Jacobean hand-carved staircase and original hand-painted sundial are just some of the period features in this grand 17th-century coaching inn. The rooms in the main building come with their own working fireplace; more modern rooms (there are 24 in total) are located in adjoining converted Georgian coach house. There's also a restaurant and a bar.

JD Young Hotel

2-4 Market Place, Harleston, IP20 9AD (01379 852822, www.jdyoung.co.uk). Rates £95 double incl breakfast.

A 15th-century coaching inn with 11 comfortable rooms. The restaurant is equally charming, with a menu of English standards that are well cooked and keenly priced, not to mention a better-than-average wine selection.

Old Bakery♥

Church Walk, Pulham Market, IP21 4SL (01379 676492, www.theoldbakery.net). Rates £75-£85 double incl breakfast.

You can't miss the Old Bakery, thanks to its impressive exterior. Inside, the 1580 listed building is pleasingly sedate, with wattle-and-daub walls, exposed internal beams and five attractive, chintz-free rooms, all en suite and some with exposed timber beams.

Diss

West of the A140 – which bisects the county from Cromer in the north to Scole in the south – a wealth of traditional Norfolk villages are packed together like peas in a pod, each with their own individual quirks and appeal. Tucked in the south-east corner of the area is Diss, a particular favourite of Sir John Betjeman. It's easy to see why. Norfolk's most southerly town is a delight, ranged around a large mere (lake) with a park on its southern side where numerous waterfowl come to feed. The town's commercial area is north of the lake, from where you get tantalising glimpses of the water from little alleyways and pubs, such as the aptly named **Waterfront Inn**. Buildings span a range of styles and periods (Tudor, Georgian, Victorian) and there are plenty of independent shops. If you're here on a Friday, don't miss the antiques and interiors auction at **TW Gaze** (Roydon Road, 01379 650306, www.twgaze.com), which could include anything from modern 20th-century furniture to medieval pieces. The auctions are regularly visited by TV programmes such as *Bargain Hunt*, *Cash In The Attic* and *Road Trip*.

The heart of the shopping area is Market Place (once the poultry market and still home to a Friday market), dominated by the giant Georgian post office. **Diss Museum** (*see p156*) is housed in the Victorian Shambles, a pretty building with Tuscan columns set on a cast-iron veranda; the impressive half-timbered Tudor coaching inn behind it is now a restaurant. A wander up Market Hill and St Nicholas Street, home to grand **St Mary's Church**, reveals more architectural delights, such as the 1854 Corn Exchange and numerous half-timbered houses and buildings,

including the impressive **Saracen's Head** (*see p159*). The **Diss Publishing Bookshop** (40 Mere Street, 01379 644612, www.disspublishing.co.uk, 9am-5.15pm Mon-Sat) resembles a boathouse and is stuffed with books, gifts and a coffee shop.

The only thing lacking is a good food and drink scene. If the pubs don't appeal, try the various restaurants in **Norfolk House Yard**, including vegetarian Les Amandines (www.amandines.co.uk) and wine bar and restaurant Weavers (www.weaversdiss.com).

Diss to Attleborough

Heading west from Diss on the A1066, it's only a few miles to the excellent **Bressingham Steam & Gardens** (*see p156*). Nearby are two churches of note, both called **St Andrew**. The tower at South Lopham is a massive, squat Norman affair, while Fersfield's version is tall and slim, surrounded by graceful yew trees and open fields.

A few miles north at **Kenninghall**, the friendly **Red Lion** (*see p159*), located opposite another appealing church, is a good pit stop. The sprawling layout of the village is ideal for a post-lunch stroll; do look round the 18th-century panelled Baptist church that's now home to the oddly named **Suffolk Potteries** (Lopham Road, 01379 687424, www.suffolkpotteries.co.uk, closed Sat, Sun).

Further west, **Brettenham** is noteworthy for its unusual red-brick estate houses and a High Gothic Victorian pile designed by Samuel Sanders Teulon that sports all the architect's best features, including a cluster of wonderfully over-the-top Gothic towers and spires. It's privately owned, but the gates are often open, so you might get a peek at the rooftop and the lake. Consolation for fans of the architect lies in the local church of **St Mary**, rebuilt by Teulon in 1852, though it's an understated example of his style, and in his bridge over the Little Ouse at nearby Rushford.

This part of Norfolk is just jammed with notable churches. Yet another impressive example is at **East Harling**: 15th-century **St Peter & St Paul** is one of the county's best Perpendicular chuches, with a number of interesting features; pick up a leaflet at the door to make sure you don't miss any. The late medieval stained glass in the east window is stunning.

More points of interest lie north of Diss. Social history enthusiasts can drop into the **Burston Strike School** (*see p156*) to pay their respects, while World War II enthusiasts can visit the **100th Bomb Group Memorial Museum** (*see p157*) in Dickleburgh. If you have kids in tow, **Banham Zoo** (*see p156*), seven miles north-west of Diss, is probably a better bet.

Banham is a hop, skip and jump from New Buckenham, a 12th-century example of town planning whose wealthy-looking but unpretentious air, as well as some fascinating buildings, reward exploration.

Ranged around a green on which sits the curious Market Cross – a tiny 16th-century building that was raised up on Tuscan columns a century after it was built – are two pubs, and a cluster of medieval cottages. For a pleasant walk, head down King Street and past a lovely group of almshouses to the remains of the 12th-century 'new' castle built by Norman baron William D'Albini as a replacement for his previous fortress at **Old Buckenham**. 'Remains' could be slightly overstating the grassy site; what was once an impressive round keep surrounded by a large castle, is now mainly a series of depressions, small mounds and ditches. The common to the east of the village has been untouched grazing land for 800 years.

A couple of miles away, **Old Buckenham** has a huge village green – the largest in England, it's claimed – a 19th-century cornmill (this used to be open on occasional weekends, but is now closed to the public).

Further east lies **Forncett St Peter**, home to a round-towered church

Mulberry Tree *see p158*

that's beautiful in both setting and design. Wander around the overgrown graveyard to admire the exterior, notably the superb Saxon tower and imposing north porch. Inside – you might need to get the key from the churchwarden – are some very convincing faux-medieval Victorian bench ends and two 15th-century engraved tomb chests. Nearby twin **Forncett St Mary** contains the quirky **Forncett Industrial Steam Museum** (*see p156*), which is open on Wednesdays and Sundays. Otherwise, the villages are unremarkable, so it's best to push on to **Tasburgh**, five miles north-east, for some bucolic rolling scenery and a walk along the banks of the River Tas, taking in the Elizabethan manor house of Rainthorpe Hall and the quaint hamlet of Newton Flotman with its fine 16th-century bridge.

Attleborough

Wymondham and Attleborough sit on the A11, seven miles from each other. Both are fairly typical Norfolk market towns, but for shopaholics and foodies, Attleborough has the edge, thanks to the **Mulberry Tree** (*see p158*), and a main road crammed with heaps of independent retailers, charity shops and tearooms. Many of the buildings are relatively new for Norfolk, the town having expanded around the railway line built here in 1840, but a few quaint oldies still exist: the whitewashed **Griffin Hotel**, a historic coaching inn on the High Street, is an elegant example of the town's medieval past. The businesses on the High Street are housed in cute bow-fronted buildings or more handsome two- and three-storey Georgian blocks, all combining to create a great example of an unspoilt Georgian market town.

The church, **St Mary,** is a knockout. Built in Norman and Early English styles, the exterior is imposing

Cultural connections

● **Holkham Beach** appears in the final scene of *Shakespeare in Love*, with Gwyneth Paltrow strolling across the expansive sands.

● American travel writer and self-confessed Anglophile Bill Bryson used to live in the old rectory at **Wramplingham**, near the market town of Wymondham since 2003. His book *At Home* (2010) was actually inspired by the house after he discovered a secret door in the attic.

● **Great Yarmouth** features heavily in *David Copperfield*. Dickens visited the town in 1849, staying at the Royal Hotel on Marine Parade.

● **Steve Coogan**'s spoof presenter Alan Partridge is a Norfolk local, broadcasting his *Up with the Partridge* show on Radio Norwich.

● Sir John Betjeman was a frequent visitor to **Diss** from the early 1960s. The town inspired his poem 'A Mind's Journey to Diss', addressed to Harold Wilson's wife Mary, who was born in the town. 'Dear Mary, yes, it will be bliss, to go with you by train to Diss', it begins.

● Although born across the border in Mendham, Suffolk, Edwardian artist **Alfred Munnings** spent much of his formative years in Norfolk, receiving formal training at the Norwich School of Art. His early paintings are filled with scenes of rural East Anglia.

● Distinguished author and academic WG Sebald set up home in the town of **Wymondham** and later the village of **Poringland**, after emigrating from Germany to work at the University of East Anglia in the 1970s. He died in a car crash near Norwich in 2001.

● Sir Arthur Conan Doyle wrote his Sherlock Holmes mystery story *The Dancing Men* while sitting in the 16th-century Hill House in **Happisburgh**.

● Parts of Stanley Kubrick's 1987 film *Full Metal Jacket* were filmed around the **Norfolk Broads**, which stood in for the paddy fields of Vietnam.

Places to visit

DISS & ATTLEBOROUGH

Banham Zoo
*Kenninghall Road, Banham, NR16 2HE
(01953 887771, www.banhamzoo.co.uk).
Open 9am-5.30pm daily (last entry 4.30pm).
Admission £20; £1-£17.50 reductions.*

From big cats to meerkats and Shire horses
to giraffes, this is traditional zoo territory, all
35 acres of it. So you get feeding sessions
and talks, close-up presentations, birds of
prey displays and plenty of other interactive
experiences, as well as a gift shop.

Bressingham Steam & Gardens ♥
*Thetford Road, Bressingham, IP22 2AB
(01379 686900, www.bressingham.co.uk).
Open Sept-Oct, Mar-Apr 10.30am-5pm daily;
June-Aug 10.30am-5.30pm (Oct closing time
may vary; check before travelling). Admission
museum & garden only £8.17; free-£7.72
reductions. For Steam Day & Gardener Day
prices, see website.*

This mix of spectacular gardens and
impressive collection of steam engines and
locomotives (including a Victorian steam
carousel and the famous 6100 Royal Scott
locomotive) shouldn't work but it does.

Banham Zoo

English Whisky Company

Possibly because tootling around the former
in one of the latter (via not one but four
narrow-gauge railway rides) is a delightful
way to admire the work and dedication that
horticulture and steam enthusiast Alan
Bloom put into the project from its inception
in the 1940s. Kids will adore the fire
museum too – almost another attraction in
its own right – while older folks might like the
memorabilia relating to TV show *Dad's Army*.

Burston Strike School
Church Green, Burston.

This tiny school in a tiny village is the site of
the longest strike in history, a 25-year boycott
of a state school that began in April 1914
when pupils of the Burston village school
walked out to protest the dismissal of their
teachers, Tom and Kitty Higdon. In 1939 the
school became a museum and archive, and
it hosts an annual festival (details posted on
Facebook). Details of how to gain access are
posted on the door.

Diss Museum
*The Shambles, 4 Market Place, Diss, IP22 4AB
(01379 650618, www.dissmuseum.co.uk). At
time of going to press the museum was closed
but set to reopen as soon as government
guidelines permit.*

This tiny museum tells the story of the
town through memorabilia including the
Old Rectory Doll's House, sepia photos and
information panels.

English Whisky Company
*St George's Distillery, Harling Road,
Roundham, NR16 2QW (01953 717939, www.
englishwhisky.co.uk). Open shop 10am-4pm
Mon-Sat; 10am-3pm Sun. Tours 11am,
12.30pm, 2pm daily.*

Take a tour lasting one hour and find out how
whisky is made (using locally grown malting
barley), then sample the first and one of the
only whiskies distilled in England. The shop
stocks the finished results, plus more than
200 other whiskies.

Forncett Industrial Steam Museum
*Low Road, Forncett St Mary, NR16 1JJ
(01508 488277, www.forncettsteammuseum.
co.uk). Open museum 11am-4pm Wed, Sun.
Admission by voluntary donation. Steam ups
May to Oct 11am-5pm 1st Sun of the month.
Admission £10; free-£9 reductions.*

A collection of large industrial steam engines (including one that used to open London's Tower Bridge).

100th Bomb Group Memorial Museum

Common Road, Dickleburgh, IP21 4PH (01379 740708, www.100bgmus.org.uk). Open Mar, Apr, Oct 10am-5pm Sat, Sun. May-Sept 10am-5pm Wed, Sun. Admission free.

Sited at the wartime base of the 100th Bomb Group and B17 Fortress Bomber, this fascinating museum – spread across a site that includes a Nissan hut, control tower and engine shed – contains an impressive collection of models and memorabilia evocatively telling the moving story of the American airmen and ground crew based here from 1943-45.

WYMONDHAM & HINGHAM

Wymondham Abbey ♥ *Church Street, Wymondham, NR18 0PH (01953 607062, www.wymondhamabbey.org.uk). Open phone or check website for details. Admission free.*

The story of the two towers (one ruined, one unfinished) of this magnificent Norman abbey, founded in 1107, is one of the most fascinating in its history, involving centuries-long bitter disputes between parishioners and Benedictine monks. But there are plenty of other tales to discover, about the gorgeous angel roofs, the two 18th-century organs, the beautiful nave made of Caen stone, the grisly death of rebel William Kett on the walls of the western tower and the glistening gilded screen built by Sir Ninian Comper as a memorial to the local men killed in World War I. The best way to see it all is on one of the regular guided tours, but you'll get a huge amount just from looking around the abbey, where various leaflets and church guides are available.

Wymondham Heritage Museum

10 The Bridewell, Norwich Road, Wymondham, NR18 0NS (01953 600205 , www. wymondhamheritagemuseum.co.uk). Open 10am-4pm Mon-Sat; 1-4pm Sun (times may change following the lifting of government restrictions). Admission £4.50; free-£3.50 reductions.

Located in the fomer Bridewell, which has seen service as various prisons, a police station and a court in its 200-year history, the museum offers an engaging history of the town.

Wymondham Abbey

Norfolk markets

Aylsham
Market Place, NR11 6EL (07765 934850, www.aylshamcountrymarket.simplesite. com). Open General market 9-11.30am Fri. Farmers' market 9am-1pm 1st Sat of mth.

The weekly Town Hall market sells a fine range of cooked foods and preserves. The deservedly popular farmers' market adds organic meat, eggs and plants to the mix. *See also p82.*

Fakenham
Corn Hall, Market Place, NR21 9AQ (01328 853653, www.fakenhamtowncouncil. org.uk/services/markets). Open Charter market 9am-3pm Thur. Farmers' market 8.30am-noon 4th Sat of mth.

Running for more than 35 years, this outdoor market is one of Norfolk's oldest Women's Institute markets, and still one of the best; the chutneys and preserves are ace. The monthly farmers' market offers cheeses from local producer Catherine Temple (see p109), locally sourced partridge, pheasant and wild venison, soups, wines, pastries and a whole host of other tempting goodies. *See also p62.*

Harleston
General market: Market Place, IP20 (01379 854519, www.harleston-norfolk.org.uk). Open 6am-4pm Wed.

The weekly general market is a traditional outdoor one. Arrive early to get the best choice of the scrumptious home-made cakes. *See also p150.*

King's Lynn
Tuesday Market Place, IP30 1JJ (01553 616202, www.west-norfolk.gov.uk). Open 9am-4pm Tue. Farmers' Market, Saturday Market Place, PE30 5DQ. Open 9am-2pm Sat.

Produce sells out fast at this popular outdoor market, so rock up early to pick up delicious own-made sausage rolls and pies, as well as Women's Institute goodies and plenty of produce direct from farms. *See also p12 and p15.*

rather than charming. But inside is a delicately carved, 15th-century oak screen that spans the church's entire 52-foot width. The panels still contain wonderful colours, as do the fragments of wall painting above the crossing arch. The windows and a stone font with humorous faces are worth examining too, and if the organ's blasting triumphantly as you explore, it makes the experience all the better.

Outside, a six-foot pyramid marks the grave of local Egyptologist Melancthon William Henry Lombe Brooke. It's not the county's only one: in the woods at **Blickling Hall** (*see p74*) in north Norfolk, a pyramid modelled on the Roman tomb of Caius Cestius contains the remains of John Hobart, the 2nd Earl of Buckinghamshire, and his two wives. It predates the 1929 tomb of Brooke by almost 140 years.

On the eastern edge of Attleborough is **Besthorpe Hall** (01953 450300). In spring thousands of bluebells carpet the grounds, but there's year-round interest for horticulture buffs in this 16th-century home of the Drury family, who gave their name to London's Drury Lane. Visiting is by appointment only.

Where to eat & drink
There's no shortage of traditional village pubs serving tasty, inventive own-cooked food in this part of the county. One worth noting is the **Burston Crown** in Burston (Mill Road, 01379 741257, www. burstoncrown.com).

Mulberry Tree♥
Station Road, Attleborough, NR17 2AS (01953 452124, www.mulberrytree. co.uk). Open noon-3pm, 5.30-10.30pm Tue-Sat. Lunch served noon-2pm, dinner served 6.30-9pm Mon-Sat.

Boutique hotel-restaurants are rare round these parts, making the Mulberry an unexpected and luxurious oasis. Food is Modern British done simply and well – mushroom and black bomber cheese wellington, smoked haddock and beurre noisette fishcake or chargrilled flat-iron steak with braised shin of beef. A variety of burgers is also on offer – all served in a space that's warm and cosy. There's a good wine list too. Upstairs are seven comfortable bedrooms (£125 double incl breakfast), decorated in a low-key, stylish manner.

Red Lion

East Church Street, Kenninghall, NR16 2EP (01953 887849, www. redlionkenninghall.co.uk). At time of going to press the pub opening hours were shorter than usual (see website for up-to-date opening hours).

A pink-painted village pub with a small bar and snug and equally tiny dining alcoves where own-cooked food is served daily. Bar snacks such as olives, houmous and pitta bread are available, as well as standards, such as local gammon and steak and kidney pudding. They host regular jam sessions, quiz nights, open mic nights and live music.

Saracen's Head

75 Mount Street, Diss, IP22 4QQ (01379 652853, www.saracensheaddiss.co.uk). Food served Mon-Sat; noon-8pm Sun (6.45pm last orders for food on Sun).

This striking timber-framed building, parts of which are more than 500 years old, is a beauty. The food's good too: traditional pub grub is given a nice twist in dishes such as peppered calves' liver, but purists will appreciate the likes of Lowestoft fish and chips and Norfolk gammon steak.

Where to stay

One of the area's best places to eat – the **Mulberry Tree** (*see p158*) in Attleborough – also has bedrooms.
   In North Lopham, **Church Farm House** (Church Road, 01379 687270, www.church-farmhouse.org) offers

North Walsham
Market Place, NR28 9BT. Weekly general market. Open 9am-3pm Thur. Monthly farmers market, last Sun of mth.

This friendly market stocks a great range of local seasonal produce, including baked goods, fish, game, salad, honey and beeswax products, pies, ready-meals and preserves. See also p108.

Norwich
Gentleman's Walk, NR2 1ND (www. norwichmarket.net). Open 9am-4pm Mon-Sat.

A fabulous, old-school daily market with more than 190 stalls, including Churros & Chorizo Spanish street food, herbs and spices, a very good cheese stall, local Aldous ice-cream, a shellfish bar and even a little deli. See also p91.

Sheringham
St John's Hall, Wyndham Street, Sheringham, NR26 8BA. Open General market Wed (Apr-Nov), Sat.

This popular market offers a wonderful selection of products: fruit and veg, plants, clothing, electrical goods, music, art and even gemstones. See also p70.

Swaffham
Market Place, PE37 7AB, www. swaffhamtowncouncil.gov.uk). Open 9am-3pm Sat; Assembly Rooms Fri.

Some 90 stalls fill what must be one of Norfolk's loveliest Georgian market squares; come for the traditional produce and prepared foods, as well as crafts and second-hand bric-a-brac. At the Assembly Rooms on Friday you can find home-made cakes, jams and pickles and other WI goodies. There's also a farmers' market on alternate Sundays. See also p168.

SOUTH NORFOLK

three rooms in the Grade II-listed farmhouse, all featuring antique furniture, rich textiles and views of the church. The sitting and dining rooms are cosy and warm, particularly when the log fire is blazing away. A candlelit evening meal is also available.

In Great Moulton, **Oakbrook House** (Frith Way, 01379 677359, www.oakbrookhouse.co.uk), formerly the village school, is now a friendly, comfortable, nine-bedroom guesthouse, with decor that's easy on the eye. Evening meals are available at the neighbouring Fox and Hounds pub.

Park Hotel

29 Denmark Street, Diss, IP22 4LE (01379 642244, www.parkhotel-diss.co.uk). Rates £85-£120 double incl breakfast.

Within walking distance of Diss town centre, the Park offers 13 individually designed rooms and a popular restaurant.

WYMONDHAM & HINGHAM

The triangular parcel of land that lies between the A11 and the A47 splits into two types of terrain: the heaths and forests of the Brecks that stretch from Attleborough to Swaffham in the west, and the more affluent villages near Norwich. The former area is great for walking and wooded adventures, while the latter has more to offer those whose outward-bound activities tend towards a post-prandial village amble rather than a long-distance hike. There are the market towns of Wymondham, Watton and Hingham, plus a slew of eminently enjoyable villages such as Shipdham, Kimberley, Bawburgh, Hethersett, Great Hockham and Great Ellingham.

Wymondham & around

Wymondham – pronounced 'Windum' – is the largest and most historically interesting town in the area, with a huge and splendid twin-towered **abbey** (*see p157*) that's visible for miles around. There are good places to eat, including the 15th-century **Green Dragon Traven** (*see p162*) and the **Station Bistro** (*see p162*) at Wymondham Station. This is also where the volunteer-run **Mid-Norfolk Railway** (01362 851723, www.mnr.org.uk) operates. Trains (sometimes with steam engines) travel the 11 miles to Dereham on weekends and bank holidays; check the website for exact days of operation. In the town centre is the pretty **Market Cross**, on Market Place, built in 1617-18 and home to the local tourist office (01953 603302, www.wymondhamtowncouncil. org/about-wymondham/tourist-information-centre). The nearby streets are lined with charity shops, independent gift and food stores – assorted tearooms, a supermarket and the **Wymondham Heritage Museum** (*see p157*). Market day is Friday, and there's also a monthly farmers' market.

The museum contains information on Robert and William Kett, leaders of the peasants' uprising in 1549 that would become known as Kett's Rebellion; the rebellion's reputed rallying point is a few miles outside town, at **Kett's Oak**, just before **Hethersett**. This large village has some interesting Tudor, Stuart and Georgian buildings, an impressive church in the form of St Remigius (14th century in origin but mainly Victorian inside) and the upmarket **Park Farm Country Hotel** (*see p163*).

A few miles north on the River Yare is **Bawburgh**, definitely worth a visit to see the cone-topped round tower, late medieval stained glass and fascinating mish-mash of building styles at the church of **St Mary & St Walstan**, and for the excellent **Kings Head** pub (*see p162*). **Ketteringham** (south of Hethersett and the A11) is worth a stop too; this estate village has some lovely neo-Tudor cottages and another church, St Peter, notable for its monuments and stained glass. From the tower you get a great bird's-eye view of stately **Ketteringham Hall**, a Tudor/mock Gothic pile owned by the family of the late Colin Chapman, one-time chairman of the Lotus car group, and now used as offices and for weddings and other functions.

Head west for the riverside mill buildings of **Barnham Broom** and the thatched cottages and Regency lodge houses of Kimberley; both are likeable, picturesque sites good for walking. If you're after some pampering, check out **Barnham Broom** hotel, golf and country club (*see p163*).

Hingham & around

The small market towns of **Watton** and **Hingham** vie for attention in a competitive fashion. The former contains a couple of oddities: a curious 1679 clocktower on the High Street and, inside **St Mary's Church**, an engaging 1639 poorbox in the form of a carved wooden grinning priest with the inscription 'Remember the poore', whose hand drops your contribution through to a bag. The round church tower is Norman, topped by a later octagonal band with some lovely stonework.

But in the battle of the picturesque, **Hingham** ❤ wins hands down, thanks to a breathtaking display of Georgian town houses that made it one of the most fashionable places in the area in the 18th century. A century earlier, people couldn't get out fast enough: the charming town sign commemorates the exodus of the many parishioners who followed in the footsteps of Robert Peck, the village's one-time vicar and Puritan, who left for America in the early part of the 17th century, founding a new

Hingham in Massachusetts. Samuel Lincoln, ancestor of Abraham, was one of the emigrants.

Today, Hingham has the appeal of a substantial village, with an interesting array of shops, pubs and restaurants. Standouts include **Lincoln's Tea Shoppe & Bistro** (*see p162*) on the smaller of the two greens; architectural salvage shop **Mongers** ❤ (15 Market Place, 01953 851868, www. mongersofhingham.co.uk, closed Sun and Wed, except by appointment), which has a wealth of wonderful stuff sprawling across gardens, sheds and a yard outside and a warren of rooms inside; and **Harrods of Hingham** (7 Church Street, 07909 333928), a community arts and crafts hub with workshops and exhibitions showcasing the work of local artists. The **White Hart Hotel** (*see p163*) is huge; you can't miss the 14th-century church of St Andrew either, thanks to its colossal 120-foot-high tower; it also has an impressive 15th-century tomb and some notable stained glass.

Another equally arresting church, **All Saints**, can be found six miles north at the village of **Shipdham** –

Wymondham Market Cross *see p160*

which is notable for being the very centre of Norfolk. The church tower is topped by a very unusual and delicate cupola made of lead and wood, which looks distinctly at odds with the solid Norman features beneath it. A few miles south of Hingham, another clutch of villages – Great Hockham and the Elllinghams – offer something of interest for the weary village wanderer. There are yet more lovely churches at Great and Little Ellingham, while **Great Hockham** is a textbook south Norfolk village if ever there was one. Thatched cottages nestle around a triangular village green; there's a primary school and popular local pub; lively village customs exist in the form of the Horn Fair in May and the dancing Clodhoppers; and on the village outskirts is a grand Queen Anne mansion, **Hockham Hall**, and a large church with some striking medieval wall paintings.

Where to eat & drink

There's a fine tearoom at **Wymondham Heritage Museum** (*see p157*) in what was the prisoners' exercise yard. In Hingham, **Lincoln's Tea Shoppe & Bistro** (The Fairlands, 01953 851357, www.lincolns-of-hingham.co.uk, closed Mon), is great for lunch or afternoon tea.

Pub enthusiasts will enjoy the food, drink and decor at the 16th-century **Honingham Buck** (29 The Street, 01603 880393, www.thehoninghambuck.co.uk) in Honingham. Country hotels **Barnham Broom** and **Park Farm** both have restaurants that offer something a bit special (for both, *see p163*).

Angel Inn
Sallow Lane, Larling, NR16 2QU (01953 717963, www.angel-larling.co.uk). Open 10am-10pm daily. Food served noon-8pm Sun-Thur; noon-8.30pm Fri, Sat.

This whitewashed 17th-century freehouse just off the A11, halfway between Thetford and Attleborough, is a regular in the *Good Pub Guide* for its changing range of well-kept real ales from Norfolk and elsewhere and its August beer festival. It's also a good place to eat, with own-cooked traditional dishes and an oak-panelled dining room that's full of warmth and original features. There are also five B&B rooms (£80 double) and camping from March to October.

Green Dragon Tavern
6 Church Street, Wymondham, NR18 0PH (01953 607907, www. greendragonnorfolk.com). Open noon-11pm Mon-Thur; noon-midnight Fri, Sat; noon-10.30pm Sun. (The pub is closing earlier than usual while government restrictions are in place.) Meals served noon-3pm, 5-8.30pm Mon-Thur; noon-4pm, 4.30-8.30pm Fri-Sun.

The oldest pub in Wymondham features beams and timber everywhere, as well as leaded Tudor windows, roaring fires in rickety bars and a pretty walled garden. Traditional food and a selection of real ales complete the picture.

Kings Head
Harts Lane, Bawburgh, NR9 3LS (01603 744977, www.kingsheadbawburgh. co.uk). Open 11am-11pm Mon-Sat; 11am-10.30pm Sun.

Winner of numerouos awards (including Norfolk Dining Pub of the Year 2020 Good Food Award Winner), the Kings Head creates excellent, beautifully presented gastropub fare, at very reasonable prices. Local produce is to the fore with suppliers are listed on the menu. The interior is charming too, with wooden settles, leather sofas, low-beamed ceilings and inglenook fireplaces. Upstairs are six boutique B&B rooms (£130-£175) and a short walk away are two self-catering apartments that can be booked by the night.

Station Bistro ♥
Station Approach, Wymondham, NR18 0JZ (01953 606433, www.stationbistro. co.uk). Open 9am-4pm Mon-Thur; 9am-4pm, 5.30pm-10.30pm Fri; 8.30am-4pm Sat, Sun.

Part of Wymondham's charming railway station, the Bistro offers cooked breakfasts, sandwiches and hot lunch dishes as well as jacket potatoes and panini. Seating is in the dining room or in a refurbished railway carriage.

White Hart Hotel

Market Place, Hingham, NR9 4AF (01953 850214, www.whitehartnorfolk.co.uk). Open noon-midnight daily. Lunch served noon-2.30pm, dinner served 6.30-9.30pm daily.

This smart restaurant with rooms is located in Hingham's most imposing Georgian building (it's the one with the deer perched grandly above the entrance porch). The setting (on two floors, with a pleasant courtyard) is warm, comfortable and informal, and the food above-par gastropub fare or you can opt for savoury or sweet tapas if you're after a lighter lunch. There are five boutique bedrooms with a hint of Provençale (£115-£155 double incl breakfast).

Where to stay

A number of pubs offer accommodation, including the **Angel Inn** (*see p162*) in Larling and the **White Hart Hotel** (*see p163*) in Hingham.

Barnham Broom

Honingham Road, Barnham Broom, NR9 4DD (01603 334157, www.barnham-broom.co.uk). Rates £165-£225 double incl breakfast.

Ideal for traditionalists looking for a very relaxing break in a top-notch country hotel, with spa and golf packages available. The 46 bedrooms and suites have been newly refurbished in a more contemporary style, and the Brasserie offers an inventive menu of dishes such as king scallops with pickled saffron cauliflower, burnt apple purée and pancetta, followed by fillet of beef, dauphinoise gratin, glazed shallot and red wine jus.

Park Farm Country Hotel

Norwich Road, Hethersett, NR9 3DL (01603 810264, www.parkfarm-hotel.co.uk). Rates £85-£415 double incl breakfast.

One for lovers of space, this Georgian building is set in 200 acres and offers well-appointed rooms, suites, apartments and lodges, ranging from standard to boutique-style, as well as a spa and gym facilities. There's also a bar and a restaurant serving Modern British food with the emphasis on local fish and meat.

Wymondham *see p160*

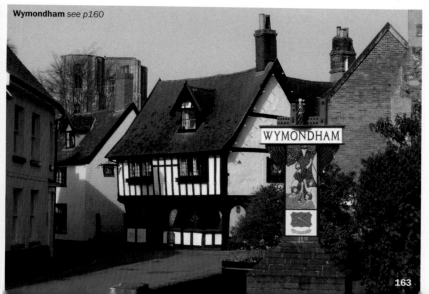

WYMONDHAM

The Fens & the Brecks

There's a bench in the WWT Welney Wetland Centre in the heart of the Fens that paraphrases a popular local saying: 'Any fool can appreciate mountains, it takes a discerning eye to appreciate the beauty of the Fens'. And it's true. As you look out across the flat, featureless terrain broken only by old windmills and new wind turbines, it's hard to imagine there's anything here worthy of more than an afternoon's exploration. But, gradually, you discover there's more to the landscape than meets, literally, the eye. Along a quiet road, acres of bright orange pumpkins, looking as if they've just landed from space, delight with their vibrant incongruity; a delightful windmill serves terrific sandwiches in a pretty tearoom; medieval churches and charming villages offer rich pickings for history and architecture fans; and even if you can't understand their fiendishly complex workings, it's easy to appreciate the Victorian engineering feats used to tame the tides at Denver. Further west, the marshy peat of the Fens gives way to the sandy heaths, pine forests, farms and Neolithic mines of the Brecks, a vast playground spanning two counties, with 370 square miles that have something for everyone.

DOWNHAM MARKET & THE FENS

Looking out across the vast open Fens that stretch west from **Downham Market**, the flatness pierced only by the occasional church spire, it's not hard to imagine that just over 200 years ago – before the area was successfully drained – much of it was a massive bog. Long before that, millennia ago, it was covered in oak forest, which became flooded after the last Ice Age and eventually rotted down to form the rich peat soils cultivated so aggressively today. Take a walk along any of the numerous paths traversing the Fens and you might trip over proof; the gradual erosion of the soil is revealing the preserved remains of ancient bog oaks, coloured in rich hues of red and blue from the minerals they have absorbed. They're just one of nature's surprises to be discovered in this rich, fertile landscape.

The Fens are also home to an impressive array of Churches Conservation Trust sites (www.visitchurches.org.uk), with three ★ that are definitely worth visiting. Two are in the village of **Walpole** on the Lincolnshire border: **Walpole St Peter** and **Walpole St Andrew**. The former is undoubtedly the big daddy of the three at 160 foot tall, and its highlights could – and do – fill a small book

Across the border

Peckover House in Wisbech, Lincolnshire (www.nationaltrust.org.uk) is that rare thing: a historic house that doesn't feel stuffy and museum-like. Imagine you're in a Jane Austen novel and take a turn in the garden too, but don't forget your fan.

(available in the back of the church). Check out the medieval bosses, among the finest in Norfolk, and the spectacular nave, complete with centuries-old paintings decorating its screens. Smaller St Andrew is celebrated for its unusual octagonal turrets. The third of the trio, **St Mary the Virgin** is at Wiggenhall and has the best collection of 15th- and 16th-century carved benches in the county, if not England.

Downham Market

The area's main settlement is Downham Market, capital of the Norfolk Fens and one of the county's oldest market towns. These days, the market (held on Fridays and Saturdays) is a lacklustre affair, with just a few uninspiring Poundbuster-style tat stalls bolstered by the occasional continental farmers' market and a fortnightly craft market on summer Saturdays, but there's still enough here to make it a good base for a weekend of pleasurable walking and sightseeing. There are some decent eating and drinking options too.

Nicknamed the 'Gingerbread Town' because of the distinctive yellow brick and rust-brown carrstone used in many of its older buildings, Downham Market sits on rising ground on the edge of the Fens and is surprisingly hilly. The main landmark is the 1878 cast-iron clock tower in the town square. A miniature Big Ben, it's a piece of pure nursery-rhyme whimsy, with distinctive black and white panels (originally green and white) and a Gothic roof with gold-leaf tracery.

The parish church of **St Edmunds** is the next building of any note. Dating from Norman times, it has some fine medieval stained glass in the tower and a 15th-century font, but is nowhere near as eye-popping as the **Castle Hotel** (*see p168*), a handsome building whose black and white

exterior is festooned with overflowing hanging baskets in summer.

Shopping options are generally old-fashioned. There are a number of farm shops not far away, with notably large ones in the villages of Hilgay and Stowbridge and on the A1122 south of town.

Walkers can access the **Fen Rivers Way** (www.countrysideaccess.norfolk. gov.uk), a 50-mile path that connects Cambridge with King's Lynn, tracing the course of rivers that drain slowly across the Fens into the Wash. It runs through the town on the west side of the Great Ouse river – get there by strolling down Bridge Street/Railway Road and past the train station.

Denver

If you follow the path south along the river for less than two miles, you'll reach Denver, home to a **windmill** turned popular teashop and a decent pub, the **Jenyns Arms** (*see p167*), where you can sit in the riverside garden and try to figure out how the fiendishly complex-looking **Denver Sluice** works. This impressive waterways control system controls river flow, diverts floodwaters and acts as a lock gate between the tidal Ouse to the north and the freshwater rivers to the south. Part of it hails from 1834, though there's been a sluice here for much longer – since 1651, when Dutch engineer Cornelius Vermuyden pioneered a scheme to drain the fenland owned by the Duke of Bedford. For another look at the Fens' unique watery landscape, visit the **WWT Welney Wetland Centre** (*see p172*), a few miles further south.

The sluice is not Denver's only claim to fame – pop into the **Downham Market Heritage Centre** to learn about the grisly Denver murderer, executed in 1837 for killing a local fortune-teller (you'd think she'd have seen it coming).

Villages nearby

As you move east from Downham Market, away from Lincolnshire and into Norfolk proper, there are perceptible shifts in the landscape – and the villages are undoubtedly prettier than their western Fens counterparts.

Take **Hilgay**, a few miles south of the town. Recorded as just one of two settlements in the Norfolk Fens in the Domesday Book, when it was an 'island' (a hilly knoll), time feels as if it has stood still here. There's a pleasing church, of course, **All Saints**, worth a look for the curious memorial to Denver-born inventor George William Manby, which contains the sad words, 'The public should have paid this tribute.' The walk to the church, which is set some way from the village, is pleasant, via an elegant avenue of mature lime trees, but you might be just as tempted to chill out on the banks of the peaceful River Wissey or stroll around **Hilgay Heronry**, a copse designated a Site of Special Scientific Interest.

Stow Bardolph, a couple of miles north of Downham Market on the A10 (the main road between Cambridge and King's Lynn), is equally enjoyable. Children will love the **Church Farm Rare Breeds Centre** (see p172), while adults will prefer the excellent **Hare Arms** (see p167), and both will be creeped out by the alarmingly life-like wax effigy of parishioner Sarah Hare adjacent to Holy Trinity Church – it's been in a mahogany cupboard in the north-west corner of the 1624 Hare Chapel since her death in 1744.

A few miles east lies another lovely village, **Barton Bendish**. It's worth a visit to examine the unusual decoration on the austere but fascinating village hall, flanked by matching houses in an elegant piece of architectural symmetry, and to pop into the gorgeous little church of **St Mary** (see p172).

Where to eat & drink

The **Andel Lodge** in Tottenhill, and **Timbers Country Lodge** in Fincham (for both, see p168) offer typical hotel dining at reasonable prices, but, given the calibre of village pubs in the area and their commitment to using good-quality Norfolk produce, you might want to follow the examples of the locals and head for their locals. **The Chequers** (7 Church Road, 01366 387704, www.thechequerswimbotsham.co.uk) in the sweet village of Wimbotsham; the **Jenyns Arms** (01366 383366, www.jenynsarms.com) in Denver; and the **Heron** (The Causeway, 01366 384040, www.theheronstowbridge.com) in Stow Bridge impress with their extensive range of ales and piles of hearty own-cooked food.

The area's restaurants and tearooms tend to cluster around Downham Market, which has assorted hotel restaurants.

Crown Hotel

12 Bridge Street, Downham Market, PE38 9DH (01366 382322, www.crowncoachinginn.com). Open 9.30am-11pm daily. Food served 6-9pm Mon; noon-3pm, 6-9pm Tue-Sat; noon-4pm Sun.

This 16th-century coaching inn has a pleasant outdoor seating area in the old carriage entrance. But if you want to avoid the smokers, best head indoors to the restaurant, which serves old-school classics such as gammon, steaks and fish cakes, and a good selection of beers and wines. You can also eat in the bar. Upstairs there are 18 rooms (£57.50-£82.50 double incl breafast).

Hare Arms

Stow Bardolph, PE34 3HT (01366 382229, www.theharearms.co.uk). At the time of going to press the pub was serving a restricted menu with shorter than usual opening hours. Check the website for up-to-date information.

A lovely garden, a roaring fire (sometimes with resident badger asleep in front of it) and great food inside, friendly staff, and a bill that doesn't break the bank – it all adds up to what is possibly the perfect pub. The extensive bar menu has plenty of vegetarian dishes and daily specials such as crab salad, but the dinner-only restaurant is the place if you want to push the boat out – it's exceedingly popular, so do book. The £14.25 Sunday roasts are highly recommended, and served all day, hurrah.

Millstone Tearooms at Denver Windmill
Sluice Road, Denver, PE38 0EG (01366 389701). Open 10am-4pm Wed-Sun.

Three generations of milling – wind, steam and electric – are visible at this fascinating windmill, dating from 1835 and now housing a traditional tearoom serving light lunches as well as home-made cakes, scones, and pastries.

Peacocks Tearoom
65 Waterside, Ely, CB7 4AU (01353 661100, www.peacockstearoom.co.uk). Open 10.30am-4.30pm Wed-Sun.

This pretty tearoom by the river in Ely, just over the Cambridgeshire border, is worth a detour. There are more than 70 teas to choose from, and the own-made cakes, including apple and cinnamon cake served warm with cream, are memorable for all the right reasons. Soup, salads and light lunches are available, as well as full-blown afternoon teas. The charming garden is perfect on warm days, and they have two delightful B&B rooms too.

Where to stay

Andel Lodge Hotel & Restaurant
48 Lynn Road, Tottenhill, PE33 0RH (01553 810256, www.andellodge.co.uk). Rates £85-£105 double incl breakfast.

Well placed for both the Fens and the Wash, Andel Lodge is a small, family-run hotel, with colourful, individually decorated rooms, a comfortable, well-stocked bar and a restaurant with a traditional – even retro – menu following the prawn cocktail or gammon steak with pineapple trend.

Castle Hotel
High Street, Downham Market, PE38 9HF (01366 384311, www.castle-hotel. com). Rates £89-£140 double incl breakfast.

This exuberent, black and white coaching inn has 12 en-suite rooms. All have character, and two have four-poster beds and jacuzzis. The decor ranges from plain to elaborate, and the photo-filled lounge bar is a great place for an aperitif before heading out for dinner.

Lakeside Caravan Park & Fisheries
Sluice Road, Denver, PE38 0DZ (01366 387074, 07790 272 978, www. lakesidedenver.co.uk). Rates from £15 per pitch.

This waterside campsite is particularly popular with fishing fans, though only the main Lakeside site takes tents. Facilities (including Wi-Fi and a children's play area) are excellent. Denver Mill is close at hand for home-made goodies, and the campsite shop sells a wide range of local produce. Self-catering options, in cottages and caravans, are available too.

Timbers Country Lodge
Lynn Road, Fincham, PE33 9HE (01366 347747, www.timberscountrylodge. co.uk). Rates £100-£140 double.

The chalet-style rooms in this converted barn complex work well if you want comfort and don't mind the somewhat corporate vibe. The restaurant has a varied menu and there's a separate vegan menu too, as well as one for the kids.

SWAFFHAM & THE BRECKS

Swaffham
If you were a fan of the Stephen Fry TV series *Kingdom*, you might remember Swaffham: the Georgian market town doubles as the show's fictional Market Shipborough. However, you might be somewhat disappointed with the real deal; judicious editing and close-cropped

Downham Market's clock tower *see p166*

THE FENS & THE BRECKS

shooting work wonders with Swaffham's dowdier aspects.

The best day to visit is Saturday, when the elegant triangular marketplace is abuzz with action. Unlike many country markets, which have been reduced to a few sad stalls, Swaffham's is thriving, with bric-a-brac, books and accessories nestling happily next to local fruit and veg and dairy products, all watched over by the statue of Ceres, Roman goddess of the harvest, who adorns the domed Market Cross.

London Street, the main drag, is home to the diminutive **Swaffham Museum** (*see p175*), which is also the tourist information centre, and a great bookshop, **Ceres** (no.20, 01760 722504, www.ceresbookshopswaffham.co.uk, closed Sun), where you can browse an impressive range of new and used books.

A handful of distinguished buildings, including the Georgian **Assembly Rooms**, some smart town houses and the grand 15th-century church of **St Peter & St Paul** (*see p175*) should keep architecture fans happy for an afternoon. There are more churches of interest in nearby villages: **All Saints** in **Necton** bears ancient and Victorian motifs and styles in a fascinating architectural mash-up; thatched **St Mary's** in **Beachamwell** features some of the best-preserved medieval graffiti in Britain and an 11th-century round tower, one of the earliest in Norfolk; and **St Mary's** in **Houghton-on-the-Hill** (*see p174*) contains some remarkable 11th-century wall paintings.

For walkers and cyclists, the long-distance **Peddars Way** (www.nationaltrail.co.uk/peddarsway), which runs for 45 miles from

Denver Sluice see p166

Knettishall Heath in Suffolk along a Roman road to Holme-next-the-Sea on the north Norfolk coast, is just a mile from the town. There are also plenty of enjoyable villages within striking distance.

A few miles to the north is **Castle Acre** ♥. One of the prettiest villages in Norfolk, with some key sights and a number of excellent places to eat and stay, it makes a great weekend base. Its attractions are manifold: the picturesque cottages and diminutive versions of Georgian town houses; the massive flint Bailey Gate and the long, manicured Stocks Green; the dramatic ruins of the Norman castle (*see p172*) and Cluniac priory (*see p173*).

Next door is **West Acre** village, where another ruined priory, the tall chimney of a lime-burning kiln, All Saints' church with adjacent 14th-century priory gate, and **West Acre Gardens** (*see p175*) provide a happy couple of hours' exploration.

South to Thetford

Heading south from Swaffham, it's not far to the attractive hamlet of **Cockley Cley**. Further on are delightful **Gooderstone Water Gardens** (*see p174*) and **Oxburgh Hall** (*see p174*), a wonderful moated manor house that has belonged to the Bedingfeld family since 1482 and is now run by the National Trust.

Further south towards the Suffolk town of Brandon, **Feltwell** is worth a stop for the church of **St Nicholas**, a strikingly elegant and imposing building with its massive Norman tower and huge, clear glass windows. In the southern Brecks, the amazing prehistoric **Grimes Graves** (*see p174*) seems to have landed from another planet altogether, while **Thetford Forest** (*see p175*) is a welcome vertical diversion for eyes that have become too used to the horizontal plane. In the underwhelming town of Thetford itself, the **Dad's Army Museum & Trail** (*see p173*) offers the chance to learn more about a part of British culture that is as popular as fish and chips. And if you haven't had enough of religious ruins by this point, **Thetford Priory** (www. english-heritage.org.uk), once one of the most important monasteries in East Anglia, also awaits. However, if you've visited Castle Acre Priory, it might disappoint: there's very little to see apart from some wall fragments and an almost-complete 14th-century gatehouse.

Finally, on the county border, **Weeting Heath** is a wonderful area of Breck heath famous for its rare stone curlews, resident between April and September. It's run by the Norfolk Wildlife Trust (01842 827615, www. norfolkwildlifetrust.org.uk).

Places to visit

DOWNHAM MARKET & THE FENS

Church Farm Rare Breeds Centre
Home Farm, Stow Bardolph, PE34 3HT (01366 382162, www.churchfarm stowbardolph. co.uk). Open Mar-Oct 10am-5pm daily. Nov-Feb 10am-5pm Thur-Sun. Admission £8.10; £5-£8 reductions.

A clean, well-tended farm where all the animals (including super-cute piglets, sheep, goats, horses and a donkey), look like happy cartoon ones. The chickens and giant rabbits in the petting pen, in particular, look as if they're straight from the pages of *Alice in Wonderland*. There is also an indoor treehouse, tractor rides, donkey treks, pig racing and other outdoor activities to keep children happy for hours.

Downham Market Heritage Centre
30 Priory Road, PE38 9JS (01366 384428, www.discoverdownham.org.uk). Open 10am-4pm Thur, Fri; 10am-1pm Sat. Admission free.

The Downham Market & District Heritage Society was formed in 1995. Today it is based at the Old Fire Station. Pop in if you're interested in the history and development of the town and, more intriguingly, the surrounding Fens.

St Mary, Barton Bendish
Broughton Long Road, Barton Bendish, PE33 9DP (www.norfolkchurches.co.uk). Open by arrangement only.

The tiny, thatch-roofed church of St Mary is a real delight. It's on the outskirts of the village; take the road to Broughton and it's down the first left-hand track, hidden by trees. Through the Norman doorway (deemed by Pevsner to be the finest in England), you enter a sparse space decorated with a 14th-century wall painting, a collection of ancient carved pieces, including a stunning table, and pure white light. It may not sound like much, but sometimes less is definitely more.

WWT Welney Wetland Centre
Hundred Foot Bank, Welney, PE14 9TN (01353 860711, www.wwt.org.uk). Open 10am-4pm daily. Admission £8.09; free-£6.90 reductions; £21.63 family. Advance bookings only for the time being and hides are currently closed in accordance with government restrictions.

The Ouse Washes, a strip of land between two drainage channels starting at the Denver Sluice and ending at Earith in Cambridgeshire, is deliberately flooded every winter to prevent unintended flooding of the Fenland fields, creating a 13-mile long ecological goldmine that's home, in part, to the Welney Wetland Centre. With heated observatories, a lovely, light-filled café, small hides and a number of trails, it's possible to spend hours here marvelling at all manner of rare and unusual water plants, fish, insects and butterflies, and, of course, the huge number and array of birds who visit and breed here. In the main observatory you can train a CCTV camera on the lagoons and banks to get terrific, close-up views of the birds.

SWAFFHAM & THE BRECKS

Castle Acre Castle
Castle Acre, PE32 2XD (www.english-heritage. org.uk). Open dawn-dusk daily. Admission free, although there's a £2 car parking fee.

There's not much left of the 11th-century castle itself, built by the baronial Warennes family (who were responsible for the

Grimes Graves see p174

St Peter & St Paul see p175

whole of Castle Acre including the town and priory), but the mighty ditched earthworks are still very impressive. The main entrance, the Bailey Gate, still stands in the village.

Castle Acre Priory 💜
Castle Acre, PE32 2XD (01760 755394, www.english-heritage.org.uk). Open summer 10am-5pm daily; winter 10am-4pm. Admission £7.90; free-£7.10; £20.50 family.

Bah, another pile of ancient religious ruins, you might think. You'd be wrong. Castle Acre is one of England's best-preserved monastic sites, with Cluniac decoration that looks way younger than its 700-plus years. It's a delight to ramble around, up and down. Don't miss the prior's personal quarters, a space that manages (along with the excellent audio guide) to give a very real sense of history and medieval monastic life.

Dad's Army Museum & Trail
Cage Lane, Thetford, IP24 2DS (07470 165795, www.dadsarmythetford.org.uk). Open Mar-June, Sept-Nov 10am-2pm Sat. July, Aug 10am-2pm Tue, Sat. Admission free.

From 1968 to 1977, Thetford doubled for Walmington-on-Sea, home town of TV's *Dad's Army*. Thousands now come to pay homage to the popular wartime-set sitco, which tells the story of the show's links with Thetford, as well as the history of the town's real Home Guard. To discover which locations were used during filming, follow the Dad's Army Trail via a leaflet that includes plenty of information and a quiz – you can download it from the website. Public walking tours start at 10.30am two Sundays a month in summer; arrive early so that you can have a good viewing of Captain Mainwaring's statue or Jones's van.

Places to visit

Gooderstone Water Gardens

The Street, Gooderstone, PE33 9BP (01603 712913, www.gooderstonewatergardens. co.uk). Open summer 10.30am-5pm daily (last admission 4pm); winter 10.30am-dusk. Admission £7; free-£6.50 reductions.

Coral Hoyos restored these beautiful gardens in memory of her parents Billy and Florence Knights, who had turned a series of boggy grazing pastures into a six-acre water garden filled with ponds, a trout stream, 13 lovely wooden bridges (discreetly numbered for easy orienteering) and a nature trail with a kingfisher hide. A small wooden tearoom (11am-4pm daily) completes the idyll.

Grimes Graves

Seven miles north-west of Thetford, off the A134, IP26 5DE (01842 810656, www. english-heritage.org.uk). Open Apr-Oct 10am-5pm Fri-Sun (currently closed until Aug 2021). Admission £6.90; free-£6.20 reductions; £17.90 family.

Everyone describes this Neolithic flint mining complex near Thetford as a lunar landscape, and so it is (give or take some scrubby grass and grazing sheep). It's the terrain that's moon-like; more than 400 shafts, pits, craters and spoil dumps are scattered around the site, where 5,000 years ago prehistoric miners dug with deer antlers for floorstone, a black flint that was ideal for making axes and other tools. It's a great spot to explore, and that's before you descend

via a 30ft ladder into a mine shaft to view the ancient underground workings. There's a picnic area and an English Heritage gift shop.

Oxburgh Hall 💙

Oxborough, PE33 9PS. (01366 328258, www. nationaltrust.org.uk). Open Summer House 11am-3.15pm daily; Gardens 9.30am-5pm daily. Winter House 11am-3pm Wed-Sun; Gardens 9.30am-4pm Wed-Sun. Admission £13; free-£6.50 reductions; £32.50 family..

You'll gasp as you come through the entrance and see the gorgeous proportions and setting of this 15th-century moated house. From the French parterre and impressive medieval brick gatehouse to the house itself, where 16th-century needlework panels created by Mary, Queen of Scots and Bess of Hardwick deservedly draw crowds, Oxburgh Hall is a real winner. Do take a walk along the battlements; the roof and chimneys are masterpieces of craftsmanship, and the views are marvellous. You can also see the priest hole, used to hide Catholic priests during Elizabeth I's reign.

St Mary, Houghton-on-the-Hill

Houghton-on-the-Hill, between North Pickenham & South Pickenham (www. houghtonstmarys.org.uk). Open Mar-Oct 2-4pm daily. Admission free.

An ivy-covered ruin in the early 1990s, this tiny flint church was saved from

Swaffham Market see p168

dereliction mainly thanks to the hard work of local churchwarden Bob Davey. In the course of restoration, a series of rare Romanesque wall paintings (dating from 1090 and among the finest in Europe) were discovered, and St Mary is now one of the most famous and most-visited churches in Norfolk. It's a serene and lovely space, and the paintings are stunning.

St Peter & St Paul, Swaffham

Market Place, Swaffham, PE37 7AB (01760 622241, www.swaffham.churchnorfolk.com). Admission free.

This grand church contains much of note. There's the marvellous medieval double-hammerbeam roof covered in carved angels, and impressive stained-glass windows, including some by William Morris & Co commemorating World War I. The elegant, early 16th-century tower was funded by churchwarden John Chapman, who, according to local legend, was the famous Pedlar of Swaffham; his carved figure, plus dog, adorn one of the pews (and he also appears on the town sign).

Swaffham Museum

4 London Street, PE37 7DQ (01760 721230, www.swaffhammuseum.co.uk). Open 10am-4pm Mon-Fri; 10am-1pm Sat. Admission £3; free-£1 reductions; £7 family.

A small social history museum, housed in a grand Georgian town house next to the market square. As well as Stone Age, Roman and Saxon artefacts, there's a gallery devoted to the discovery of the tomb of Tutankhamun by Swaffham-born Howard Carter. The gift shop and Swaffham Tourist Information Centre are housed here too (same opening hours).

Thetford Forest

01842 815434, www.forestry.gov.uk/england.

Spread across some 80 square miles, Thetford Forest is the largest lowland pine forest in Britain, and a joy to explore. The carefully managed woodlands are home to all sorts of rare breeds, including red squirrels, bats and woodlark, some of them visible from the vast network of trails that criss-cross the forest. Head for the High Lodge Forest Centre for maps, activity sheets and suggested trails.

West Acre Gardens

West Acre, PE32 2BW (01760 755562, www. west acregardens.co.uk). Open Feb-Nov 9.30am-5pm daily. Admission free.

Located a mile outside West Acre, this garden centre doesn't feel like a garden centre at all. You're left to wander round the walled domain of this old Norfolk manor house and the display gardens are a delight, with mixed borders, shrubs, roses, bamboo, Mediterranean beds and even a shade garden.

Nine Norfolk climbs

Appleton Water Tower
Sleep in an octagonal Victorian water tower near Sandringham, courtesy of the Landmark Trust. *See p22.*

Beacon's Hill
Norfolk's highest point, a whopping 338ft above sea level. *See p69.*

Cathedral Church of St John the Baptist
Take a tower tour for a breathtaking view of Norwich, the surrounding countryside and, on a clear day, the sea. *See p92.*

Cathedral of the Broads
Climb the 100ft tower of St Helen's Church, Ranworth, and see the Broads the way the birds do. *See p123.*

The dunes at Winterton-on-Sea
Exhilarating fun in the sand on the north-east Norfolk coast. *See p103.*

Grimes Graves
Exercise your knees on a neolithic lunar landscape near Thetford Forest. *See p174.*

Happisburgh Lighthouse
This candy-striped lighthouse, the oldest working lighthouse in East Anglia, is deemed to be one of Norfolk's seven wonders. *See p104.*

Old Hunstanton cliffs
Feast your eyes on the stripy millennia of rock, but don't climb the cliffs; erosion is a big problem here so climb the path to the top and admire the view. *See p23.*

Oxburgh Hall
Climb the circular staircase to the priest's hole and battlements in this 15th-century moated manor house. *See p174.*

Where to eat & drink

Award for best pub name has to go to Cockley Cley's **Twenty Church Wardens** (01760 721439), which gets packed to the gills on Sunday – perhaps by churchwardens enjoying a well-earned half. The rambling **Olde Windmill Inn** (01760 756232, www.oldewindmillinn.co.uk) in Great Cressingham is popular for its great choice of real ales and proper pub grub; it also has rooms. In Swaffham, **Strattons Hotel** (*see p180*) is the place for a special occasion; while **Mother Hubbard's** (91 Market Place, 01760 721933, www.mother-hubbards.com) offers giant portions of fish and chips, and **Rasputin** (21-22 Plowright Place, 01760 724725, closed Sun, Mon) is Norfolk's first and only authentic Russian restaurant.

CoCoes
4 Ash Close, Swaffham, PE37 7NH (01760 723845, www.strattons-hotel.co.uk). Open for lunch until 2pm.

Guests at Strattons Hotel (*see p180*) wanting to take home some of the excellent jam served with their breakfast will love this bright café-deli, adjacent to the hotel. Eat-in selections include own-made cakes, tarts (savoury and sweet) and inventive snacks, such as Norfolk fish cakes with fennel coleslaw, while the deli offers freshly baked bread, Norfolk cheeses, preserves and pâté and superior picnic ingredients.

Market Cross Café Bar
15A Market Place, Swaffham, PE37 7AB (01760 336671). Open 9am-4pm Mon-Thur; 9am-5pm Fri; 8.30am-5pm Sat; 9.30am-3.30pm Sun.

This licensed café is a nice alternative to Swaffham's plethora of pubs. Breakfast, brunch and lunch are all served by amiable staff in a small, warm and welcoming space.

Thetford see p171

Eight Norfolk breweries

Beeston Brewery
Fransham Road Farm, Beeston, PE32 2LZ (01328 700844, www.beestonbrewery. co.uk). Open phone for times.

This small craft brewer in west Norfolk, established in 2006, uses locally grown barley from Branthill Farm on the Holkham Estate to brew award-winning beers with names like *Squirrels Nuts* and *Worth the Wait.*

Fat Cat Brewery
98-100 Lawson Road, Norwich, NR3 4LF (01603 624364, www.fatcatbrewery.co.uk).

Norwich's much-loved Fat Cat pub (see p97) expanded to include a cask ale brewery in 2005. Beers include *Fat Cat Bitter*, which mixes speciality malts from the continent with classic English pale malts, *Stout Cat*, *Tom Cat*, *Wild Cat* and *Marmalade Cat.*

Fox Brewery
22 Station Road, Heacham, PE31 7EX (01485 570345). Open Pub noon-11.30pm daily. Tours by arrangement only. Admission free.

Based at the Fox & Hounds pub in Heacham, near Hunstanton, the Fox has up to 20 beers ranging across all styles and strengths, including fruit beers and seasonal ales. The light *Heacham Gold* was its first ale and remains a firm favourite for its sweetish malty taste with citrus undertones. Also popular is *Nelson's Blood.*

Humpty Dumpty Brewery
Church Road, Reedham, NR13 3TZ (01493 701818, www.humptydumptybrewery.com). Open Shop Easter-Oct noon-5pm daily. Tours by arrangement only.

This charming brewery and shop sells its own award-winning cask- and bottle-conditioned beers (*Little Sharpie* and *Broadland Sunrise* among them) plus brewing and beer paraphania and produce from other local suppliers.

Ostrich Inn ★
Stocks Green, Castle Acre, PE32 2AE (01760 755398, https://ostrichcastleacre. com). Open 10am-11.30pm daily. Lunch served noon-3pm daily. Dinner served 6-9pm Mon-Sat.

In a perfect spot opposite a perfect green in a perfect Norfolk village, the 16th-century Ostrich Inn is a great eating and sleeping spot. The current owners have been here since 2009 and have renovated the four handsomely decorated rooms (£90-£110 double) with tasteful touches. The landscaped garden has an enclosed play area complete with sand pit and beach hut. Inside, it's all warm woodwork and copper and gold hues, and the food is delicious.

Where to stay
Plenty of choice in all styles and price brackets means you should find the accommodation you want in this area.

There are country hotels such as **Greenbanks** (01362 687742, www. greenbankshotel.co.uk) in Wendling

and Great Danes (01366 328443, www. thegreatdanes.co.uk) in Beachamwell. Fans of pubs with rooms might prefer the **Ostrich Inn** (*see p178*) in Castle Acre.

Self-caterers could consider the two cottages in Narborough run by **Church Farm Holiday Homes** (07801 641570, www. churchfarmholidayhomes.com). And if you really want to go to town – and there are 18 people in the party – **Cliff Barns** (0870 850 5468, www. kateandtoms.com/houses/cliff-barns) in Narborough is a cross between a private house and a hotel, decorated in a rumbustious style described as 'Rancho-Deluxe – an irresistible mix of Mexican hacienda and American hunting lodge'. Catering can be provided too.

George Hotel

Station Street, Swaffham, PE37 7LJ (01760 721238, www. georgehotelswaffham.co.uk). Rates £92-£115 double incl breakfast.

Strattons Hotel see p180

Wagtail Brewery

New Barn Farm, Old Buckenham, NR17 1PF (01953 887133, www.wagtailbrewery.com).

This specialist in bottle-conditioned beers uses only vegetable-based finings, so is that rare thing, a supplier of wholly vegan beers. Lovely old-style labels hark back to days of yore, and the beers are equally traditional, from popular *Ale-next-the-Sea* to *Devil's Doorbell*. Outlets include the Real Ale Shop (*see p34*) near Wells.

Why Not Brewery

17 Cavalier Close, Dussindale, Thorpe St Andrew, Norwich, NR7 0TE (01603 300786, www.thewhynotbrewery.co.uk). Open phone to check times.

Colin Emms set up his tiny brewery in his back garden on the outskirts of Norwich in 2005, and now produces six beers, among them the smooth, full and malty *Chocolate Nutter*. Unsurprisingly, it has a nutty bitter chocolate and roasted grain in its aftertaste.

Woodforde's Brewery

Slad Lane, Woodbastwick, NR13 6SW (01603 720353, www.woodfordes.co.uk). Open Shop & visitor centre 10am-4.30pm Mon-Fri; 11am-4.30pm Sat, Sun.

Norfolk's most famous brewery produces a dozen beers and one dry cider from its rural setting north-east of Norwich. Multi award-winning *Wherry* is the populist one, with a floral aroma and fruity flavour; *Admiral's Reserve* is the most complex, providing a rich and rounded taste with subtle fruit undertones. Regular tours can be booked online (from £15).

And if you don't like beer...

Whin Hill Cider

The Stables, Stearman's Yard, Wells-next-the-Sea, NR23 1BW (01328 711821, www. whinhillcider.co.uk). Open Shop July, Aug 10.30am-5.30pm daily. Easter-June, Sept, Oct 10.30am-5.30pm Sat, Sun.

This appealing cider producer grows apples on its orchard at Stanhoe, ten miles south-west of Wells-next-the-Sea. The apples are then pressed into golden nectar in an 18th-century barn and outbuildings off the main car park in Wells. Single-variety apple juices, ciders (standard and sparkling) and perry are for sale.

This elegant building just off Swaffham's market square may be a chain, but don't discount it as a possible sleeping option. The 28 rooms are sizeable and the public areas comfortable, with free Wi-Fi and good amenities in both.

Horse & Groom

40 Lynn Street, Swaffham, PE37 7AX (01760 725935). Rates £55 double.

It might not be terribly inspiring and is no longer functioning as a pub, but there's a friendly welcome and the nine clean bedrooms are cheaper than most.

Strattons Hotel ♥

4 Ash Close, Swaffham, PE37 7NH (01760 723845, www.strattons-hotel. co.uk). Rates from £159-£235 double incl breakfast.

The pick of the crop in Swaffham, Lee and Vanessa Scott's flamboyantly decorated boutique hotel is stuffed to the gills with sumptuous touches: lush velvet drapes, Persian rugs, overstuffed armchairs, rococo gilt mirrors and bright, bold colours everywhere – anyone for shocking pink handmade wallpaper? Stay in the

Castle Acre Priory *see p173*

Boudoir, Fantouche or one of the other imaginatively-named rooms. The award-winning Modern European restaurant makes everything on the premises, from bread to after-dinner chocolates, and is admirably conscientious about supporting small local businesses. Although prices for both food and 14 rooms are high, a meal or stay here makes for a memorable event. There are also two one-bedroom apartments, based in what was the printing workshop and let on a self-catering basis. The on-site café-deli, CoCoes (*see p176*) is a treat too.

Castle Acre Priory *see p173*

Further reference

USEFUL ADDRESSES

www.bbc.co.uk/norfolk
www.edp24.co.uk Norfolk news and sport.
www.english-heritage.org.uk
www.heritageopendays.org.uk
www.literarynorfolk.co.uk
www.metoffice.gov.uk
www.nationalrail.co.uk
www.nationaltrust.org.uk
www.norfolkbroads.com
www.norfolkbroadscycling.co.uk
www.norfolkchurches.co.uk Fantastic round-up of Norfolk churches.
www.norfolk.gov.uk Norfolk County Council official website.
www.norfolkwildlifetrust.org.uk
www.ordnancesurvey.co.uk
www.sustrans.org.uk
www.thegoodpubguide.co.uk
www.thetrainline.com
www.visitbritain.com
www.visitengland.com
www.worldheritageuk.org

COAST & COUNTRYSIDE

www.bbc.co.uk/coast
http://camping.uk-directory.com
www.classic-sailing.co.uk
www.cpre.org.uk Campaign for the Protection of Rural England.
www.mcsuk.org Marine Conservation Society
www.nationalparks.uk
www.nationaltrail.co.uk
www.naturalengland.org.uk
www.ngs.org.uk National Gardens Scheme.
www.river-swimming.co.uk
www.ramblers.org.uk
www.rya.org.uk Royal Yachting Association.
www.sas.org.uk Surfers Against Sewage.
www.surfingengland.org
www.ukclimbing.com
www.ukgolfguide.com
www.walkingbritain.co.uk
www.walking-routes.co.uk
wildaboutthebritishisles.uk
www.wildswimming.com
www.woodlandtrust.org.uk Woodland Trust.

HOLIDAY HOME COMPANIES

Baby-Friendly Boltholes *www.babyfriendlyboltholes.co.uk.*
The Big Domain *www.thebigdomain.com. Big houses.*
Boutique Retreats *www.boutique-retreats.co.uk.*
Landmark Trust *01628 825925, www.landmarktrust.org.uk.*
The Little Domain *www.thelittledomain.com.* Small, romantic one-bedroom properties.
Living Architecture *www.living-architecture.co.uk.*
Superior Cottages *www.superiorcottages.co.uk.*
Unique Home Stays *01637 881942, www.uniquehomestays.com.*

TOURIST INFORMATION CENTRES

More details can be found at **www.visitnorfolk.com**. The main tourist offices are listed below.
Great Yarmouth 01493 846346
King's Lynn 01553 774297
Norwich 01603 989500
Wymondham 01953 604721

FICTION

John Betjeman *A Mind's Journey to Diss, East Anglian Bathe, Lord Cozens Hardy, Norfolk.*
Daniel Defoe *Robinson Crusoe* Defoe travelled through Great Yarmouth for his Tour Through the Whole Island of Great Britain, and used it as the point from where Crusoe sets off.
Charles Dickens *David Copperfield* Great Yarmouth is a key location.
Charles Kingsley *Hereward the Wake* Set in the Fens.
Sir Henry Rider Haggard *Colonel Quaritch*, VC Set around Norfolk.
Edward Storey writes fiction and non-fiction based on both his personal experiences and on Fenland legends and superstitions.

NON-FICTION

Benjamin Armstrong His diary details life in the Norfolk village of Dereham in the mid 19th century.
Adrian David *Hoare Standing up to Hitler: Story of Norfolk's Home Guard and Secret Army* Popular account of Norfolk's contribution to the war effort.
Nikolaus Pevsner *Norfolk 1: Norwich & North East, Norfolk 2: South & West* Classic explorations of Norfolk's architecture.
Matthew Rice *Building Norfolk* An illustrated history of Norfolk's architecture.

POETRY

John Clare *The Fens* Description of the Fenland.
RN Currey *King's Lynn* Currey refers to King's Lynn as the 'town that history could have made into a city'.
Sir Walter Raleigh *Walsingham.*
Michael Rivière *On Lady Katherine Paston's Tomb at Oxnead* Contemplates the demise of Oxnead Hall and the Paston family.
John Taylor *A Very Merry-*

John Taylor *A Very Merry-Wherry-Ferry Voyage* Recalls stopping at Cromer on a journey from London to York, and being mistaken for pirates by the townsfolk of the day.

FILM & TV

45 Years (Andrew Haigh 2015) The Norfolk Broads

Alan Partridge: Alpha Papa (Declan Lowney, 2015) Cromer Pier Annihilation (Alex Garland, 2018) Holkham Beach

Atonement (Joe Wright, 2007) Walpole St Andrew was used as a stand-in for Dunkirk.

Dad's Army (1968-1977) Much of this wartime comedy series was filmed in Thetford Forest.

Full Metal Jacket (Stanley Kubrick, 1971) The Norfolk Broads were used instead of Vietnam in many scenes.

Kingdom (2007-2009) Various locations around Swaffham and Wells-next-the-Sea were used.

Lara Croft: Tomb Raider (Simon West, 2003) Elveden Hall was used as a location for the Croft family home.

Never Let Me Go (Mark Romanek, 2010) Holkham Beach

Shakespeare in Love (John Madden, 1998) Holkham Hall and Estate feature in the last scene.

The Duchess (Saul Dibb, 2008) Cley-next-the-Sea

The Personal History of David Copperfield (Armando Iannucci, 2019) King's Lynn

MUSIC

The Darkness *Black Shuck* The name of this song is a reference to the ghostly black dog, said to roam Norfolk.

Ernest John Moeran Moeran spent the early part of his career as a composer compiling and arranging over 150 traditional Norfolk folk songs, often sitting in country pubs waiting for old men to start singing and noting them down. This work heavily influenced his later compositions.

ART

John Alfred Arnesby Brown His landscape paintings include *View of Norwich* (from the Bungay Road) 1934-1935.

John Sell Cotman Part of the Norwich school, Sell Cotman is known for his paintings of the area, such as Norwich Market-Place 1809.

Alfred Munnings spent much of his formative years in Norfolk, and trained at the Norwich School of Art.

FOOTPATHS/WALKS

Peddars Way & Norfolk Coast Path *www.nationaltrail. co.uk/peddarsway.*

Weavers' Way *www.ramblers. org.uk/ info/paths/name/w/ weavers.htm* A 56-mile walk from Cromer to Great Yarmouth.

Index

Picture credits

Pages 2 AndrewSproule/Shutterstock.com; 2, 9, 59, 78, 90, 91, 119, 131, 136 yackers1/Shutterstock.com; 3, 113, 181 Richard Bowden/Shutterstock.com; 3, 120 Helen Hotson/Shutterstock.com; 4 DavidYoung/Shutterstock.com; 12, 13, 120, 121, 122, 123, 128 Leonard Smith; 13 tony mills/Shutterstock.com; 13, 15 Clive117/Shutterstock.com; 14, 16, 30, 33, 51, 53, 57, 59, 70, 71, 88, 89, 91, 100, 101, 102, 135, 137, 144, 157, 163, 169, 170, 173, 174, 175, 177 Alys Tomlinson; 25 Andy333/Shutterstock.com; 29 Jon Kempner/Shutterstock.com; 29 Original Bob/Shutterstock.com; 29, 48, 50, 51, 75 Sam Robbins; 32, 102 Philip Bird LRPS CPAGB/Shutterstock.com; 33 MyriadLifePhoto/Shutterstock.com; 33 StevenDocwra/Shutterstock.com; 37 Pamela Farrell; 40, 180 Martin Charles Hatch/Shutterstock.com; 41, 46, 142, 143 RSPB; 42 Patrick James Gosling/Shutterstock.com; 49 Clare Louise Jackson/Shutterstock.com; 55 Peter Brown; 56 david muscroft/Shutterstock.com; 62, 71 Phil Silverman/Shutterstock.com; 63 heardinlondon/Shutterstock.com; 65 Chris Lawrence Travel/Shutterstock.com; 67 Seferix/Shutterstock.com; 70 Alena Veasey/Shutterstock.com; 72 Chris Humphries/Shutterstock.com; 74 Chapelle/Shutterstock.com; 75 Chris Pierre; 75 Nicola Pulham/Shutterstock.com; 77 Abdul N Quraishi - Abs/Shutterstock.com; 80 Chris Herring; 85 Radomir Rezny/Shutterstock.com; 86 Jacek Wojnarowski/Shutterstock.com; 90 Action Images; 92 James Austin; 93 Nigel Young; 95 Calrdonian Air Surveys Ltd; 96 orfolk Photography/Shutterstock.com; 116 Christopher Keeley/Shutterstock.com; 121 Fexel/Shutterstock.com; 121 James Norfolkboy/Shutterstock.com; 124 S.m.u.d.g.e/Shutterstock.com; 138, 172 English Heritage; 139 Kemaro/Shutterstock.com; 147 Richard Hayman/Shutterstock.com; 150 Edwin Rosier/Shutterstock.com; 156 Jason Wells/Shutterstock.com; 161 Peter Moulton/Shutterstock.com; 177 Dronegraphica/Shutterstock.com; 177 Maria Schepers/Shutterstock.com..

The following images were supplied by the featured establishments: pages 7, 21, 28, 35, 44, 76, 105, 107, 121, 125, 136, 141, 152, 154, 156, 178, 179.

Credits

Crimson credits
Editor Felicity Laughton
Picture research Ben Rowe and Mihaela Botezatu

Maps Contains OS data © Crown copyright and database right (2021) Licence number:100049681.

Production Designer Patrick Dawson
Design Mytton Williams

Managing Director Andy Riddle

Sales & Marketing Diane McEntee and Tania Ross

Acknowledgements
This edition of *Time Out Norfolk* was edited by Felicity Laughton. Felicity thanks the staff at Time Out London for their help, especially Ben Rowe and all contributors to previous editions of *Time Out Norfolk & Suffolk* whose work forms the basis of this guide.

Photography credits
Front cover Pawel Bulejak

Back cover
Left: Radek Sturgolewski/Shutterstock.com;
Centre left: Alena Veasey/shutterstock.com;
Centre Right: Richard O'Donoghue/Shutterstock.com;
Right StevenDocwra/Shutterstock.com.

Interior Photography credits, *see "Picture credits" on page 191.*

Publishing information
Time Out Norfolk 3rd edition
© TIME OUT ENGLAND LIMITED 2021
June 2021

ISBN 978 1 914515 01 9
CIP DATA: A catalogue record for this book is available from the British Library

Published by Heartwood Publishing
www.heartwoodpublishing.co.uk on behalf of Time Out England.

Distributed by Grantham Book Services
Distributed in the US and Canada by Publishers Group West (1-510-809-3700)

Printed by Ashford Colour Press, Gosport, UK.